CATHOLIC SOCIAL ACTIVISM

T0386066

Catholic Social Activism

Progressive Movements in the United States

Sharon Erickson Nepstad

NEW YORK UNIVERSITY PRESS

New York

NEW YORK UNIVERSITY PRESS
New York

www.nyupress.org

References to Internet websites (URLs) were accurate at the time of writing. Neither the author nor New York University Press is responsible for URLs that may have expired or changed since the manuscript was prepared.

Library of Congress Cataloging-in-Publication Data
Names: Nepstad, Sharon Erickson, author.
Title: Catholic social activism : progressive movements in the United States /
Sharon Nepstad.
Description: New York : NYU Press, 2019. | Includes bibliographical references and index.
Identifiers: LCCN 2018043750| ISBN 9781479885480 (cl : alk. paper) |
ISBN 9781479879229 (pb : alk. paper)
Subjects: LCSH: Catholic Church—United States. | Christian sociology—Catholic Church. |
Church and social problems—Catholic Church.
Classification: LCC BX1406.3 .N47 2019 | DDC 261.8088/282—dc23
LC record available at https://lccn.loc.gov/2018043750

New York University Press books are printed on acid-free paper, and their binding materials are chosen for strength and durability. We strive to use environmentally responsible suppliers and materials to the greatest extent possible in publishing our books.

Manufactured in the United States of America

10 9 8 7 6 5 4 3 2 1

Also available as an ebook

For Claude

CONTENTS

When NYU Press editor Jennifer Hammer initially approached me about writing this book, I thought that she had the wrong person. I explained that I am not a theologian. I am not a church historian. I am not a Catholic Studies scholar. I'm not even Catholic personally. She approached me because I have been writing about Catholic activists for the past twenty-five years, but I have done so as a sociologist of religion and a social movements researcher. Jennifer, in her wisdom, explained that my perspective as a sociologist could be an asset rather than a liability. Numerous books have been written about official church teachings, but I have always been far more interested in how laypeople put these teachings into action in their daily lives—something we call "lived religion." While other books convey the Roman Catholic hierarchy's stances on various social and political issues, this book captures what happens on the ground, in parishes and religious communities throughout the nation. This is important, I argue, because religious activism at the grassroots level has had a trickle-up effect, pushing bishops, cardinals, and pontiffs to respond to these pressures from below.

To capture this experience of lived religion in contemporary American Catholicism, I have chosen to focus on progressive activism around six issues: (1) labor; (2) peace, war, and militarism; (3) gender equality; (4) poverty, political repression, and revolutionary struggles; (5) immigration; and (6) environmental degradation. Obviously, this does not comprehensively cover all progressive Catholic social movements. I have not included important efforts to abolish capital punishment; to end police brutality in communities of color; to promote gay, lesbian, bisexual, and transgender rights; and to fight sexual abuse within the church. Why have I chosen to focus on these six issues? This is where wide-scale organizing has occurred within American Catholicism and where the movements have taken on a distinctively Catholic character rather than merely being part of a broader (and mostly secular) political coalition. It is in such movements that we see how people embody their religious beliefs.

Others will notice that my focus is primarily on the actions of lay-people. As a result, I have omitted highly active groups within religious orders, such as "Nuns on the Bus" or Sisters who have undertaken corporate responsibility campaigns that pressure gun manufacturers and oil companies to adopt socially responsible practices. While recognizing the importance of these initiatives, I maintain that it is also valuable to focus on "rank-and-file" Catholics, not only those who represent the institutional church. It is often in these semiautonomous lay spaces (or spaces where laypeople, clergy, and members of religious orders collaborate as equals) that we see new insights occurring and tactical innovation emerging.

In exploring progressive movements on these six issues, I relied on various data sources. In the cases of the Plowshares movement, the Central America solidarity movement, and the Sanctuary movement of the 1980s, I drew on in-depth interviews that I conducted in previous research projects, using a purposive sample of roughly seventy-five activists. These interviews were semistructured and typically lasted between one and a half and two hours. Using standard social science methods, I recorded and transcribed the interviews and then coded them to inductively discern patterns and themes. In addition to these interviews, I used original sources and archival documents, including Catholic Worker newsletters, court transcripts from Plowshares trials and Sanctuary movement trials, as well as activist autobiographies and writings. Finally, I drew on a wide array of secondary sources to compile historical accounts of these movements.

Clearly, I am not presenting new data in this book. Neither am I attempting to build new theories of religion and social movements. Rather, like a *bricoleur*, I have utilized various data sources to offer a broad overview of the wide-ranging movements that defined the progressive wing of American Catholicism in the twentieth and twenty-first centuries. My purpose is not to document untold stories but to weave together narratives of various movements that have collectively created a distinctive religious tradition and a distinctive style of activism. While many still see the Roman Catholic Church as inherently conservative, I cast a spotlight on progressive, indeed sometimes radical, Catholic activists who were architects of a new style of resistance and whose stories have often been overlooked in accounts of mainstream Catholicism. My purpose is to show how laypeople have had a political impact within their own country but also a religious impact within their own church. The stories presented in this book are not new, but they are worth preserving and retelling.

Introduction

I was working in my office on a warm spring day in 2014 when I received a phone call from a friend who was working in Guatemala. There was urgency in her voice as she told me that a young woman named Ana was in trouble with gangs in Guatemala City.[1] Ana's family feared for her life. They had good reason to be fearful: they had firsthand experience with gang violence. They were reaching out to me, asking if we could take Ana to live with us because we, too, are part of their family.

I have two daughters whom I adopted from Guatemala. In 2013, after a highly complicated investigation, our birth family searcher was able to locate the girls' families. As we got to know them and visited them, we learned more about the reasons they had relinquished their children for adoption. Our younger daughter, Malaya, comes from a family that is extremely indigent. At the time they conceived Malaya, they were living in a squatter settlement of shanty homes, patched together from sheets of corrugated tin. They constantly feared eviction, and they often did not have enough to feed their children. Malaya's birth father told me that he worried that Malaya might starve to death. Her parents wanted her to have a life where she did not lack the basic necessities and could get an education that they are not able to provide.

Our older daughter, Linnea, was born in Guatemala City to a family of greater economic means. Yet, due to Guatemala's unstable economy, the family still finds it difficult to make ends meet, despite the fact that her older siblings had advanced education and professional positions. However, the reason that Linnea was given up for adoption was because of the violent environment her birth family lives in—a section of Guatemala City that is deemed a "red zone," denoting severe violence and crime. Even taxi drivers won't take passengers into the neighborhood. Just days before Linnea was born, her seventeen-year-old birth brother was shot and killed by local gang members. Now the family worried that Ana, Linnea's birth sister, would meet a similar fate. They asked if we would open our home to Ana if they could get her across the US border.

As it turned out, Ana did not come to live with us. But other children and teenagers from Central America did make the journey that summer, traveling unaccompanied for thousands of miles to enter the United States. I watched in amazement during the summer of 2014 as they poured across the border. Within a few months, the US Border Patrol had detained nearly 60,000 children.

Quickly, these children became a political battlefield. Republicans blamed President Obama, claiming that his policy of not deporting "Dreamers" (i.e., individuals whose parents brought them illegally into the country as children) was encouraging this influx. Democrats also used the immigration crisis to court potential Hispanic constituents, promising reform but delivering few tangible changes. As political leaders debated how this situation should be handled, numerous US Catholic agencies went quietly to work, getting the children released from the detention centers and reuniting them with family members or placing them in foster care.

Catholic leaders and laypeople also began speaking out about the conditions that compelled so many people to risk everything by embarking on this journey north. Many people assumed these children left because of poverty. There is indeed significant poverty in the region. According to the World Bank, 66 percent of Hondurans subsist on less than $1.25 per day. About 53 percent of Guatemalans and 35 percent of Salvadorans share that fate.[2] Yet generally the very poorest are not the ones to migrate, since traveling to the United States can be expensive, as most spend thousands of dollars to hire coyotes or guides to help them cross the border. One of the main factors driving these migrations is the chronic violence in Central America—much of it the result of gangs that emerged from the region's brutal civil wars during the 1970s and 1980s. Thus, while Catholics in the United States provided immediate assistance to these refugee children, they also tried to address the root problems that drove so many out of their homelands.

Many Americans may find it surprising that the US Catholic Church has taken such a progressive position on immigration and led the efforts to help these Central American children. After all, many assume that the Catholic Church is inherently conservative, based on its stance on contraception, abortion, homosexuality, and divorce. In reality, there is a long-standing tradition of progressive Catholic movements in the United States, which have addressed a variety of issues from labor, war, and environmental protection to human rights, exploitive development practices, women's rights, and bellicose foreign policies. These Catholic social movements have helped to shift the church from an institution that had historically supported incumbent governments and political elites to an institution that has sided with the oppressed and the vulnerable.

This book focuses on these progressive Catholic movements and how they have shaped the religious landscape of the United States. It provides an introduction to the movements but, more important, it shows how they have provoked controversy and stirred debate, often prompting Catholic leaders to take a stand and to articulate the theological bases for social justice. These theological and ethical views, known as Catholic Social Thought, have been developed in a variety of church documents.[3] Yet, as I argue throughout the book, there is an iterative dynamic at play: progressive Catholic movements have shaped church teachings, while church teachings have inspired and motivated grassroots activism as well. This book introduces and explores both the social teachings and the movements that have shaped the progressive wing of US Catholicism.

Historical Development of Catholic Social Thought

Because the purpose of this book is to introduce Catholic Social Thought and examine how laypeople live out these principles, it is essential to briefly explain how these teachings developed. Although Catholics have articulated ethical principles in response to sociopolitical challenges since the church's inception, such teachings were systematically developed in the nineteenth century in response to an unregulated form of industrial capitalism that generated suffering and poverty for many factory and mine workers. Since Europe was at the core of the industrial world at that time, it is no surprise that the early pioneers of socially engaged Catholicism were Europeans.

Yet the Catholic Church was not always concerned about workers. In the decades leading up to the release of the first papal encyclical,

Rerum Novarum, published in 1891, the European Catholic Church was still recovering from changes incurred by the French Revolution, which included loss of land, prestige, and various political privileges. Many Catholic leaders were in a reactive mode, suspicious of movements oriented toward social equality and labor rights; instead, the European Catholic Church saw wealthy elites as its allies in a politically tumultuous and unpredictable world.

What happened to change the conservative, perhaps even reactionary, Catholic Church in Europe? What shifted the church from an institution that clung to its medieval past to one that, by the end of the nineteenth century, advocated for social progress? Some key individuals helped to shift the church, denouncing the injustices that factory workers faced. Since there were virtually no labor laws in place to protect workers, they experienced low wages, a twelve-hour workday, child labor, unsafe work conditions, and the constant threat of industrial injuries. Moreover, the Industrial Revolution had not been kind to members of the working class: it forced them into overcrowded slums, where crime and unsanitary conditions were widespread, and it destroyed their family life as parents and children alike toiled for long hours in the factories. Earning subsistence wages, these families continually lived in survival mode, with little hope of ever improving their economic situation.

One of those who responded to these oppressive conditions was Archbishop Wilhelm Emmanuel von Ketteler (1811–1877) from Mainz, Germany. Ketteler insisted that this suffering was not God's will or punishment for alleged sin. Instead, he argued that it was a reflection of an unjust and exploitive economic system. He asserted that improving labor conditions and establishing living wages could solve the major social ills of that era, including poverty, crime, violence, and family disruption. Toward that end, Archbishop Ketteler called upon the church to be the champion of the working class, and he encouraged his parishioners to organize labor unions.[4] He even donated his own money to help establish worker associations.[5]

Other European Catholics were also advocating for workers' rights during this period. In France, there were aristocratic laypeople, such as Charles de Montalembert (1810–1870) and Albert de Mun (1841–1914), who believed that social justice and economic reform must be at the heart of the church's agenda. Similarly, Frédérick Ozanam started a Catholic charity called the St. Vincent de Paul Society, which served the immediate needs of the most destitute and continues to do so today. Yet Ozanam was adamant that charity was not enough: he insisted that Catholics should work to change the social and economic systems that produced this poverty. In England, Cardinal Henry Edward Manning (1808–1892) became a leading advocate of socially engaged Catholicism. Because the church had previously ignored the suffering of factory workers, he worried that the working class would embrace atheistic Marxism. In response, Cardinal Manning supported labor unions, workers' rights, and state-sponsored social assistance programs. More significantly, he used his position within the church to support the indigent: in the 1860s, he canceled plans to build a new cathedral, instead using the funds to build twenty schools in impoverished neighborhoods.[6]

These leaders began to slowly shift the church away from its tradition of supporting the sociopolitical status quo. Yet laypeople played an important role in this process as well: between 1865 and 1870, they formed "Christian-social associations." These groups operated independently from the church and called for better wages, an end to child labor, reduced working hours, and the right to organize. Within a few years, the Christian-social associations in Germany had 22,000 members, constituting the largest workers' group in the entire country.[7] Thus laypeople helped to highlight the links between religion and workers' rights, ensuring that these issues were prominent within the minds of church leaders, including the pope.

All these efforts made a difference. In 1891, Pope Leo XIII released *Rerum Novarum*, literally translated as "Of New Things" but more commonly entitled "The Condition of Labor." This encyclical affirmed the right to private property, thereby rejecting socialism as a solution, yet it prioritized laborers over capitalism. Pope Leo XIII insisted that employers have a moral obligation to pay a just wage, to ensure a safe work environment, and to allow workers the freedom of association. While this does not sound radical, it marked an important change for a church that had for many centuries endorsed systems of social inequality as God's will.

The release of *Rerum Novarum* inspired workers and fostered a more politicized form of Social Catholicism in Europe and the United States. In Europe, Catholics such as Sicilian-born Luigi Sturzo (1871–1959) embodied this new religious orientation. Sturzo, an ordained priest and sociologist, had seen firsthand the exploitation of his fellow Italians at the hands of local elites. Like other socially engaged Catholics, he encouraged the formation of worker and student associations. He also urged Catholics to get directly involved in electoral politics, translating religious principles into policy. Sturzo himself was elected mayor of his hometown, setting a new example of Catholic political action.[8] In the United States, Monsignor John Ryan (1869–1945) promoted workers' rights through two notable books: *The Living Wage*, published in 1906, and *Distributive Justice*, published in 1916. Ryan encouraged political action, including collaboration with various secular reform groups. He served on the national board for the American Civil Liberties Union— the first priest to do so. And in 1913, he wrote legislation for a minimum wage for women and children, which was passed in the state of Minnesota.[9] Both men set an example of taking Catholic Social Thought straight into the political arena by encouraging involvement in policy and legislation.[10]

Key Themes in Catholic Social Thought

Rerum Novarum marked the formal start of Catholic Social Teachings. As the previous discussion illustrates, such teachings emerged as a result of multiple forces, including grassroots action and pressure from Catholic laity and leaders who were affected by these social issues. Many more encyclicals and official church documents followed, addressing problems such as the nuclear arms race, war, revolutionary movements, environmental concerns, and human rights. Although each document addresses a particular social concern, a number of common themes run through these teachings.[11]

One of the first and clearest themes within Catholic Social Thought is the *dignity of humans*. Because humans are created in the image and likeness of God, each person is to be treated with profound respect throughout the entire life course. For many Catholics, although not all, this emphasis on the inestimable worth of human life has led to a stance opposing abortion, euthanasia, and capital punishment. Yet another central aspect of dignity is that all humans are to be treated equally. Thus all forms of social inequality—such as racism or class oppression—must be opposed.

A second theme is *the common good*. Catholic Social Thought seeks to counter the rampant individualism that pervades much of Western culture, balancing individual rights with a concern for the well-being of the broader community. Each person has the obligation to improve the lives of others, including future generations, even if we personally receive no direct benefit from these improvements. Hence Catholics should support education programs, for example, even if they themselves do not have children, since education is foundational for the advancement of individuals as well as society as a whole.

The third theme of Catholic Social Teaching is *solidarity*. This concept recognizes that humans flourish in social relationships and in community. Moreover, it is an acknowledgment that we are all highly interdependent for our physical, social, and cultural needs. Solidarity often begins as an internal attitude, a sense of connection to others. At times, however, it may require external action on behalf of others. It reflects the idea so well articulated by Dr. Martin Luther King Jr.: "An injustice anywhere is a threat to justice everywhere."[12]

A fourth theme is known as the *option for the poor and the vulnerable*. A test of any society's ethics is how well its most vulnerable populations are faring. According to Catholic Social Thought, the church's mission is one of service to the poor and the marginalized. This service includes meeting their spiritual and physical needs but also addressing the underlying causes of their suffering. Where social, political, and economic structures are harming people, the faithful must side with the oppressed, working to change the exploitive systems.

Fifth, Catholic Social Thought affirms the *rights of workers*. The church takes the stance that the economy is to benefit workers, not the other way around. Moreover, it maintains that work should be more than simply a way to pay bills; it should be a meaningful way to contribute to society. To respect the dignity of work and workers, the church advocates for fair wages, safe working conditions, and the right to organize.

Sixth, the theme of *peace and reconciliation* is also prominent within Catholic Social Thought. Peace means more than the absence of conflict; it means the presence of just relations and social institutions. Without security and stability, human communities cannot flourish. Hence the church calls upon its members to be peacemakers, seeking to transform conflicts nonviolently.

The final theme deals with the *preservation of creation*. The environmental crisis that the world currently faces is, at its core, a moral issue. The issue is about whether humans are being responsible stewards of the earth's resources and whether they will protect the environment for future generations. The church teaches that caring for the earth is an essential component of the Catholic faith.

Sources and Methods of Catholic Social Thought

In this book, I use the term "Catholic Social Thought" to refer to the Catholic Church's ethical principles about human nature, purpose, and social justice—particularly in the realm of politics and the economy. These ethical principles have been formed from two streams of influence: (1) the body of *official* Catholic teachings, as articulated in papal encyclicals, statements by national and regional bishops' councils, and so forth (which is called Catholic Social Teaching); and (2) *unofficial* contributions from Catholic thinkers, movements, and groups. Yet precisely how do Catholic leaders come to these views? How do Catholic movements generate positions on social, political, and economic problems? Catholic thinkers rely on four different sources to help them formulate their stances. These include scripture (or revelation), reason (also referred to as "natural law"), tradition, and experience.

Naturally, Catholic leaders turn to scripture as the basis for their ethical positions. For instance, justice is a major theme throughout the Judeo-Christian scriptures and the basis for Catholic social ethics. Yet the Hebrew and Greek terms for justice can be translated in multiple ways, including mercy, loving-kindness, fidelity, or legal justice. Furthermore, the question arises regarding how to translate these ideas to current issues. Hence Catholic leaders focus on how the Hebrew (e.g., Old Testament) prophets denounced any practices that harmed the most vulnerable members of society, including widows, orphans, the socially outcast, and the poor; how Christ interacted with others, including notorious outcasts such as tax collectors and adulterers; and the acts of the apostles.[13] The premise is that scripture reveals God's intentions for the world and the godliest methods of responding to conflict and injustice.

An additional source of inspiration is human reason. We can derive a set of ethics by using human knowledge to assess the roots of complex social problems. In particular, Catholic theologians rely on "natural law reasoning." The basic premise is that God created humans with intelligence and the capacity to engage in rational, thoughtful analysis. Using these skills, as well as the innate knowledge embedded in our hearts and minds, people can observe the world and make good judgments regarding ethical responses to social problems.[14] Theologian Thomas Massaro described natural law this way:

> Normally, Christians think of God's will as coming to us through Scripture, such as the contents of the Ten Commandments. A key claim of natural law theory is that nature is another path by which we learn God's will in a less direct way than through revelation. By closely observing the structures of nature, including our own bodies and the healthy instincts and inclinations built into our minds, we gain knowledge of the natural order God intends. For example, our innate desire to preserve our lives suggests the divine prohibition against suicide and, by extension, murder and wanton destruction of wildlife. Our natural desire to live peacefully in society is cited as evidence to support all the rules of social order (to avoid stealing, lying, adultery, etc.) that contribute to social stability.[15]

A third source that Catholic leaders draw on is tradition, or all previous Christian teachings. This can include other papal encyclicals but also writings from earlier periods in church history.[16] For example, some Catholic leaders have cited the writings of the church fathers, from the second through fifth centuries; these include figures such as Clement of Alexandria, Tertullian, Basil the Great, Ambrose of Milan, Augustine of Hippo, and Jerome. These individuals wrote about greed, private property, and participation in war, among other matters, providing a historical basis for Catholic social ethics.[17]

The final source of inspiration comes from human experience. Catholic social teaching encourages people to carefully observe a situation, make a judgment about what is occurring, and then take action. This process is sometimes referred to as the "circle of praxis" or the "hermeneutical circle." The process involves four steps. First, Christians gain experience by directly getting involved in the issue, becoming acquainted with those who suffer from a particular social ill. Second, people are to engage in social analysis—that is, they should ask about the causes of these problems. This may require consultation with experts who have studied and gathered data on these issues. Third, the faithful should engage in theological reflection, determining a biblically appropriate response. Fourth, individuals should plan a course of action and implement it. It is through such human experience that social ethics are clarified.

Lived Religion

Catholic laypeople have contributed to Catholic Social Thought through their experiences in progressive movements. Indeed, it has often been through their activism that they have formulated the biblical and theological bases for their social ethics. This type of religious action is the primary focus of this book. In other words, the book will not focus on whether various Catholic Social Teachings are accurate interpretations of scripture or theologically correct positions. Rather, it will focus on how lay Catholics in the United States have lived out their religious beliefs through daily acts, including engagement with various social, economic, and political issues.

Within academic circles, this is known as a lived religion approach. Sociologist Meredith McGuire defines lived religion as "how religion and spirituality are practiced, experienced, and expressed by ordinary people (rather than official spokespersons) in the context of their everyday lives."[18] This is not the same as popular religion or folk religion. The term "popular religion" emerged among historians of the Protestant Reformation who examined how the theology of Reformers was being translated into local congregations. These historians noted that there often was a gap or slippage between the official theology of Protestant Reformers and the daily practices of Protestant church members. Within this gap, lay Protestants had a degree of autonomy to reconfigure religious beliefs and practices to suit local circumstances. Hence popular religion denotes the scope of practices beyond officially sanctioned religion; such popular religious practices may, in fact, resist and oppose official religion.[19] The term "lived religion" is not synonymous with "popular religion." Although scholars of lived religion also emphasize the autonomy of lay actors and activities that occur on the margins of ecclesial institutions, lived religion is simply a way of capturing the daily experiences of the "person in the pew" and how such individuals act on their religious beliefs.

A lived religion approach requires attention to religious organizations as well as religious participants, to theology as well as practice, to texts as well as daily rituals.[20] It examines how religious teachings are imagined and reimagined in the context of family, community, work, and politics. As religious studies scholar Robert Orsi put it, "The key questions [of lived religion] concern what people *do* with religious idioms, how they use them, what they make of themselves and their worlds with them. . . . The study of lived religion focuses most intensely on . . . hot cultural moments—at the edges of life, in times of social upheaval, confusion, or transition, when old orders give way and what is ahead remains unclear—that [is where] we see what matters most in a religious world."[21]

This book asks: How have American laypeople responded in such hot cultural moments, including moments of war, severe economic trouble, human rights abuses, and encounters with immigrants fleeing these problems? How have they interpreted official church documents and translated them into progressive political action? And how have their actions influenced religious leaders and official church teachings?

I must emphasize, however, that due to laypeople's independent agency, American Catholics will interpret and act on Catholic Social Teachings in divergent ways. While the focus of this book is on Catholics in progressive social movements, there are Catholics who have understood the same teachings as promoting conservative causes. To illustrate this point, we can look at two responses to the papal encyclical *Quadragesimo Anno*, also known by its English title *Forty Years After: On Reconstructing the Social Order and Perfecting It Conformably to the Precepts of the Gospel*. This encyclical, which was issued in 1931 by Pope Pius XI, reinforced the Catholic Church's commitment to workers' rights while underscoring the responsibilities of the rich. And, in the midst of the Great Depression, it condemned the huge gaps between the wealthy elites and the suffering masses. The document called for livable wages and the "uplifting" of the proletariat while simultaneously defending the right to private property. It argued that the world's economic problems could only be solved through a reconstruction of the social order, grounded in the principles of justice.[22] Pope Pius XI insisted that this new social order must be an alternative to the political threats of that era: it must offer a path to economic improvement and social justice while avoiding the problems of communism and class warfare, predatory liberal individualism, and fascism.[23]

Many American Catholics responded to the pope's call, but their interpretation of these ideas varied widely.[24] On the progressive side, the Catholic Worker movement, founded by Dorothy Day and Peter Maurin in 1933, took action by establishing farming communes. Maurin argued that there were several reasons why radical agrarianism could be a realistic alternative. First, farm communes could address the immediate needs of people struggling through the Great Depression because the farms could provide food. Second, a radical agrarian life could ease the technological unemployment produced by industrial economies, thereby contributing to a more stable social order. Third, subsistence farming and craftwork centered the forces of production on need rather than desire. This could restore the values of cooperation while providing fulfilling and meaningful labor.[25] Although the farming communes were largely a failure, they demonstrated a progressive interpretation and application of *Quadragesimo Anno*.[26]

On the conservative side, other American Catholics had a different interpretation of this encyclical. Edward Keller—a priest in the order of the Holy Cross who taught economics at the University of Notre Dame—argued, "The encyclicals do not condemn our economic system of free enterprise, but instead give a strong moral foundation for such a system."[27] In his book *Christianity and American Capitalism*, Keller emphasized that the Catholic Church had rejected socialism, but nothing in the church's social teachings condemned the basic institutions of American capitalism: private property, freedom of competition, and free enterprise. The encyclicals only condemned unregulated and unlimited competition, which he argued did not exist in the United States.[28] In fact, Keller maintained the belief that American capitalism was ethically admirable because it bestowed excess wealth to some, who could then use this wealth to establish new companies that would provide more jobs. Although he never called for an end to unions, he did argue that they were potentially dangerous since they had a monopoly of power that, through strikes and other forms of collective action, could paralyze industry, thereby hurting workers and their families.

Building on the ideas of Keller in the mid-twentieth century, other Catholic thinkers promoted religious justifications of free-market capitalism. For example, in 1990, Father Robert Sirico and others founded the Acton Institute, which offers a moral defense of economic liberty and capitalism.[29] Sirico and his supporters cite other encyclicals not covered in this book, such as the 1991 encyclical *Centesimus Annus*, which condemned Marxism and the dictatorial regimes that practiced it.

In short, while Catholic Workers aimed to fulfill the mandates of *Quadragesimo Anno* by re-creating an economic order rooted in small-scale sustainable agriculture, Edward Keller and Robert Sirico aimed to reconstruct the economic order by promoting large-scale capitalism. This underscores the importance of a lived religion approach, examining how a church's ethical teachings are implemented in everyday life. It is clear that progressive Catholics do not have hegemonic control over these issues, and I encourage readers to also explore works on conservative Catholic social movements to gain a more holistic understanding of the American Catholic landscape. Nonetheless, covering all Catholic social movements in the United States is beyond the scope of this book. In this book, my aim is to challenge the assumption that religion is an inherently conservative, status quo–enforcing institution. In addition, I highlight the progressive and sometimes radical history of American Catholics, whose stories have for too long remained on the margins of public awareness.

It is these stories that are depicted in subsequent chapters, as captured in the experiences of laypeople who put into action their understanding of Catholic social ethics. The focus is on American Catholic lived religion vis-à-vis six political issues in the twentieth and twenty-first centuries. Chapter 1 explores the Catholic Worker movement and the United Farm Workers union, which fought for workers' rights. Chapter 2 examines American Catholic peace activism to end war, particularly in Vietnam, and to stop the nuclear arms race. The focus of chapter 3 is on Catholic feminist activism and the struggle for gender equality. Chapter 4 addresses poverty, political violence, and human rights abuses in Central America and the US movements in solidarity with those Nicaraguans, Salvadorans, and Guatemalans who were seeking liberation. Immigrant rights are the topic of chapter 5, which focuses on the US Sanctuary movement of the 1980s and the New Sanctuary Movement that emerged at the start of the twenty-first century. Chapter 6 looks at Catholic activism for the preservation of the environment. These six issues—labor rights, militarism and war, women's rights, poverty and political repression, immigration, and the environment—are indeed the hot points of contemporary times. Following Orsi's lead, I believe that in exploring these moments of social upheaval, we gain new insight into the beliefs and practices of progressive US Catholics.

1

Dignity and Just Treatment of Workers

Prior to the eighteenth century, most Europeans and North Americans lived in rural settings. Many were small farmers, producing food for their own families and selling or trading whatever surplus they were able to generate. Others were craftsmen and craftswomen, using basic tools and simple machinery to produce goods within their homes. These were typically family businesses, with parents and children working together for their survival. The average citizen did not have much; incomes were so meager that most could hope for little more than providing basic food and shelter for their families. Malnourishment and illness were common.[1]

With the introduction of the steam engine and mass production, factory owners recruited the peasantry to leave behind their agrarian existence to find employment in urban centers. Factories were expanding quickly, and men, women, and children were hired to provide labor for the burgeoning industrial economy. Proponents of industrialization proclaimed that mechanization and mass production would transform the economy and everyday life, providing a wide variety of manufactured goods. Life during the Industrial Revolution was, indeed, transformed. But for many, it did not bring improvements. For the typical factory worker, daily existence was brutal. Most worked between ten and fourteen hours a day, six days a week. Moreover, the work was tedious. Skilled artisans, who had taken pride in their craftsmanship, found themselves performing the same monotonous task, over and over, on the assembly line. Former peasants missed the variety of jobs involved in running a family farm and the independence of setting one's own schedule. The pay was also substandard. Men earned poverty-level wages; women and children were paid even less. With parents and children spending sixty to seventy hours a week in factories, family life was utterly destroyed.[2] Additionally, conditions within factories were deplorable, with industrial accidents occurring frequently, including mine explosions, factory fires, and equipment injuries. Tens of thousands were killed from these accidents, hundreds of thousands more were injured and maimed, yet employers seldom provided compensation for workplace deaths or injuries.[3]

These dangerous and exploitive conditions prompted some Catholic leaders to speak out. They argued that the church must support laborers or else risk losing them to other movements of that era. This chapter examines some of the historical trends, events, individuals, and experiences that pushed Pope Leo XIII to release *Rerum Novarum* in 1891. It further provides an overview of the second papal encyclical, *Quadragesimo Anno* (known as "The Reconstruction of the Social Order"), released in 1931 by Pope Pius XI. I conclude the chapter by exploring how these teachings on labor were interpreted and put into practice by the Catholic Worker movement and the United Farm Workers movement.

Historical Context Leading Up to *Rerum Novarum*

The Communist Manifesto and the Emergence of Marxism

As industrialization expanded, so too did the suffering of factory workers. But this suffering was not passively accepted. By the mid-nineteenth century, workers were forming unions and proposing various solutions to their plight. In 1847, a group of radicals commissioned Karl Marx and Friedrich Engels to write a manifesto that would explain the roots of workers' misery, propose a solution to this exploitive dynamic, and offer a call to arms.

According to Marx and Engels, the source of industrial workers' misery is found in the inherently conflicted relationship between the *bourgeoisie*, who own all the means of producing goods (such as factories and industrial machinery), and the *proletariat*, who do not own the means of production and therefore can only earn a living by selling their labor in exchange for wages. On the one hand, the bourgeoisie and the proletariat have an interdependent relationship: factory owners need workers to run the equipment and staff the assembly line, while workers need the factory owners to supply them with jobs. On the other hand, the bourgeoisie and the proletariat do not have equal influence. Since they own the business and equipment, the bourgeoisie have the upper hand—especially because there were virtually no labor laws at the time to protect workers' rights.

This unequal power relationship meant that the bourgeoisie had the capacity to hire or fire workers, to set their wages, and determine their work tasks and hours. This often resulted in various forms alienation. Specifically, Marx described how industrial workers—who once were their own bosses on the family farm, where they undertook a wide variety of tasks on their own time frame—were now subjected to the efficiency-focused assembly line. The production process was broken into discrete acts that could be performed as quickly as possible with little training. To use a contemporary illustration, someone working for an automobile factory would not make an entire car but would be assigned to one task—such as screwing in a bolt or attaching a single piece of electrical wiring—which leads to *alienation from the act of working*. Work should be pleasurable, but the monotonous, repetitive nature of the assembly-line made work drudgery. The proletariat is also *alienated from the product of one's labor*. Prior to the Industrial Revolution, farmers and craftsmen created various goods through their own full efforts. They made shoes or furniture and felt a sense of pride in their final product, which reflected their skill. In contrast, in assembly-line production, factory workers do not see the finished product and thus do not feel the same attachment to the product. This is further linked to *alienation from workers' own potential*. Working long hours in a factory doing mind-numbing work, members of the proletariat have no time or energy to develop their skills, talents, and intellectual abilities. Finally, members of the proletariat are *alienated from their fellow workers*. Since the bourgeoisie want to keep labor costs down, they will, according to Marx, promote division and competition among workers. They can do this by actively encouraging the development of a large population of poor people so that they have a ready supply of workers from their "surplus army of labor." When this occurs, workers may be less willing to organize and rebel, since they know they can easily be replaced. The bourgeoisie may also encourage divisions along racial, ethnic, gender, or religious lines. This keeps workers focused on their differences rather than uniting and organizing together due to their common experiences of oppression.

In addition to these various forms of alienation, Marx described several ways in which the bourgeoisie can exploit their workers. First, the bourgeoisie, who are motivated to maximize profits, routinely required their workers to put in long hours. This, combined with child labor practices, meant *the destruction of family life* for factory employees. Parents and children alike left home in the early morning hours and returned late at night, with no time or energy to devote to one another. Second, workers were *dehumanized*, seen as little more than tools in the production process or appendages of the machinery. And, if a tool breaks, no one mourns; they simply replace it with another tool. So, too, is the injured worker tossed out without a second thought, without concern about how this will affect the well-being of his or her family. Third, the *bourgeoisie can steal the surplus value created by workers*. In other words, they can force workers to produce more goods in the same amount of time without increasing their pay; the extra product generated can be sold without the cost of labor, thereby increasing the profit. As an illustration, imagine that a textile factory worker is paid $10.00 an hour and is required to sew four shirts in that time frame, making the cost of labor for each shirt $2.50. Then one day, the factory owner announces that the hourly wage will remain the same, but now each worker must sew five shirts in an hour. The labor cost per shirt is subsequently $2.00, enabling the bourgeoisie to collect more profit since the labor costs are lower. Instead of compensating workers for the value created by their labor, the bourgeoisie steal the compensation that workers are rightfully owed.

The fourth form of exploitation occurs when the bourgeoisie promote *false consciousness*. This term refers to the intentional promotion of ideas that will keep the proletariat from rebelling. The primary manifestation of false consciousness is religion, according to Marx and Engels. In their view, religion is a set of ideas that teaches the poor and the oppressed that their lot in life is part of God's will. They will suffer in this life, but if they are faithful and submit to God's divine plan, they will be rewarded in the afterlife with eternal salvation. In contrast, if the proletariat rebel, this is tantamount to rebelling against God—which results in eternal damnation. Hence religion acts as a drug that temporarily eases the pain of workers' suffering, allowing workers to believe that their acceptance of this difficult life will eventually yield a great reward. As Marx put it, "Man makes religion, religion does not make man. . . . Religious suffering is, at one and the same time, the expression of real suffering and a protest against real suffering. Religion is the sigh of the oppressed creature, the heart of a heartless world, and the soul of soulless conditions. It is the opium of the people."[4]

So what was Marx's solution to this situation of exploitation? Marx maintained that workers had to abolish religion so that they could see the true nature of their oppressive situation. If they eliminated religion, the proletariat would no longer believe that their suffering was a divine mandate; they would see that it was a result of the exploitive system set up by the bourgeoisie to increase their own wealth and power. As this false consciousness disappears, a new *class consciousness* will develop. With this new consciousness, workers will recognize this human-made system can be changed but only through the organized and united efforts of the proletariat, who would rise up to violently overthrow the system, eliminating the bourgeoisie's control of the "means of production." Once the bourgeoisie were ousted, business would be regulated by the state to eliminate any exploitive dynamics. In other words, the revolutionary movement of the workers would result in socialism. Over time, as class consciousness deepened and workers recognized the importance of just relations and work that promotes human dignity for all, the state would no longer be needed to regulate industry and business; the state would simply wither away, leaving a classless form of society known as communism.

European Catholic Responses: Archbishop Ketteler and the Fribourg Union

Marx's analysis resonated with industrial workers throughout central Europe. It also caught the attention of some European Catholic leaders, who shared Marx's concerns about the exploitation and impoverishment of workers, but who could not accept his views on religion. These leaders called upon the Catholic Church to respond to these injustices; otherwise, the church risked becoming socially obsolete.

One of the most notable responses came from Wilhelm Emmanuel von Ketteler, archbishop of Mainz, Germany. By 1869, Archbishop Ketteler formally proposed solutions to the dilemmas of industrial capitalism, which he asked the assembly of German bishops to endorse. His solutions included paying a sustainable wage, abolishing child labor, establishing limitations on the length of the workday, proposing Sundays off, closing unhealthy or unsafe work spaces, separating men and women in the factories, and providing care for injured workers.

A series of violent events that erupted in the 1870s brought a new urgency to Archbishop Ketteler's proposals. Europe's sense of stability was rattled by the onset of the Franco-Prussian War and the Commune de Paris, a worker uprising. These events generated new interest in socialism among the working class. To counter this trend, clergy and laity decided to organize worker clubs within the church that would bring together the proletariat and the upper class for social events, prayer, and discussion of such political and economic questions. One of the first was the Parisian Society of Catholic Worker Circles (L'Oeuvre des Cercles Catholiques d'Ourvriers), which was formed in 1870. Within a few short years, there were several hundred clubs in France, with a total of 50,000 members. Catholic youth organizations, serving as feeder organizations for the worker circles, also flourished during this period. By the 1880s, the youth clubs had roughly 140,000 members.[5] Over time, these "circles" became an important place for Catholics to study and discuss pressing social issues.

Similar study groups were forming in Austria, Switzerland, and Italy. One of these groups was known as the Fribourg Union, which formed in October 1884 when four laypeople asked to meet with the bishop of Lausanne, Gaspard Mermillod, at his home in Fribourg, Switzerland. The group later expanded to include several dozen theologians and laypeople, who continued to meet annually, from 1885 to 1891, to discuss a Catholic response to capitalism and socialism.

From these meetings, five central themes emerged. The first theme is that *charity is an insufficient solution*. Bishop Mermillod emphasized that charity provided only temporary relief and that the problem of poverty could only be addressed through the establishment of social justice. The second theme dealt with the issue of *just wages*. The Fribourg Union argued that work must be viewed not merely as a commodity but as a personal act of value. Hence a just wage rewards the value of human labor, and it also must be sufficient to maintain a family living in modest conditions. The third theme deals with *the role of the state*. The Fribourg Union held that the state does not need to be involved in work environments unless workers are being oppressed. In these circumstances, the state must intervene to stop abuses and ensure the basic livelihood of workers. The fourth theme focuses on the issue of *private property*. The Fribourg Union sought a middle ground between capitalists, who believed in the inalienable right to private property, and socialists, who opposed it. The Fribourg Union participants argued that people did have the right to private property, but that it was a limited right that could not interfere with humans' right to subsist.

The fifth and final theme emphasizes a *corporately organized society*. This refers to a vision of the economy not organized according to one's relationship to the means of production but based on people's common social functions. Hence craft workers would form a natural set of ties and relationships, which could be seen as a corporation that looked after common interests of its members. This corporative approach was also applied to factories, where workers and factory owners were encouraged to see one another as a professional family, since they work collectively to produce goods. This "professional family" would then meet with similar groups in the same area to form a regional council, composed of both the bourgeoisie and the proletariat. The regional council would establish rules to govern their work spaces and would also form an endowment to provide loans, retirement benefits, and insurance for workers so that they could also benefit from the profits of the industrial economy. Members of the Fribourg Union argued that the proposed corporative model would be a suitable alternative to unbridled capitalism, to state intervention, and to socialism.[6]

The Fribourg Union members communicated their ideas to the Vatican. Pope Leo XIII subsequently met with Bishop Mermillod in 1888, and the pope asked for a written copy of all their work. These ideas influenced Leo's thinking as he drafted *Rerum Novarum*.

The Rise of Labor Unions in the United States

Catholic leaders in the United States were, like their European counterparts, also figuring out how they should respond to the growing injustices that workers faced in the new industrial economy. In the late 1870s, the US economy was seriously distressed. Unemployment rates hovered around 20 percent, and underemployment rates were as high as 40 percent. Wages declined and poverty rates increased. The Catholic Church's response was one of charity. Organizations such as the St. Vincent de Paul Society provided some relief to the poorest.[7] However, by the 1880s, many workers believed that charity was merely a short-term measure that did not address the underlying problem. What workers really needed was a transformed economic system.

As a result of this conviction, more American workers joined labor unions. One of the most prominent US labor unions of that era was the Knights of Labor, founded by Uriah Smith Stephens in 1869 in Philadelphia. This union started out fairly small, claiming only 28,000 members in 1880. However, it expanded rapidly once the Knights of Labor appointed Terence Powderly, an Irish American Catholic, as their Grand Master Workman. Powderly envisioned one large union that would encompass all workers, regardless of sex, ethnicity, or religion. He made the Knights of Labor more inclusive than other unions, welcoming skilled as well as unskilled laborers. As a result, it drew in railroad workers, coal miners, and steel and quarry workers. Moreover, the organization transformed itself, acting less as a fraternal organization and more as a union, negotiating contracts and occasionally organizing successful strikes. The Knights of Labor articulated a clear agenda, including the abolition of child labor, the establishment of an eight-hour workday, and a graduated income tax. By 1886, 20 percent of all workers—approximately 800,000 individuals—were members of this union.[8]

Yet not all Catholic leaders supported this burgeoning union. Some were concerned about the secretive nature of the organization. The Knights of Labor representatives argued that they had to keep membership confidential to protect workers from retribution and sanctions that might be inflicted if their bosses knew of their involvement. Catholic leaders, however, worried that this secrecy was similar to the Masonic tradition and customs, which they had officially condemned in 1734.[9] Moreover, some church leaders opposed the Knights of Labor's use of strikes, which sometimes resulted in violence. Other Catholics were opposed to the union for ideological and theological reasons: they feared that unions were working to establish Marxist-style socialism and that Catholic union members would be collaborating with non-Catholics and even atheists. On this basis, a few religious leaders, such as Archbishop James Roosevelt Bayley of Baltimore, publicly denounced the union; others, including Bishop James Healy of Portland, Maine, denied members the sacraments. Archbishop Eleazar Taschereau convinced the Vatican to condemn the Quebec Knights of Labor. Yet Taschereau wanted more: he appealed to the Vatican to make the condemnation universal.[10]

Other Catholic leaders endorsed the union. This was evident in 1886, when the US bishops voted on whether to condemn the US Knights of Labor: only two of the twelve bishops supported the proposal. Archbishop James Gibbons of Baltimore went a step further: while at the Vatican in 1887, he delivered a statement that defended the rights of workers, arguing that union participation was one of the few means they had to improve their conditions and preserve their humanity. The statement, signed by numerous US archbishops, asked Vatican officials to refrain from condemning the Knights of Labor. These archbishops stated that such a condemnation would have a negative effect, alienating the working class and depicting the Roman Catholic Church as unsympathetic to the plight of the poor. After significant deliberation, the Vatican agreed with Gibbons, declaring that the Knights of Labor were acceptable as long as they refrained from speaking about socialism and communism. This was a turning point, marking a new Catholic stand on labor issues.[11]

All these historical factors—the worsening conditions for industrial workers in Europe and North America, the growing influence of Marxism, and the expansion of labor unions and workers' circles—pushed the Roman Catholic Church to respond. Several personal experiences also led Pope Leo XIII to address labor issues. Earlier in his career, he had served as the papal nuncio in Brussels, where he was exposed to the effects of advanced industrial economies. He had traveled to London, Cologne, and Paris, where he encountered those who were suffering from unregulated capitalism. Then, after being appointed pope, he met with 10,000 laborers who traveled to Rome on pilgrimage, and he was moved by Cardinal Manning's support for striking dockworkers in Great Britain in 1889. These experiences instilled in Pope Leo XIII a deep conviction that the church should offer a theological and social response. Ultimately, the response came in the encyclical, *Rerum Novarum*.

Main Themes of *Rerum Novarum*

Rerum Novarum conveyed the key social views of Catholic Church, which can be summarized in six themes. The first theme focuses on the *dignity and rights of workers*. In the encyclical, Pope Leo reiterated that workers were suffering greatly within industrial capitalism. He denounced these conditions, stating, "It is neither just nor humane so to grind men down with excessive labor as to stupefy their minds and wear out their bodies."[12] Instead, the pope called upon employers to treat their workers with respect, refusing to view them as commodities in the production process. He also underscored employers' responsibilities: ensuring that their workers had sufficient rest and time off so that they were not overburdened beyond their capacity, and paid a wage that allowed workers to support their families at a basic level. A laborer, he argued, was entitled to a wage that "will enable him, housed, clothed, and secure, to live a life without hardship."[13] In return, workers had an obligation to perform their labor conscientiously. They must not engage in sabotage or use violence in the workplace. The pope emphasized that while there are inequalities in people's talents and abilities, all people have equal dignity in the eyes of God.

The second theme deals with the *rights and duties of property owner-ship*. Pope Leo clearly rejected the socialist stance, stating that people have the right to private property. This includes workers, who would benefit from owning property, since it would add to their dignity and alleviate their wage dependency. However, the right to property must always be viewed within the context of the common good, to which all people—rich and poor—should contribute. The encyclical stated, "Whoever has received from the divine bounty a large share of temporal blessings has received them for the purpose of using them for the perfecting of his own nature, and, at the same time, that he may employ them, as the steward of God's providence, for the benefit of others."[14]

Third, Pope Leo affirmed *workers' right to organize*. He maintained that it was acceptable, even commendable, for workers to join unions to advance their interests. He also argued that the state should protect this right of association.

Fourth, the encyclical calls for *collaboration rather than class struggle*. On this point, the pope emphasized that Marx was wrong: class conflict is not inevitable. In fact, he argued that the bourgeoisie and the working class have an interdependent set of interests: "Each needs the other: capital cannot do without labor, nor labor without capital. Mutual agreement results in the beauty of good order, while perpetual conflict necessarily produces confusion and savage barbarity."[15] Of course, such harmony only occurs if employers treat their workers fairly and if workers fulfill their duties without malice or hostility. Under these circumstances, Pope Leo XII believed that it is possible for these classes to peacefully coexist.

The fifth theme deals with *the role of the state* in class struggles. Because the balance of power between capitalists and laborers is not equitable, it is necessary for the state to ensure the well-being of all. The encyclical states, "And the more that is done for the benefit of the working classes by the general laws of the country, the less need will there be to seek special means to relieve them."[16] The government should provide public aid to families in extreme poverty and protect the right of workers to form unions. Governments should only intervene, however, when a particular class is threatened or harmed.

The sixth theme deals with *the role of the church* in class struggles. This was largely a reaction to the anticlerical sentiments of the time, following the French Revolution. Leo emphasized that contemporary social issues have a moral dimension, to which the church must respond. Moreover, he stated that the Catholic Church's primary role is to educate people to act fairly and justly. In that role, the church can be a force for reconciliation between workers and their employers. Additionally, the church should improve the plight of the poor through "works of mercy" and religious societies that address the needs of the suffering.[17]

The publication of *Rerum Novarum* was important for several reasons. First, it established that the church could no longer operate with a medieval, precapitalist mentality. Second, it marked the public emergence of a Catholic social conscience. Third and most significant, the encyclical mandated that workers must be treated with dignity. Leo XIII insisted that the poor should not be demeaned or judged harshly, since most lived in intolerable conditions undeservedly. The pope also noted that God's favor is inclined toward the poor, and therefore those who support the poor in attitude and action are behaving in a godly manner.

Yet the encyclical was by no means a radical statement. *Rerum Novarum* called for a moderate path between laissez-faire capitalism and socialism. It warned against the excesses and exploitive potential of capitalism as well as the oppressive dangers of communism. Additionally, the pope underscored the importance of promoting and preserving harmony in the social order. The poor were to stand up against injustice, but they must refrain from violence. They could form unions but not strike. Therefore, even though this was a major turnabout from the Catholic Church's earlier position that endorsed social inequality as a reflection of God's will, it was a carefully stated middle ground. It did not call for a radical reconstruction of the social order.

Quadragesimo Anno ("On Reconstruction of the Social Order")

Over the next decades, *Rerum Novarum* was the foundation for Catholic labor views. Yet the twentieth century yielded new events, forcing the church to revisit the matter. Among the most influential events of this period were the Russian Revolution of 1917 and the subsequent formation of the Soviet Union. Suddenly, the concerns about socialist states were not just a possibility but a reality. In addition, the world was plunged into the Great Depression, which led to global economic turmoil. And capitalism was stronger than ever, expanding into new parts of the world. In some regions, such as Austria and Italy, political leaders proclaimed that they were following the corporative vision for society that Pope Leo XIII had articulated. That corporatist plan, unfortunately, was used to justify a fascist state. Hence Pope Pius XI felt that a new encyclical was needed to clarify a few points that were open to misinterpretation. He released *Quadragesimo Anno* in 1931, forty years after the publication of *Rerum Novarum*.

There are four central themes in *Quadragesimo Anno*. The first two deal with the concepts of *social justice* and *social charity*. "Social justice" was a term that Pius XI used frequently. The adjective "social" was intended to distinguish the term from legal justice or individual-level justice. The main premise is that all people deserve to be treated fairly, to receive what they are rightly due, and to have access to basic necessities. Intrinsically linked to this is the concept of social charity. Unlike individual-level charity, such as giving to the poor, social charity emphasizes institutional dimensions that promote justice and harmonious social relations. As Marvin Krier Mich put it, "Social charity emphasizes a more positive orientation of benevolence, of wishing another well, not simply that they receive their 'due.' The pope's motivation in coining the phrase 'social charity' was to keep love, *caritas*, as the central moral virtue in Catholic social teaching, but not let it be reduced to almsgiving."[18]

The third theme of *Quadragesimo Anno* is the principle of *subsidiarity*. Pius XI emphasized the common good, particularly in societies that were losing midlevel organizations, leaving a polarized situation in which individuals and the state coexist, with little in between. Such conditions were contributing to growing state power and increasingly individualistic mentalities. Pius XI wished to promote the establishment of intermediary groups—such as vocational organizations, civic groups, and employer-employee councils—that could foster a community-oriented mind-set. These groups would minimize the need for state intervention in political and economic matters, which he felt were best addressed at the local level.[19]

The final theme of this encyclical is *owner-worker councils*. Building from the principle of subsidiarity, Pius XI called for the creation of autonomous, self-governing employer-worker councils that would have the power to set wages and regulate workplace conditions. Pius XI believed that this would promote harmonious class relations and minimize hostility.[20]

Many labor groups considered this last proposal unrealistic, since it did not acknowledge the power inequalities that exist between capitalists and their employees. The pope also proposed that workers should be able to purchase shares in the company, but, again, this appeared naive to some workers, who found this possibility unlikely, since minimum-wage workers could barely support their families. Few would have the resources to buy company stock. Yet some Catholic observers maintained that, properly implemented, this idea of employer-employee councils could effectively empower workers.[21]

Lived Religion and Labor Movements

The Catholic Worker Movement

Leo XIII and Pius XI had specific proposals for dealing with labor challenges. But how did laypeople respond to these social teachings? How did Catholics address the suffering caused by the burgeoning industrial economy? Among US Catholics, there have been diverse responses to these two encyclicals. On the one hand, some individuals have interpreted them conservatively, arguing that the popes were advocating a free-market system with minimal state intervention.[22] On the other hand, some US Catholics took this as an indication that they should strongly support labor movements. In the latter camp was Dorothy Day, who—along with Peter Maurin—formed the Catholic Worker movement in 1933.

BACKGROUND

Peter Maurin and Dorothy Day came from quite different backgrounds. Maurin was born in 1877 to a farming family in southern France. He was the oldest of twenty-two children and left home at age sixteen to join the Christian Brothers, a Catholic teaching order. After nine years, he left the order to devote himself to the work of Le Sillon (The Furrow)—a faith-based organization that supported unions and cooperatives and opposed militarism and nationalism. When the organization shed its religious roots to pursue secular politics, Maurin emigrated to Canada, where he homesteaded in Saskatchewan for a couple years and then took a variety of jobs, from laying railroad tracks to working in steel mills and coal mines. He eventually ended up working as a handyman at a Catholic boys' camp in upstate New York, where he received room and board, sleeping in the barn with the horses, as well as access to the chaplain's library.[23] During this time, Maurin had virtually no possessions and very little money. This experience led him to conclude that a life of material simplicity was liberating because it afforded him the freedom to pursue other endeavors and a life of prayer and study.

During these itinerant years, Maurin read widely and was referred to by some as the "hobo-philosopher."[24] He had numerous influences, including Peter Kropotkin's anarchism, Emmanuel Mounier's personalism, Leon Bloy's antibourgeoisie philosophy, Saint Francis of Assisi's emphasis on simplicity and voluntary poverty, and Hilaire Belloc and Eric Gill's distributist philosophy.[25] Maurin synthesized these ideas into a vision of how Catholic ideals could be manifested in social and personal life. Marc Ellis describes this vision:

> To an urban-industrial society in the midst of depression, Maurin proposed embracing a village economy, where crafts, farming, and a personal way of life could be established. . . . [I]t is centered in a simplicity that

Maurin called voluntary poverty. . . . Maurin's vision of community was neither evolutionary nor progressive, and the appetite of modernity in pursuit of power held no allure for him. Instead, Maurin's vision was to live in harmony with others, to share what manual and intellectual labor produced, to be silent and to worship in community. Maurin's sense of commitment was also a dissent. He did not share the hopes of secular radicals, for they were seeking to increase and distribute the material abundance of industrial life to a humanity freed from the spiritual. The basis of Maurin's commitment, in contrast, was renunciation and sacrifice exemplified in the life and crucifixion of Jesus. In this life of spirit and sacrifice Maurin saw the only possibility of recapturing the integrity of the person and bringing about authentic social reform.[26]

Maurin frequently traveled to New York City to use the library and to preach his views in Union Square. That is where he met George Schuster of *Commonweal* magazine, a Catholic publication, who told him that he must meet Dorothy Day since they held such similar ideas. Schuster gave him Day's address and told him to get in touch with her.

Dorothy Day was born in Brooklyn Heights in 1897, making her twenty years younger than her Catholic Worker cofounder. Her family was officially Episcopalian, but her journalist father was a religious skeptic. When Day was a young child, they moved from New York City to the San Francisco area, where her father had accepted a position with a newspaper. However, when the earthquake of 1906 struck, the newspaper went out of business. The family then moved to Chicago, where Dorothy completed high school and won a scholarship in 1914 to the University of Illinois at Urbana. In the course of her studies there, she read about labor history. She was indignant at workers' suffering and admired those who had formed unions and pushed for an eight-hour workday. As a result of these convictions, she joined the Socialist Party but found the meetings boring. Within a couple years, Day left the university, moved to New York, and looked for employment as a reporter. After months of being told that urban reporting was not an appropriate job for a woman, Day finally landed a position at *The Call*, a New York socialist paper. She quickly became involved in the city's radical political circles. As she recalled, "There was much to do—meetings to attend to protest against labor, capital, the high cost of living, war-profiteering, entering the war, not entering the war, conscription, anti-conscription to fight against unions. Food riots came . . . and interviews galore."[27] One of those interviews was with Leon Trotsky, a key founder of the Soviet state, who was living in exile in New York. Eventually, Day took another reporter position with the leftist magazine *The Masses*. She also got involved in the Anti-Conscription League and the suffrage movement; it was her involvement in the women's movement that led to her first arrest and experience in jail. In short, Day was deeply involved in secular radical politics.

In other ways, too, Dorothy Day was not a likely candidate to convert to Catholicism.[28] In her twenties, she had a relationship that resulted in an unwanted pregnancy and an abortion. She also had a short-lived marriage that ended in divorce. Then she spent four years in a common-law relationship with Forster Batterham, a biologist with a love of nature and radical politics. He was opposed to institutions such as religion, marriage, and family. Though he was deeply in love with and committed to Day, he was adamant that their relationship "was a comradeship rather than a marriage."[29]

Given her radical politics and her nontraditional lifestyle, how did Day become a Catholic? During these years with Batterham, Day was increasingly drawn to prayer and the church. She began attending Sunday morning Mass. She also longed for a child but she was convinced that the abortion several years earlier had left her infertile. In June 1925, she was elated to discover that she was pregnant. In her biography, *The Long Loneliness*, she wrote:

> For a long time I thought that I could not bear a child, and the longing in my heart for a baby was growing. My home, I felt, was not a home without one. The simple joys of the kitchen and garden brought sadness with them because I felt myself unfruitful, barren. No matter how much one was loved or one loved, that love was lonely without a child. It was incomplete.[30]

To Day, the pregnancy was a miracle, the fulfillment of her most sincere desire. When her daughter, Tamar, was born in March 1926, Day's conversion process was irreversible. She wrote:

No human creature could receive or contain so vast a flood of love and joy as I often felt after the birth of my child. With this came the need to worship, to adore. . . . I had heard many say that they wanted to worship God in their own way and did not need a Church in which to praise Him, nor a body of people with whom to associate themselves. But I did not agree to this. My whole experience as a radical, my whole makeup, led me to want to associate with others, with the masses, in loving and praising God. Without even looking into the claims of the Catholic Church, I was willing to admit that for me she was the one true Church. She had come down through the centuries since the time of Peter, and far from being dead, she claimed and held the allegiance of the masses of people in all the cities where I had lived. They poured in and out of her doors on Sundays and holy days.[31]

As Day prepared to baptize her daughter in the Catholic Church and become a Catholic herself, her partner grew increasingly opposed to her religious orientation. While Day hoped he would develop some sympathy and eventually marry her, he was resolute that he would do no such thing. Eventually, these differences led to the demise of their relationship. Day was left to raise Tamar by herself.

In the subsequent years, Day synthesized her religious beliefs and her political convictions. She was still unequivocally committed to social justice, to transforming the political and economic system in the United States, and to writing. Yet she found it difficult, since radicals were suspicious of her religiosity and many Catholics advocated little more than charity. She searched for a way to cultivate a Catholic commitment to social justice. She found it when Peter Maurin arrived at her home and proposed that they start a movement together. Quoting Lenin, he told Day, "There is no revolution without a theory of revolution." If they wanted a Catholic-based revolution, they needed a newspaper that would publicize Catholic Social Thought and propose ways to implement these teachings in light of the Depression and workers' suffering. He suggested that Day, with her writing experience, could serve as the editor of this paper. Day was captivated by the idea and quickly transformed her kitchen into an editorial office. Maurin suggested that they call the paper the *Catholic Radical.* Day argued that the paper's title should reflect their targeted audience. Mimicking the communist *Daily Worker*, Day insisted that they call their publication the *Catholic Worker*. They decided to sell the paper for a penny a copy to ensure that it was affordable to all. On May 1, 1933, they launched the paper, selling it to the thousands of workers and radicals who gathered in Union Square in New York City to celebrate Labor Day.[32] The front-page editorial read:

> For those who are sitting on park benches in the warm spring sunlight.
> For those who are huddling in shelters trying to escape the rain.
> For those who are walking the streets in the all but futile search for work.
> For those who think that there is no hope for the future, no recognition of their plight—this little paper is addressed.
> It is printed to call their attention to the fact that the Catholic Church has a social program—to let them know that there are men of God who are working not only for their spiritual, but for their material welfare.
> filling a need
> It's time there was a Catholic paper printed for the unemployed.
> The fundamental aim of most radical sheets is the conversion of its readers to radicalism and atheism.
> Is it not possible to be radical and not atheist?
> Is it not possible to protest, to expose, to complain, to point out abuses and demand reforms without desiring the overthrow of religion?
> In an attempt to popularize and make known the encyclicals of the Popes in regard to social justice and the program put forth by the Church for the "reconstruction of the social order," this news sheet, *The Catholic Worker*, is started.[33]

The rest of the paper addressed concerns that would be at the center of the Catholic Worker struggle in years to come: child labor, racism, strikes, and the need for direct action.[34]

In one of the earliest editions of the paper, Day and Maurin announced the three purposes of the Catholic Worker movement. The first was discussion and clarification of thought regarding Catholic views on various social issues. This would happen through roundtable discussion and through articles in the Catholic Worker paper. The second aim was to establish houses of hospitality where the destitute and homeless could be fed and given shelter. Maurin pointed out that a fifth-century Church Council had ordered bishops to set up such houses of hospitality in each parish. These were open to the poor, orphans, the elderly, and immigrants; these houses fulfilled Christ's teaching in which he explained, "For I was hungry and you gave me something to eat, I was thirsty and you gave me something to drink, I was a stranger and you invited me in, I needed clothes and you clothed me, I was sick and you looked after me, I was in prison and you came to visit me. . . . Truly I tell you, whatever you did for one of the least of these brothers of mine, you did for me."[35] The third aim was what Maurin called the "green revolution": moving to rural areas to establish farming communes that would be economically self-sufficient and provide places for work and study.[36]

DIALOGUE ON LABOR ISSUES

These ideals quickly materialized. The paper's circulation was growing, with 150,000 copies distributed each month by 1936.[37] Within the pages of the paper, Day and other Catholic Workers debated the ideas about labor that Leo VIII and Pius XI had articulated. The following excerpt illustrates this dialogue, revealing that laypeople did not always readily accept the encyclical positions. They often pushed for stronger stances and more direct forms of action. As Day wrote in 1946:

> In the great clean shining factories, with good lights and air and the most sanitary conditions, an eight-hour day, five-day week, with the worker chained to the belt, to the machine, there is no opportunity for sinning as the outsider thinks of sin. No, it is far more subtle than that, it is submitting oneself to a process which degrades, dehumanizes. To be an efficient factory worker, one must become a *hand*, and the more efficient one is, the less one thinks. Take typewriting, for instance, as an example we all know—or driving a car, or a sewing machine. These machines may be considered good tools, an extension of the hand of man. We are not chained to them as to a belt, but even so, we all know that as soon as one starts to think of what one is doing, we slip and make mistakes. One is not supposed to think. to think is dangerous at a machine. One is liable to lose a finger or a hand, and then go on the scrap heap and spend the rest of one's life fighting for compensation for one's own carelessness, as the factory owners say, for not using the safety devices invented and so

plentiful, for the benefit of the workers. The existence of those same safety devices is an example of the truth of what I write.

Supernatural selfishness *is* in order here, and a hatred of such work that degrades and dehumanizes. We must hate evil. I am not arguing for class war, for resistance at the point of machine guns, for barricades (which go, by the way, with the city streets). There must be some probability of success; that is one of the conditions for a just war. But I am in favor of the nonviolent techniques of the strike, the withdrawal of labor, violence will be inflicted, but let it not be on the part of the worker. . . . One must lay down one's life for one's brothers, they say, we must sacrifice even to the shedding of blood. Of course they do not stop there. But they do regard the shedding of one's blood as so essential that I have seen the workers goading the police to bring about this violence so satisfying to man, who has not been taught the use of his spiritual weapons so that he may take heaven by violence, and make it more possible to praise and worship God here and now thus beginning one's heaven on earth to what extent it is possible.

The basic ideal of family life is to "multiply the number of the elect." Let this be brought home to the working classes, for they in particular are equal to the acts of generosity, devotion and self denial which such an ideal demands.

What about wages, housing, the mother working, the father withdrawn for long hours from the home, so that under our present civilization a child might as well not have a father. And are not the clergy "laying burdens too heavy for them to bear," on the shoulders of the workers, and themselves not willing to lighten them by lifting a finger, to change the conditions of their life. . . . If the workers are lost to the church, who will be held responsible?[38]

ACTION IN SUPPORT OF LABOR

Day argued that religious declarations in support of workers were not enough. *Action* must be taken to improve workers' lives and restore their dignity. She put her beliefs into action in 1949, when a small union of grave diggers went on strike against the Archdiocese of New York. Cardinal Spellman took a harsh position: he called the grave diggers communists, refused to meet or speak with them, and used seminarians to break the strike. The grave diggers swore that they were not communists but simply laborers who were not receiving a fair wage for their labor. Dorothy Day took the side of the grave diggers, joining their picket outside the cardinal's office.

Although Day had sided with the laborers, she reached out to Cardinal Spellman. She had always been deferential and respectful to the cardinal, who was well known for his anticommunist views and his strict insistence on obedience to church authorities. Day asked the cardinal to meet with the grave diggers. She implored him to respond compassionately, seeing them not as communists but as men who desired dignity and a livable wage. The cardinal did not respond, but his staff member Monsignor Edward Gaffney did. He called Day to his office and ordered her to change the name of the movement, which sounded too communist, or stop publishing the paper. She told Monsignor Gaffney that she would have to discuss it with her co-editors, who promptly rejected the idea. Although she reaffirmed her own obedience to the bishop, she wrote, "We are all ready to receive respectfully and give practical heed and application to all scientific, scholarly criticism and correction of spiritual errors. . . . [W]e cannot simply cease the publication of a review which has been built up, with its worldwide circulation of 63,000."[39] She also reminded the church leaders that the Vatican's newspaper had stated that there are inherent problems in both the American and Soviet economies and thus Catholics are not innately capitalists. Eventually, the archbishop dropped his order to change the movement's name. Dorothy Day and her colleagues had not backed off their commitment to workers. In fact, Day continued to address these issues throughout her life.

HOUSES OF HOSPITALITY

Day, Maurin, and the growing number of Catholic Worker activists supported the struggle for a new economic order, but it was clear that the daily needs of workers could not be ignored. Day implored people to perform what Pope Leo XIII called the "works of mercy." In an essay in the *Catholic Worker*, she wrote:

> It is no use turning people away to an agency, to the city or the state, or the Catholic Charities. It is you yourself who must perform the works of mercy. Often you can only give the price of a meal, or a bed on the Bowery. Often you can only hope that it will be spent for that. Often you can

literally take off a garment if it only be a scarf and warm some shivering brother . . . to combat the growing dependency on the part of the State to take the job which our Lord Himself gave us to do.[40]

After she wrote about her commitment to "works of mercy," a number of people approached Day, expressing their need for food and shelter. Within a few months, she had an apartment with space for ten women, followed by other housing for men. By 1936, the demand was so great that the Catholic Worker moved into two buildings on Mott Street in New York's Chinatown. By 1937, the Catholic Worker house was feeding 400 people daily, and the number doubled in the following year.[41] By 1941, there were 41 houses of hospitality throughout the United States.[42] Over the decades, there would be more than 200 houses of hospitality in North America, Europe, Australia, and New Zealand.

Yet these houses of hospitality were about more than offering food and shelter to the destitute. These works of mercy were also about treating people with dignity, as the papal encyclicals called for, and about social charity—treating people with love, *caritas*. Although Day agreed with Pope Pius that the state should intervene when a situation is dire, she believed that laypeople ought to take responsibility to care for those in need. She felt that individuals would be more empathetic and nurturing than the state. One story particularly illustrates this. Dorothy Day recounted how a social worker had asked her what the New York Catholic Worker's caseload was. Day stated that the people they served were guests, not "cases." When the same social worker asked how long individuals were permitted to stay, Day replied, "Since there are no jobs, we let them stay forever. They live with us, they die with us and we give them a Christian burial. We pray for them after they are dead. Once they are taken in, they become members of our family. Or rather they were always members of our family. They are our brothers and sisters in Christ."[43]

Naturally, Day never intended for such social charity to be an end in itself. It was always seen as a necessary but insufficient response to the exploitive nature of industrial capitalism. Such works of mercy responded to immediate needs, but social action would create the social justice of which Pope Pius XI spoke. Hence, action on behalf of workers' rights, such as strikes and pickets (social justice), was the essential counterpart to houses of hospitality (social charity). One Catholic Worker described it in the following way:

> We use the analogy of a truck out of control. The driver is not in the seat, the emergency brake is off, and the truck is going down a hill, rolling over people. There are dead and wounded behind the truck. The dead need to be buried, a work of mercy. The wounded need to be tended to, a work of mercy. But the truck keeps rolling over people. Who is going to get in the truck and hit the brake? . . . So we need people behind the truck to tend to the wounded and bury the dead and we need people to maybe get in front of the truck or try to jump inside. I think that's the balance of what the Catholic Worker . . . is trying to do—to recognize that we've got this . . . violent apparatus, and the brake is off and the driver is out and we have a responsibility to respond to that as best we can.[44]

WITHDRAWING FROM CAPITALISM: FARMING COMMUNES

Another way that Catholic Workers lived their religious convictions was to withdraw from the capitalist system by returning to the land to engage in subsistence farming. These farming communes, sometimes referred to as "agronomic universities," were Maurin's way of encouraging Christian communalism—his envisioned alternative to the exploitive industrial economy.[45] This would provide employment but also a chance to live in harmony with the land and with one another, thereby creating an example of a "sustainable human society."[46]

The first experiment with this so-called green revolution took place on Staten Island. The second, more ambitious farming commune was near Eaton, Pennsylvania. Initially full of hope, the farm members quickly became embroiled in conflicts. There were tensions over who would complete the daily chores and maintenance tasks, with many people preferring to talk about farming rather than actually doing it. At one point, there was a physical altercation over an egg that one resident had set aside for himself and another had taken. These types of arguments ultimately led to the failure of the farms. Day took some consolation from the fact that the farming experiment had a few benefits. She wrote, "We might not have established a model community but many a family got a vacation, many a sick person was nursed back to health, crowds of slum children had the run of the woods and fields for weeks, and groups of students spent happy hours discussing the green revolution. . . . We aimed high, too high. But at least we were able, as Peter said, to 'arouse the conscience.'"[47]

The United Farm Workers Movement

Several decades after Day and Maurin launched the Catholic Worker, another labor movement was under way. This one was fighting for the rights of predominantly Mexican American farmworkers in California. The movement was cofounded by César Chávez and Dolores Huerta, both devout Catholics who came from farmworker communities.

BACKGROUND

Chávez was born in 1927 near Yuma, Arizona, where his family had a small farm. They lost their land during the Depression, forcing them into a life as migrant workers. Following the crops for work, Chávez changed schools frequently; he attended thirty-seven different schools by the time he finished eighth grade. At that time, his father had been injured in an accident and was unable to work. Chávez decided to forgo high school, instead working in the fields to help support his family. At age nineteen, he joined the navy, serving two years before returning to the San Jose area to marry, begin a family, and work. It was there that he met Father Donald McDonnell, who taught Chávez about the Catholic Church's views on labor. Chávez recalled:

> He told me about social justice and the Church's stand on labor and reading from the encyclicals of Pope Leo XIII, in which he upheld labor unions. I would do anything to get the Father to tell me more about labor history. I began going to the Bracero camps with him to help with the Mass, to the city jail with him to talk to the prisoners, anything to be with him.[48]

Father McDonnell quickly recognized Chávez's leadership potential. In 1952, McDonnell recommended him to Fred Ross, who—along with Dolores Huerta—was setting up a local chapter of the Community Service Organization (CSO). Ross was trained in Saul Alinsky's method of community organizing, which includes listening to the local population to determine its needs, identifying grassroots leaders and training them, conducting research on injustices, implementing campaigns that galvanize support, and evaluating and adapting movement strategies until the community's goals are accomplished.[49] Chávez was hired by the CSO and worked with the organization for a decade, focusing on voter registration campaigns, citizenship classes, combating discrimination in education and employment, and exposing police brutality.[50]

The other founder of the United Farm Workers was Dolores Huerta, who was born in 1930 in a small mining town in northern New Mexico. Her parents divorced when she was three, and her mother moved with her children to the farming community of Stockton, California. Huerta graduated from high school, got married, had two children, and subsequently went through a divorce. After working several unfulfilling jobs, she went to Stockton College, earning a teaching degree. She was employed as an elementary school teacher for a while but found that many of her students, who were children of migrant farm laborers, did not have the most basic necessities. She decided to devote herself to improving their living conditions by working with the CSO.[51] It is there that she met Chávez.

Chávez and Huerta both wanted to focus their organizing efforts on farmworkers. But, by the early 1960s, they found that the CSO's work was taking on an increasingly middle-class character. Chávez reflected:

> For more than ten years I worked for the CSO. As the organization grew, we found ourselves meeting in fancier and fancier hotels and holding expensive conventions. Doctors, lawyers and politicians began joining. They would get elected to some office in the organization and then, for all practical purposes, leave. Intent on using the organization for their own prestige purposes, these "leaders," many of them, lacked the urgency we had to have. When I became general director I began to press for a program to organize farm workers into a union, an idea most of the leadership opposed. . . . In March of '62 I resigned and came to Delano to begin organizing the Valley on my own.[52]

Chávez and Huerta immediately began building a farmworker organization using the skills they developed through the CSO. Although they left behind secure jobs, they believed this task was essential, since farmworkers were one of the most exploited groups in the country. Because US labor laws intentionally excluded them, farmworkers had no legal right to a federal minimum wage and no prohibition on child labor. Growers were not required to comply with government mandates for safe working conditions.

Many labor groups were skeptical about Chávez and Huerta's prospects, since other unions, with significantly more resources, had tried to organize farmworkers without any success.[53] Chávez himself was fully aware of the significant obstacles they faced. He observed, "The power of the growers was backed by the political power of the police, the courts, the state and the federal laws and by the financial power of the big corporations, the banks and utilities."[54] Nonetheless, they scheduled hundreds of house meetings, where farmworkers spoke about their concerns. Through these meetings, they eventually built the National Farm Workers Association.

UFW ACTIONS: STRIKES, PILGRIMAGES, FASTING, AND BOYCOTTS

This new organization had an opportunity to take action in September 1965, when it was asked to join a strike against table grape growers, started by the mostly Filipino Agricultural Workers Organizing Committee (AWOC). Although Chávez and Huerta were not convinced that their organization was ready, they let the workers decide. The membership voted to join the strike. Chávez then asked for a second vote requiring all participants to commit to nonviolent forms of struggle. That vote passed, too. "La Huelga" (the strike) was under way. Shortly thereafter, AWOC and the National Farm Workers Association merged to form the United Farm Workers (UFW).

To support the strikes and increase pressure on the growers, Chávez and Huerta turned to other forms of action. They organized pickets at the fields, carrying banners with the image of the Virgin of Guadalupe, an important symbol within Mexican American Catholicism. But the growers, led by the DiGiorgio Corporation, countered by filing a court order to restrict the pickets. The strikers grew discouraged, believing that the growers had the upper hand. Chávez held a meeting to discuss the UFW's next move, but no one had suggestions. He described what happened next:

A couple hours later, three ladies came to see me. . . . [T]hey said, "We don't understand this business of the court order. Does it mean that if we go picket and break the injunctions, we'll go to jail?" "Well, it means that you go to jail and we'll be fined," I said. "What would happen if we met across the streets from the DiGiorgio gates, not to picket, not to demonstrate, but to have a prayer, maybe a Mass?" they asked. "Do you think the judge would have us arrested?" . . . "You just gave me an idea!" I said, and I was away and running.

I got Richard and had him take my old station wagon and build a little chapel on it. It was like a shrine with a picture of Our Lady of Guadalupe, some candles, and some flowers. We worked on it until about 2:00 in the morning. Then we parked it across from the DiGiorgio gates where we started a vigil that lasted two months. People were there day and night. . . . People came by the hundreds. . . .

[One day] something very dramatic happened. When the trucks brought the workers from the fields to eat at the company mess hall, about eight women decided to come to where we had the vigil instead of going into the mess hall. The supervisors got the trucks in the way to keep them from coming, but the women went way out through the vines and wouldn't be stopped. They knelt down and prayed and then went back. That was the beginning. The same evening about fifty women came. The next evening, about half the camp was out, and from then on, every single day, they were out there. Every day we had Mass, held a meeting, sang spirituals, and got them to sign [union] authorization cards. Those meetings were responsible in large part for keeping the spirit up of our people inside the camp and helping our organization for the coming battle. It was a beautiful demonstration of the power of nonviolence.[55]

Such religious rituals were important because the strike was a long struggle, filled with harsh and repressive actions on the growers' part. One year into the strike, the Schenley Company sprayed some of the picketers from the air with a toxic pesticide. Although the growers claimed it was accidental, Chávez and Huerta decided to respond to this horrific act. They chose a *peregrinacio*, or pilgrimage, which was a familiar religious custom for Mexican American Catholics. They started the pilgrimage in Delano, the heart of the farming region, and ended it in Sacramento, the state capital. It culminated on Easter Sunday, as a crowd of 8,000 supporters greeted the marchers.[56] The pilgrimage drew national attention to the farmworkers' plight and garnered support for their cause.

While events like the pilgrimage marked high points in the UFW's morale, there were also low points when farmworkers were harassed by the police and the growers' security forces. During those times, some in the movement talked about abandoning nonviolence, thinking they might have more success if they resorted to violence. Chávez was deeply concerned about this, and thus he embarked on a penitential fast on February 15, 1968. For the next twenty-five days, he consumed nothing but water, calling upon union activists to remain committed to nonviolence. Each evening, a local priest would celebrate a liturgy, and UFW members would visit with Chávez. Senator Robert Kennedy visited on the last day of the fast, showing his support for the movement. Some people called the fast a publicity stunt, but Chávez noted its religious meaning: "The fast is a very personal and spiritual thing, and it is not done out of recklessness. It's not done out of a desire to destroy myself but is done out of a deep conviction that we can communicate to people, either those who are against us or for us, faster and more effectively, spiritually, than we can in any other way."[57]

The final tactic that the UFW employed was an international boycott of table grapes—one of the main crops and sources of profit for the California growers. Yet boycotts are only effective if a sizable number of people participate. Toward that end, the UFW sent volunteers to cities throughout the United States and Canada.[58] These volunteers worked with local churches, student groups, and labor and progressive organizations, who mobilized their members to boycott table grapes and the large grocery chains that marketed them. Huerta described the strategy:

> For several months, we had picket lines at about 25 to 30 stores and turned thousands of customers away. A lot of the managers had come up through the unions and were very sympathetic to us. In response to consumer pressure, the store managers began to complain to their division heads, and soon they took the grapes out of all their stores, 430 of them.[59]

Chávez also sought support from other Catholic groups for the strike and boycott. In the spring of 1966, he visited the Catholic

Worker house in New York and met with Dorothy Day. They had an instant affinity, since they each saw their work as grounded in religious faith, and both were deeply committed to nonviolence. As a result of this connection, Day traveled to California in 1969 to take part in a picket outside the grape fields. She returned for additional visits in subsequent years. During her last visit, Day was arrested for picketing; she spent two weeks in jail with other UFW activists. Throughout this period, she published articles in the *Catholic Worker* to help build support for the farmworkers. She described how children worked long hours in the fields and how one striker tried collecting pay that was due to him, only to be threatened by the grower with a rifle. She called upon readers to "remember these things, you whose mouth waters for table grapes. Remember the boycott and help the strikers. . . . It is the first breakthrough to achieve some measure of Justice for these poorest and most beloved of God's children."[60]

Eventually, the UFW took a more targeted approach to the boycott, concentrating its organizing efforts on ten cities that constituted the largest grape markets. When the growers tried to make up for their losses by increasing their shipments to European markets, the UFW was prepared, with volunteers who organized boycotts in England, Sweden, Finland, Denmark, Norway, and the Netherlands. Entire shipments of grapes were left on docks to rot.[61] Simultaneously, Dolores Huerta appealed to the Central Labor Council, the meatcutters union, and the seafarers union to totally blockade California grapes.

These efforts paid off. The boycotts significantly impacted the growers' profit margin, compelling twenty-six growers to sit down at the negotiating table. Huerta served as the UFW's first contract negotiator, earning a reputation as persistent and determined. In July 1970, the growers recognized the union and signed collective bargaining contracts.[62] By 1973, UFW membership reached 60,000. In 1975, California passed the Agriculture Labor Relations Act.[63] The UFW would continue organizing over the next decades, tackling a variety of issues, including the use of pesticides that adversely affect the health of farmworkers. Although it experienced setbacks along the way, the movement empowered a group of laborers, achieved union recognition, and established important legislative policies to protect farmworkers.

Conclusion

Lived religion is often about experimentation, a process of trial and error, as laypeople try different ways to put their convictions into action. In both the Catholic Worker and the United Farm Workers movements, there were important gains as well as setbacks. The Catholic Worker farm communes, for example, were largely a failure, and the UFW struggled to keep the union's membership and power intact over subsequent decades.[64] Nonetheless, both these movements made important contributions.

One of the most significant contributions of the Catholic Worker movement was that it offered a visible example of laypeople generating their own solutions to social ills. Day did not sit passively, expecting that the words of the encyclicals were enough to bring about change. In fact, she was disappointed that the Catholic Church leadership did not ask more of the laity. Day wrote, "So little is expected of laypeople, the moral theology we are taught is to get us into heaven with scorched behinds. What kind of an unwilling, ungenerous love of God is this?"[65] In another moment, she described reporting on a communist hunger strike in Washington, DC, and feeling disappointed that Catholics were doing virtually nothing:

> I stood on the curb and watched them, joy and pride in the courage of this band of men and women mounting in my heart, and with it a bitterness too that since I was now a Catholic with fundamental philosophical differences, I could not be out there with them. I could write, I could protest, to arouse the conscience, but where was the Catholic leadership in the gathering of the bands of men and women together, for the actual works of mercy that the comrades had always made a part of their technique in reaching the workers?[66]

Day offered a new model of Catholic activism—blending direct action with daily works of mercy.

A second contribution was that Dorothy Day and the Catholic Workers demonstrated an alternative way of interacting with the destitute. While church leaders spoke of the dignity of all and the need for social charity, Catholic Workers lived the ideals of *Rerum Novarum* and

Quadragesimo Anno on a daily basis. How was this evident? Those who came to the houses of hospitality were treated as guests, not "cases." They were treated with love, not disdain, even when they were full of hostility and anger resulting from their suffering and wounded spirits.[67] Catholic Worker guests were never proselytized, but simply accepted. Although some people critiqued the movement for not doing enough to reform the homeless, Catholic Workers maintained that love was what their guests needed most. Dorothy Day was successful in this regard, as was evident at her funeral in November 1980, when a homeless man named Lazarus came forward. Crying, he proclaimed, "That fine lady gave me love."[68]

A third important contribution was Day and the Catholic Workers' example of pushing back against the Catholic hierarchy when they were not in agreement with their leaders' views. Although Day was always deferential to the bishops and archbishops, she nonetheless would challenge them when she felt their actions were incompatible with the gospel and Catholic Social Teachings. The grave digger strike illustrated this, demonstrating that laypeople can be part of the deliberations of the church, not merely passive recipients of church proclamations. In the words of Christian ethicist Marvin Mich Krier, Dorothy Day "was not afraid to disagree with the hierarchy . . . on social issues, such as the morality of war and the grave digger strike of 1949. Her positions, moral influence, and following made her a visible countervailing force within the Catholic community and part of its 'unofficial' tradition."[69]

Day and the Catholic Worker movement offered a radical Catholicism that made connections between capitalism, militarism, poverty, nationalism, and war. Although this chapter has focused on the movement's views of labor and economics, Day was also a committed pacifist who opposed war as a method of dealing with international conflict. In fact, she is often referred to as the "mother of American Catholic pacifism."[70] The Catholic Worker tradition of war resistance will be explored more fully in chapter 2, but here it is important to note that Day believed that only love could cast out fear and only nonviolent forms of resistance would honor God and preserve the dignity of humans.[71] She also recognized that expanding militarism in the United States was linked with issues of poverty, both by directing resources away from education and social programs and through the growing US role in third world struggles of the poor and oppressed. In short, Day was essential in promoting dialogue and action that revealed the links between these issues, as well as promoting a radical, progressive set of Catholic social ethics.

César Chávez, Dolores Huerta, and the United Farm Workers also made important contributions. Unlike Dorothy Day, who came from a middle-class background, Chavez and Huerta demonstrated that workers themselves can be effective leaders for change. They do not need church officials or individuals with formal education to establish organizations, implement strategies, and achieve gains. While Day was expressing solidarity with workers, Chávez was part of the working class himself, which enabled him to connect easily with other farm laborers and win their trust.

Chávez and Huerta also demonstrated the effectiveness of nonviolent strategies. Through their disciplined and creative use of strikes, boycotts, and pilgrimages, they proved that nonviolence is not merely a moral principle; it is a powerful tool for change that, at the end of the day, could put money in the pockets of workers and food on the table. Chávez famously stated, "Nonviolence is not inaction. It is not discussion. It is not for the timid or weak. . . . Nonviolence is hard work. It is the willingness to sacrifice. It is the patience to win."[72] Chávez illustrated the compatibility of Christian nonviolence, which is grounded in concepts of love and human dignity, and effective union organizing.

2

Peace, Nonviolence, and Disarmament

While labor issues were a major concern for US Catholics in the first half of the twentieth century, the second half was marked by concerns over international conflicts. As World War II came to a close, humanity faced the reality of living in a world with nuclear weapons. The immense destructive capacity of atomic warfare was evident in Hiroshima and Nagasaki, where approximately 200,000 died within weeks of the bombings and an additional 140,000 died within five years. Many others suffered long-term effects of massive radiation exposure, including malignant tumors, various forms of cancer, ophthalmological disorders, neurological disorders, and birth defects.[1] The unmatched power of these weapons meant that the United States had become the world's dominant military force. But within a few years, the Soviet Union also developed nuclear capabilities, launching the world into an arms race.

Alongside the nuclear arms race, conventional wars were erupting across the globe. This included the Korean War, the Vietnam War, and numerous liberation struggles for independence from colonial powers. Moreover, Cold War tensions were on the verge of turning into hot conflicts, as East Germany erected the Berlin Wall and the United States considered using nuclear weapons during the Cuban missile crisis of 1962. In short, the world was embroiled in conflicts, and the leader of Roman Catholicism at that time, Pope John XXIII, understood that the church could no longer sustain its isolation from the world. Hence the pope inaugurated a new period of aggiornamento, or updating of the church. In 1963, he began by addressing issues of war, nuclear weapons, disarmament, and the arms race in the encyclical *Pacem in Terris*, or "Peace on Earth."

Reassessing the Just War Tradition

Pacem in Terris marks an important moment of rethinking the church's centuries-old stance on war, known as just war theory. This tradition was initially developed in the fourth century, when Constantine, a Roman emperor from AD 306 to 337, converted to Christianity. Many scholars have concluded that, up until this time, the Christian church was pacifist.[2] The writings of early church fathers—including Origen, Ireneaus, Tertullian, Hippolytus of Rome, Cyprianus, Arnobius, and Lactantius—indicated that they opposed Christian participation in war.[3] Early theologian Tertullian wrote, "Only without the sword can the Christian wage war: for the Lord has abolished the sword."[4] And Justin, in dialogue with Trypho in approximately 160 CE, stated, "We ourselves were well conversant with war, murder, and everything evil, but all of us throughout the whole wide earth have traded in our weapons of war. We have exchanged our swords for plowshares, our spears for farm tools."[5] Additionally, there is evidence that Maximilianus of Tebessa was the first documented Christian conscientious objector, who was executed for his refusal to serve in the military in 295.[6] In short, there is substantial evidence to support the claim of pacifism in the early church.[7]

Yet when the emperor Constantine converted, he faced a dilemma: How could he reconcile his role as head of the military (with the responsibility of protecting his citizens) with the church's teaching that the taking of human life is wrong? Greek philosopher Aristotle and Roman philosopher Cicero found a way to overcome this tension by establishing criteria to discern what constitutes a just war and how combat should be conducted to minimize harm.[8] An explicit set of principles was established in the Catholic tradition by Augustine of Hippo (354–430) and Ambrose (340–397) and later refined by Thomas Aquinas.[9] These principles, which are known as just war doctrine, specify the conditions that (1) justify the declaration of war (*Jus ad bellum*), (2) indicate how combat should be conducted (*Jus in bello*), and (3) describe how to establish justice in the aftermath of war (*Jus post bellum*).

Let us begin by exploring the conditions for declaring war. The first condition is *just cause*: war can only be used as a means of addressing a serious public threat, such as an invasion of an outside force or massive human rights violations such as genocide. Second, only *legitimate state authorities*—that is, those responsible for protecting their citizens—can declare war, since war is only to be used for public purposes, not private ones. Third, a war must be motivated by *right intentions*. War cannot be motivated by ethnic or sectarian hatred, revenge, material gain, or power.

Moreover, combatants must not hold an attitude of self-righteousness; they must be fully cognizant of their opponents' humanity and regretful for the loss of life. Fourth, war cannot be declared unless there is a *probable chance of success*. It is not appropriate to wage war, which inevitably leads to suffering and loss, if the likelihood of winning is low. Fifth is the principle of *proportionality*. This refers to the standard in which the good that will be accomplished through war must outweigh the suffering that war will cause. If the evil generated through combat is greater than the good to be achieved, then war is not justified. Sixth, war can only be waged as a *last resort*. The use of military force is not permissible until all other options (including negotiations, diplomacy, and nonviolent pressure) have been exhausted.

Religious leaders within the just war tradition view war as an evil that is sometimes necessary to protect people from greater harm. However, to minimize the evil, they set standards regarding how war should be waged. First, soldiers must act in accordance with the principle of *distinction*, which requires that civilians not be targeted. Second, all actions must comply with the principle of *minimum force*. The force of any attack must be limited to the amount that will achieve the military's objective—nothing more. Third, soldiers must act according to the principle of *proportionality*: no attacks should occur if the number of civilian casualties outweighs any military advantages that are gained. Fourth, there must be *fair treatment for prisoners of war*. Any soldiers from the opposing side who surrender or are captured do not pose a threat, and therefore torture, neglect, and other forms of mistreatment are not permitted. Fifth and finally, no weapons may be used that are evil or atrocious (*malum in se*)—for example, mass rape or weapons whose effects cannot be controlled.

These principles have been the basis for the Roman Catholic Church's stance on war over the centuries. So why did Pope John XXIII release an encyclical that addressed the issue of war once again? In large part, the pope was compelled to speak to a world that was endangered by nuclear weapons. A growing number of theologians, laypeople, and ethicists argued that the advent of the atomic era had changed everything, rendering many of the just war principles obsolete, since there is no way to wage war in compliance with the principles of *Jus in bello*. Nuclear, chemical, and biological weapons cause excessive damage and do not distinguish between combatants and civilians. Similarly, the principle of proportionality is nearly impossible to accurately assess. As one commentator noted, "How does one measure into the future the continuing hazard of exploding landmines and bombs, drug addiction, alcoholism, mental illness, physical crippling, suicide?"[10] In short, the invention of nuclear weapons has made it virtually impossible to uphold humanitarian principles and ensure right intention. This new political and military reality required a new response from the church.

Pacem in Terris: Central Themes

Pope John XXIII began the encyclical with an overview of the changing circumstances within the global community. He observed that numerous nations were struggling for independence from colonial powers. Many of these newly independent countries were establishing constitutional governments that recognized fundamental human rights. Such developments also led to an increasingly interdependent set of international relations and economic ties such that "each country's social progress, order, security and peace are necessarily linked with the social progress, order, security and peace of every other country. The fates of all nations are linked. We are one human family."[11]

The pope additionally noted that any conflicts that arise ought to be addressed through diplomacy and negotiation rather than warfare. The world craves peace, he stated, but authentic, lasting peace must be "founded on truth, built according to justice, vivified and integrated by charity, and put into practice in freedom."[12]

After these introductory comments, the encyclical is divided into several sections, the first of which describes the human rights and moral duties that are required to create just and peaceful societies. This includes respecting the physical rights of all people (such as the right to food, clothing, shelter, and medical care), cultural and religious rights (such as freedom of worship), and political and economic rights (such as the right to work in humane conditions, to receive just wages, to emigrate, to participate in public affairs, and to have free speech).[13]

The encyclical's second section focuses on the responsibilities of governments, public authorities, and citizens. According to the pope, governmental leaders receive their authority from God, and thus citizens ought to respect and comply with them. However, with such authority comes responsibility for the common good, addressing the material and emotional needs of their citizens, especially for the least fortunate. Governmental leaders must establish political institutions and practices that enable every citizen to exercise his or her rights. John XXIII also argued that just governments should have a written constitution and a charter of human rights. The encyclical recommends that governments divide their power among executive, legislative, and judicial branches. However, the pope did recognize the limits of state authority, noting that no government can command matters of conscience. Any policy or order that is in contradiction to moral law is not binding on individuals.

In the third section, John XXIII encouraged relationships among nations that are characterized by four traits: truth, justice, liberty, and solidarity. Truthful international relations promote objective media reporting, the right to self-development, and the elimination of prejudicial views. Just relations include respecting the traditions of racial and ethnic minorities and honoring all people's inalienable rights. Liberty means that wealthier nations will give freely to less developed countries, without the intent of seeking dominance and control. Liberty also means that no country has the right to oppress another nation or unjustly meddle in its affairs. Solidarity entails recognizing the rights of refugees to emigrate and calling upon developed nations to reduce the material inequalities in the world. Nations should also foster friendly relations with other countries to reduce fear and hostility.

In the fourth section of the encyclical, the pope addressed the nuclear arms race, which he argued is the opposite of solidarity, since it generated fear and distrust. A lasting peace can only be established, he argued, when there is mutual trust and collaboration; authentic justice can never be established through nuclear warfare. Stockpiling nuclear weapons may function as a deterrent to war, yet it takes much-needed resources away from other human development programs. Moreover, a nuclear attack could potentially eliminate all human life. For these reasons, weapons of mass destruction should be banned and a disarmament process should begin. International disputes should be addressed through negotiation and diplomacy, not through war or the threat of annihilation.

What role does the layperson have in this quest for disarmament, peace, and justice? This is the topic of the encyclical's final section. John

XXIII implored everyone, not just Catholics, to become involved in public life, influencing civic and political organizations from the inside. He argued that peace would not be achieved by "an equal balance of armaments" but by working for the good of all humanity.[14]

Lived Religion and US Catholic Peace Movements

Pope John XXIII released *Pacem in Terris* in response to the escalating political tensions of his era, but there had long been discussion among lay Catholics about war and peace. In fact, such conversations occurred in the United States decades before the release of the encyclical, suggesting that lived religious action may have helped push the Vatican to formally articulate a stance on these issues.

Catholic Association for International Peace

The beginnings of contemporary American Catholic peace movements can be traced to the 1920s and Dr. John Ryan, a social reform advocate. Ryan had learned about England's Catholic Council for International Peace during a trip to the United Kingdom in 1922. When he returned to the United States, he hoped to form a similar group that would lobby Congress on issues of militarism and war. After meeting with prominent Catholic leaders over the subsequent years, Ryan was able to fulfill this vision in 1927, when the Catholic Association for International Peace (CAIP) was formed. The primary purpose of the CAIP was peace education, not direct action, and thus it focused mainly on producing publications that were distributed to Catholic organizations and institutions. Because most of these publications endorsed the just war doctrine, CAIP can hardly be considered a progressive force for peace. In fact, CAIP ultimately supported World War II and continued the tradition of Catholic patriotism during periods of war.[15] As Ryan stated in his pamphlet "The Right and Wrong of War":

> The extreme pacifist position, that war as such is always wrong because it involves violence, does not deserve formal discussion. With the position of some recent Catholic authorities, that in our day war is practically never justified because of its awful consequences, I have considerable

sympathy; but if Hitler and his government intend to substitute paganism for Christianity not only in Germany but in foreign territories which they have annexed in the last two years and if they are aiming at world domination, then I have no hesitation in saying that a successful war against this immoral Nazi program would be the lesser evil. In other words, such a war would be justified, despite the enormous ensuing destruction of life and property.[16]

The Catholic Worker and Noncooperation with Civil Defense Drills

Most American Catholics shared Ryan's sentiment. One notable exception was Dorothy Day and the Catholic Worker movement. As described in chapter 1, the early years of the Catholic Worker movement were devoted to labor issues and works of mercy, addressing the crushing poverty of the Depression era. Catholic Workers called for a social revolution that would transform the exploitive aspects of the industrial economy, yet they insisted that this revolution be waged nonviolently. This commitment to nonviolence and the struggle against militarism became a more prominent theme for the movement as aggression and fascism developed throughout the 1930s. Day wrote, "For . . . years we have been opposing the use of force—in the labor movement, in the class struggle, as well as in the struggles between countries. . . . By working for a better social order in our own country, by working for the 'tranquility in order,' which is the definition of peace, we are working for peace."[17]

The Catholic Worker movement's commitment to pacifism was, in part, inspired by the theological writings of Paul Hanly Furfey, a priest and sociology professor at the Catholic University of America. Furfey called upon Catholics to reject the "Constantinian Compromise" of just war and return to the pacifist roots of the early Christian church. Then, when the Spanish Civil War erupted in 1936, the Catholic Worker announced its position in its newspaper, prompting a series of articles on the theological basis for Catholic pacifism. Some of these were written by Monsignor Barry O'Toole and Father John Hugo, who argued that Catholics should fight social evils through "weapons of the spirit."

Not all Catholic Workers were persuaded, and many accused Day of dividing the movement. Tensions culminated when Day published an article in the *Catholic Worker*, calling for conscientious objection and encouraging young men to refuse to register for the draft. The New York Chancery rebuked Day. She agreed that she did not have the right to tell others what to do, but she underscored that "we had to follow our own consciences, which later took us to jail; but our work in getting out the paper was an attempt to arouse the consciences of others."[18] Once the attacks on Pearl Harbor occurred and the United States entered the war, Day found that the majority of American Catholics did not agree with her views. In fact, the newspaper lost many subscribers: the circulation of the *Catholic Worker* declined from 130,000 monthly copies in 1939 to only around 50,000 monthly copies by 1944.[19]

In the beginning, the Catholic Workers' pacifism was primarily a theological stance. Yet Dorothy Day had a long-standing history of political action, and thus it didn't take long before she was resisting militarism with more than her words. The first widely publicized action occurred in 1954. Instigated by Ammon Hennacy, who had newly joined the movement, a number of Catholic Workers refused to cooperate with New York City's air-raid drills, which were intended to prepare the population for a nuclear attack. Under the Civil Defense Act, all citizens were legally required to participate, taking cover in designated shelters when the alarms went off, simulating an air raid. Even though such measures would not provide any viable protection in the event of a real attack, the drills were designed to encourage acceptance of the arms race and provide a (false) sense of protection. To challenge this militarism, seven Catholic workers—including Day and Hennacy—refused to take shelter.

During the following year's drill, in June 1955, twenty-three activists from the War Resisters League and the Fellowship of Reconciliation joined the Catholic Workers' act of noncooperation. In 1956, they again refused to participate in the drill and were sent to jail for five days. Year after year, they repeated the action, telling New York's Civil Defense director, "Civil defense, after all, is an integral part of the total preparation for nuclear war. We, on the other hand, are convinced that the only secure defense is for people to refuse to participate in any way in the preparations for war."[20] In 1960, when the sirens went off, nearly 2,000 protesters assembled in Central Park, enjoying a picnic instead of cowering in fear of a nuclear attack. The protest was covered by various news agencies, marking it the largest direct action against nuclear arms at that point in time.[21] Eventually, when city personnel realized that they couldn't enforce drill participation with so many protesters, they suspended the policy.[22]

PAX

The air-raid drills inspired a number of American Catholics, who called for a formal organization devoted to Catholic approaches to peace and war. Toward that end, they revived PAX (later the US branch of Pax Christi International) in the early 1960s. The main focus of PAX was lobbying the church hierarchy to adopt a strong peace position. The organization had a prime opportunity, since Pope John XXIII had convened the Vatican II Council where 2,400 bishops from all geographic regions were gathered to discuss ways of modernizing the Roman Catholic Church. Moreover, the council meetings coincided with the release of *Pacem in Terris*. Yet this encyclical's peace-building emphasis was not without controversy, since many Vatican II participants still subscribed to the just war doctrine. PAX activists hoped to persuade religious leaders to relinquish this doctrine once and for all, to definitively condemn nuclear weapons, and to support the right to conscientious objection.

In the fall of 1965, members of PAX and the Catholic Worker traveled to Rome, where the Vatican II Council was being held. These activists took a twofold approach. Some, including Dorothy Day, fasted and prayed, speaking directly with Catholic leaders about these issues. Others—including Eileen Egan, Gordon Zahn, Jim Douglass, Thomas Merton, and Jean and Hildegard Goss-Mayr—wrote a statement that articulated an ethic of peace and nonviolence.

PAX members' efforts yielded mixed results. On the matter of war, the council fathers stated, "As long as the danger of war remains and there is no competent and sufficiently powerful authority on the international level, governments cannot be denied the right to legitimate defense once every means of peaceful settlement has been exhausted."[23] In other words, the council was not willing to depart from the just war doctrine. The PAX lobbyists were more successful in getting the church to support conscientious objectors to war. There was some opposition to this proposal—primarily from Cardinal Spellman, the head of the military ordinate for the US armed forces, who wanted a provision that would make military service mandatory. He also wanted to underscore that civil authorities were the ones who determined whether a draft was necessary and that Catholics must respect and comply with their decisions. The council did not agree with Cardinal Spellman, choosing instead to endorse the right of individual conscience on matters of military participation.[24] The final success came when the bishops included a statement on war in *The Pastoral Constitution on the Church in the Modern World*, which read: "Every act of war directed to the indiscriminate destruction of whole cities or vast areas with their inhabitants is a crime against God and humanity, which merits firm and unequivocal condemnation."[25] Hence these Catholic lay activists were able to push the religious hierarchy to take a stance on peace, war, and disarmament—even if it was not as strong of a stance as they had hoped for.

The Vietnam War

As the Vatican II Council was meeting, the conflict in Vietnam was heating up. Tensions had been simmering since North Vietnam had defeated the French colonial administration in 1954 and set up a communist-led regime headed by Ho Chi Minh. In South Vietnam, the French relinquished control to the provisionally appointed premier, Ngo Dinh Diem. In 1955, Diem appointed himself president, with the support of US military advisers. Yet discontent rapidly expanded among the South Vietnamese, due to Diem's nepotism and corruption. Moreover, Diem viciously cracked down on communist sympathizers in the late 1950s, arresting and torturing tens of thousands. As a result, the North Vietnamese communist group known as the Viet Cong undertook a series of terrorist attacks, aiming to unite the North and South. By 1959, the Central Committee of the Vietnamese Communist Party voted to wage an armed struggle to overthrow the South Vietnamese regime. With this vote and subsequent infiltration of Viet Cong fighters into the South, the Vietnam War began. It escalated further when Diem's opponents in South Vietnam formed the National Liberation Front, aiming to undermine Diem's control.[26]

American involvement exacerbated the war, as President John F. Kennedy increased aid to the South Vietnamese regime in the early 1960s. This occurred just as the Diem family became a growing problem and liability. Diem's brother Ngo Dinh Nhu was known to be an opium addict, and his wife, Madame Nhu, used her position to promote Catholic causes and to ridicule Buddhists, who were the majority religious group. Regime corruption had prompted strikes and protests throughout the country. One of the most dramatic protests occurred when a Buddhist monk, Thich Quang Duc, immolated himself on a busy Saigon intersection in June 1963.[27] Photos of the burning monk were printed on the front pages of newspapers worldwide. Shortly thereafter, several other monks followed Duc's example, and resistance exploded throughout South Vietnam. The Diem regime responded by sending out its paramilitary troops, who raided Buddhist temples, injured thirty monks, and arrested more than a thousand others. The Diem regime defiantly defended its actions, with Diem's sister-in-law, Madame Nhu, stating that she would applaud another "monk barbecue show."[28] The South Vietnamese military, however, was concerned about the growing unrest and the regime's inability to contain it. Consequently, it assassinated Diem in the fall of 1963.

Three weeks after Diem's death, President Kennedy was assassinated. Lyndon B. Johnson, the newly appointed president, chose to expand aid to South Vietnam even further, in hopes of promoting political stability. Then, in the summer of 1964, the US Congress passed the Gulf of Tonkin Resolution, which enabled Johnson to undertake military action against North Vietnam and to fight the Viet Cong in South Vietnam. The situation quickly morphed into an international conflict as the president authorized the deployment of 100,000 US troops in 1965 and an additional 100,000 deployments in 1966. By 1967, there were nearly half a million US soldiers in Vietnam.[29]

The US military not only used ground troops to wage the war but also employed toxic chemicals and herbicides. For example, it used the herbicide Agent Orange to destroy the dense jungles where the Viet Cong operated. This resulted in serious environmental damage, as well as significant health problems for the local populations.[30] The military also used napalm, a flammable gel that sticks to skin, causing severe burns. Moreover, it engaged in heavy bombing raids, ultimately detonating more bombs in Vietnam than it had in Japan during World War II. These bombings killed civilians and combatants alike, and casualty rates rose rapidly.

CATHOLIC RESISTANCE TO THE VIETNAM WAR

As news reports documented the growing human costs of the Vietnam War, and photographs of napalm-burned children were printed in newspapers throughout the United States, people began questioning the legitimacy of the war. In the summer of 1963, shortly after the Vietnamese monks' immolations, four New York Catholic Worker volunteers were discussing how they should respond. These four—Tom Cornell, Chris Kearns, Carlotta Ribar, and Bob Steed—decided to stage a ten-day picket outside the New York apartment of the Vietnamese permanent observer to the United Nations. This marked one of the earliest US public protests against the war. The picketers called upon others to join them in daily afternoon pickets, culminating in 250 antiwar activists demanding an end to US support for the Diem regime.[31]

There were frequent articles about the Vietnam War in the Catholic Worker's newsletter. However, since the Catholic Worker was never a single-issue movement, it continued to address the plight of workers, and its volunteers were devoted to daily works of mercy for the homeless and destitute throughout this period. Some young Catholic Workers wanted an organization that would focus primarily on war resistance. Therefore, in 1964 they formed Catholic Peace Fellowship (CPF). Under the leadership of Jim Forest and Tom Cornell, and advised by Cistercian monk Thomas Merton, the organization focused on the moral aspects of the Vietnam War, the Christian tradition of nonviolence, and Catholic social teachings on peace and war.[32]

Draft Card Burnings

It did not take long before Cornell and Kearns put the Catholic Peace Fellowship on the activist map. When they attended a protest at the Whitehall Military Induction Center in Manhattan in July 1965, Kearns burned his draft card in protest of the Vietnam War. When *Life* magazine published a photo the following month of Kearns setting his draft card on fire, Congress quickly passed legislation that made such acts punishable by a fine of $10,000 or five years in prison. In October that same year, Catholic Worker David Miller let Congress know that the new legislation was not a deterrence to war resistance: he destroyed his draft card and became the first person to be prosecuted under the new laws.[33] A few weeks later, Cornell and four others burned their draft cards in Union Square. Before committing the act, Cornell stated, "The mutilation of human beings in Vietnam has become a civic virtue; now, the mutilation of a scrap of paper becomes a grave crime against the state. The grave crime, we are told, is not the destruction of life but the destruction of a piece of paper."[34] The five young men were arrested as Vietnam War supporters chanted, "Burn yourselves instead!"[35] Eventually, roughly 3,500 men destroyed their draft cards.[36]

With this open defiance of federal conscription law, a new style of Catholic resistance was forged called "prophetic witness." Historian Penelope Adams Moon describes this particular form of resistance:

Prophetic anti-war witness employed drama, theatre, and action to jolt the public conscience and force American Catholics to assess the intersection of their civic and religious identities. . . . While religious and non-religious resisters alike expressed moral outrage over the war and used moral language to justify burning draft cards, the sacrificial nature of draft card burning, particularly in light of the recently-passed law, held special appeal for some Catholic activists. As Christ died to save humankind, so Catholic resisters believed they sacrificed their personal wellbeing to save others and witness to Christ's love. More than a means of questioning the legality of the draft or avoiding military service, CPFers hoped that burning one's draft card could help eradicate the social injustice of the draft and bring an end to the killing in Vietnam. The adoption of prophetic witness by Catholic activists spurred a tactical shift in the antiwar movement. While the prophetic action built on the pioneering protest of Catholic Workers during civil defense drills, Catholic draft card burnings in the 1960s transcended the symbolic nature of McCarthy-era Catholic Worker civil disobedience. In refusing to go into fallout shelters during scheduled civil defense exercises, Catholic Workers had condemned the drills because they perpetuated a culture of violence. Like the sit-ins they inspired in the 1960s, Catholic Worker civil defense protests were, fundamentally, consciousness-raising actions aimed at forcing Americans to reevaluate their political decisions and admit the evil of nuclear weapons. By destroying their draft cards, however, Cornell, Miller, and Kearns went beyond denouncing the immorality of the draft and of war; they jeopardized the government's ability to rely on the draft and consequently, its ability to continue waging war in Vietnam. They aimed to cripple the machinery of war, not simply broaden disdain for it. If adopted by enough people, draft card burning could physically bring an end to the war, saving both American and Vietnamese lives in the process. This was more than nonviolent civil disobedience; it was nonviolent resistance.[37]

Immolations

The draft card burnings began a period of tactical experimentation and innovation among radical Catholic activists. The most controversial tactic during this time was immolation. Although Vietnamese Buddhist monks had used this form of protest, it did not occur in the United States until March 1965, when Alice Herz—an eighty-two-year-old Jewish Quaker who had fled Nazi Germany—took her own life in Detroit, Michigan. She stated that the immolation was an act of protest against "a great country trying to wipe out a small country."[38] Later that year, on November 2, 1965, yet another immolation occurred. This time it was thirty-two-year-old Norman Morrison, the director of a Quaker community in Baltimore, who set himself on fire at the Pentagon, directly in front of the office window of Secretary of Defense Robert McNamara. One week later, Roger LaPorte, a twenty-two-year-old former Columbia University student who had dropped out to volunteer at the New York Catholic Worker house, immolated himself outside the Dag Hammarskjöld Library at the United Nations. Before dying the next day in the hospital, LaPorte stated the motivation behind his act: "I'm a Catholic Worker. I'm against this war, all wars. I did this as a religious act."[39]

The Catholic hierarchy reacted swiftly to LaPorte's immolation. New York's Cardinal Spellman immediately condemned the act as suicide and a grave sin. Yet many radical Catholics did not agree. Jesuit priest Daniel Berrigan refused to view LaPorte's action as suicide, explaining that such acts are about taking on the suffering of others so that this suffering would break through the veil of invisibility. Although forbidden by his superiors to speak publicly on the matter, Father Daniel Berrigan defied these orders, giving the homily at LaPorte's funeral. At the service, Berrigan asked, "What if the death did not reflect despair, but a self-offering attuned to the sacrifice of Christ? Would not such a presumption show mercy to the dead as well as honor the living?"[40] Berrigan's words infuriated Cardinal Spelman, who staunchly supported the Vietnam War as the best way to preserve a Catholic-friendly state that was threatened by atheistic communism. Spellman demanded that the Jesuits expel Berrigan from New York. Jesuit leaders complied with the cardinal's request, sending Father Berrigan to Latin America to work on the editorial board of a Jesuit missionary magazine.

Dorothy Day and other prominent Catholic peace advocates reacted with ambivalence. Day was sympathetic to these individuals who were willing to sacrifice their own lives to publicize the plight of Vietnamese citizens. Yet she could not accept their acts, which she thought negated the principles of nonviolence.[41] Nonetheless, her public statements were words of compassion and mercy. Day wrote:

> Roger LaPorte . . . embraced voluntary poverty and came to help the Catholic Worker because he did not wish to profit in this booming economy that the Wall Street Journal speaks of so gloatingly. . . . Roger LaPorte was giving himself to the poor and the destitute, serving tables, serving the sick, as Saint Ignatius of Loyola did when he laid down his arms and gave up worldly combat. . . . And now he is dead—dead by his own hand, everyone will say, a suicide. But after all, there is a tradition in the Church of what are called "victim souls." . . . In this month's *Theology Digest*, Father Karl Rahner, S.J., has an article called "Good Intention." Roger "intended" to lay down his life for his brother in war-torn Vietnam. The article is about purifying one's intention and how complex and elusive a thing an intention is and how often other motives of which we are unaware are at work. There will undoubtedly be much discussion and condemnation of this sad and terrible act, but all of us around the Catholic Worker know that Roger's intent was to love God and to love his brother.[42]

Draft Board Raids

The immolations did not mark the end of the controversial tactics that radical Catholics were developing to resist the Vietnam War. Within a short time, other actions would stir further debate. Although none were as divisive as immolations, the next tactics—draft board raids—were also highly contentious. They began when Philip Berrigan, a Josephite priest and brother of Jesuit Daniel Berrigan, called on Catholics not merely to express opposition to the war but to actually obstruct it. Philip Berrigan and Catholic Worker Tom Lewis contemplated various campaigns but ultimately decided to subvert the conscription system. Lewis explained how they came to this choice:

> We, Phil Berrigan and myself, had already been in the military. As far as our burning draft cards, it didn't make any sense because we really weren't liable. It was a gesture with no personal risk. . . . So I was searching along with Phil for a really creative, positive response to what was happening. . . . I had great respect for people who were considering immolating themselves—yet there had to be some kind of alternative to that. Then, of course, [there was] Dorothy Day and her philosophy about filling the jails to put a lot of pressure on the system. . . . So it was the consideration of being in jail, which led to the other thing: What do you do to get locked up? We decided to do something really strong and the connection with draft cards was very important. . . . So we came up with . . . the idea of doing *something* with the draft records. Doing something, we decided, was pouring blood on them, keeping the symbolism, the Christian symbolism of blood, as something of bloodletting and also something of reconciliation.[43]

In October 1967, this plan was enacted when Tom Lewis, Phil Berrigan, David Eberhardt, and the Reverend James Mengel raided Baltimore's Custom House. Once they entered the building and encountered the receptionist, Father Philip Berrigan, wearing his clerical collar, stated that he was there to check on the draft status of his parishioners. When the receptionist refused to give him access to the draft files, he and the others pushed their way in. Berrigan described the incident:

> Three of us broke through this little gate and entered the draft board proper, yanking open draft files and pouring our blood on them. This lasted about a minute, because the secretaries were furious, grabbed us from behind, and locked their arms around our waists. We didn't resist or try to break loose. We sat down and waited to be arrested. Jim Mengel, having made a last minute decision to not pour blood, handed out copies of the New Testament. The enraged clerks threw them back in his

face. Afterward, we were accused of frightening the secretaries, but I don't remember them showing fear. They were enraged, and when they testified against us they were still angry. We had invaded the state's sanctuary, poured our blood over . . . its sacred files. We had damaged property, a crime far greater than destroying human life.[44]

The four men were arrested and convicted. As they awaited their sentencing, they were released on bail. During this time, Philip Berrigan plotted the next draft board raid. Eight other radical Catholics volunteered to join him, including his brother Daniel Berrigan, who had returned from his exile in Latin America. In May 1968, the nine resisters entered the draft board office in Catonsville, Maryland. There they pulled out 600 conscription files, brought them to the parking lot, and set them on fire, using homemade napalm—the jellied form of petroleum that had burned so many children in Vietnam. They released a public statement that read: "We destroy these draft cards not only because they exploit our young men but also because they represent misplaced power concentrated in the ruling class in America. . . . We confront the Catholic Church, other Christian bodies, and synagogues of America with their silence and cowardice in the face of our country's crimes."[45]

The event was the front-page story in many national newspapers, which published the now-famous photo of the "Catonsville Nine" praying in front of the burning files. During the trial, the judge ordered the jury to not consider the nine defendants' testimony, stating that their motivation was irrelevant; the jury was merely to decide whether they had committed a criminal act. The verdict came back quickly: the Catonsville Nine were convicted on charges of interference with the Selective Service Act of 1967, destruction of Selective Service records, and destruction of US government property. They all received a three-year prison sentence.[46]

Undoubtedly, the judge gave a sentence that he thought was harsh enough to deter anyone else from raiding a draft board. But this bold new form of war resistance inspired others. Scholars estimate that between 53 and 250 raids occurred between 1967 and 1971.[47]

How did mainstream American Catholics respond to these actions? There was a wide range of reactions: outrage and condemnation, admiration, qualified support, empathetic discomfort, and confusion. Sitting in jail after the first raid, Philip Berrigan addressed some of the reactions, particularly from his own parishioners. In his "Letter from a Baltimore Jail," imitating Martin Luther King Jr.'s "Letter from a Birmingham Jail," Berrigan wrote:

> Some of you have been sorely perplexed with me; some of you have been angry, others despairing. One parishioner writes of quarreling with people who thought me mad. After all, isn't it impudent and sick for a grown man (and a priest) to slosh blood . . . on draft files; to terrorize harmless secretaries doing their job; to act without ecclesiastical permission and to disgrace the collar and its sublime office? . . . You had trouble with blood as a symbol—uncivilized, messy, bizarre. . . . You had trouble with destruction of property, with civil disobedience, with priests getting involved, and getting involved this much. Let's face it: perhaps half of you had trouble with us acting at all.[48]

For many US Catholics, this was a remarkable departure from the traditional patriotic sentiments promoted within their parishes. Even those who were critical of the war wondered whether acts of property destruction were going too far.

The same ambivalence was present among Catholics in the peace movement. Some, such as Tom Cornell, praised this tactical shift. He stated:

> The burning of the Catonsville files signals a shift in tactics, from nonviolent protest to resistance to revolution. . . . The Catonsville Action . . . was designed so that no one would be in danger of physical harm nor otherwise violated. It was aimed at things, at property that is violating young men and causing immense grief, suffering and death around the world, property that has no right to exist, but which current folklore invests with a certain mystical inviolability. The participants in the action made no effort to conceal their identities. They know what penalties they face and do not shrink from paying the price. . . . Some of our friends were shocked by the Catonsville Action, primarily, I suspect, because of the terrible price that is likely to be exacted. Do they think revolution comes for the asking, or that its victims are always anonymous? Even a nonviolent revo-

lution, or rather, especially a nonviolent revolution will demand blood, our blood, not theirs, and that's the difference.[49]

Other prominent Catholics were less certain. Thomas Merton expressed his doubts:

> The napalming of draft records by the Baltimore [*sic*] Nine is a special and significant case because it seems to indicate a borderline situation: as if the Peace Movement too were standing at the very edge of violence. . . . The Peace Movement may be escalating beyond peaceful protest. In which case they may also be escalating into self-contradiction. What were the Berrigans and others trying to do? It seems to me that this was an attempt at prophetic nonviolent provocation. It bordered on violence and was violent to the extent that it meant pushing some good ladies around and destroying some government property. The evident desperation of the Baltimore Nine has, however, frightened more than it has edified. The country is in a very edgy psychological state. Americans feel terribly threatened. . . . In such a case, the use of nonviolence has to be extremely careful and clear.[50]

Catholic Worker laypeople had mixed responses. Dorothy Day, for instance, initially approved of the actions, describing the raids as a "very strong and imaginative witness." Soon thereafter, her opinion shifted due to concern that unintended violence could occur, especially with young radicals who were less disciplined. Day also feared that draft board raiders were unprepared for the psychological toll of prison.[51] One draft board raider, Jim Forest, summarized her stance: "In the end, she didn't agree with what we had done, but she treasured us and supported us, wrote about us, published our things in the newspaper. . . . But she also made it clear that this was not her idea of the best way to bring the change that we wanted."[52]

Catholic Resistance to the Nuclear Arms Race: The Plowshares Movement

In addition to resisting the "hot war" in Vietnam, progressive American Catholics were also resisting the Cold War that propelled the nuclear arms race. One group, which included Philip and Dan Berrigan, took direct inspiration from the draft board raids; the activists contemplated ways to apply the same dramatic and provocative tactics to challenge the production of nuclear weapons. This group of laypeople and clergy, known as the Plowshares movement, engaged in symbolic moral witness by enacting the words of the Old Testament prophet Isaiah: "They shall beat their swords into plowshares and their spears into pruning hooks. Nations shall not lift up sword against nation. Nor shall they train for war anymore."[53] Toward that end, Plowshares activists entered weapons production sites or military installations to damage weapons of mass destruction in campaigns that they called "acts of disarmament." They hoped to render these weapons inoperable, but they also aimed to challenge Catholic complacency on matters of militarism and war.

The idea of the Plowshares movement began in the late 1970s during a vigil held outside the General Electric (GE) plant in King of Prussia, near Philadelphia. A local activist had initiated the vigil when he discovered that the GE plant was making first-strike nuclear weapons. At that time, the US military's official policy was mutually assured destruction (MAD)—a policy whereby the United States kept pace with the Soviet Union's military capacities to assure reciprocal annihilation. Military strategists argued that this would deter a Soviet attack. Yet the production of these new weapons indicated something different: the United States had shifted to a first-strike policy whereby immensely powerful nuclear weapons could be launched that would decimate an enemy's military sites, impairing its ability to retaliate.[54] General Electric was producing the first-strike warheads known as the Mark 12A reentry vehicles.

For months, activists held a vigil outside the GE plant, protesting the "business of genocide." One of those activists was John Schuchardt, who noticed that there was limited security at Plant No. 9, where the Mark 12A was being produced. As he watched the employees file through the plant's back entrance, he realized that it would be quite simple to enter the building. He later stated:

[We knew] these weapons were not defensive; they are criminal and genocidal. I thought, if we believe this, then what is our responsibility? Here we are vigiling but is it possible that a group of us could go in and bring this production line to a halt? These warheads have all these electronic components that would be very vulnerable to a hammer blow. . . . When I [started] talking about this . . . it was a practical question of how we could render this electronic equipment harmless. We thought we could take in some hammers. I wasn't putting two and two together until the Isaiah passage when we realized, yes, this really will be hammering swords into plowshares."[55]

After months of planning, eight people launched the first Plowshares campaign. On September 9, 1980, the eight arrived at the King of Prussia GE plant, having fabricated false employee identification cards to facilitate their entrance during the morning shift. Two of the activists, Sister Anne Montgomery and Father Karl Cabat, distracted the security guard, enabling the other six to enter the facility. The guard quickly sent notification that several individuals had entered the plant without authorization. Montgomery and Cabat tried to calm him, stating that there was nothing to be worried about because they were nonviolent. Meanwhile, the other six—including Father Daniel Berrigan, Philip Berrigan, Dean Hammer, Elmer Maas, Molly Rush, and John Schuchardt—quickly located a room where some of the warheads were stored. Remarkably, the security door was unlocked. They began hammering upon the warheads and then pouring their blood, which they had brought into the facility in baby bottles. Within minutes, they were arrested. From jail, they released a press statement that read:

We commit civil disobedience at General Electric because this genocidal entity is the fifth leading producer of weaponry in the U.S. To maintain this position, GE drains $3 million a day from the public treasury, an enormous larceny against the poor. We also wish to challenge the lethal lie spun by GE through its motto, "We bring good things to life." As manufacturers of the Mark 12A reentry vehicle, GE actually prepares to bring good things to death. Through the Mark 12A, the threat of first-strike nuclear war grows more imminent. Thus GE advances the possible destruction of millions of innocent lives. . . . In confronting GE, we choose to obey God's law of life, rather than a corporate summons to death. Our beating of swords into plowshares is a way to enflesh this biblical call. In our action, we draw on a deep-rooted faith in Christ, who changed the course of history through his willingness to suffer rather than kill. We are filled with hope for our world and for our children as we join in this act of resistance.[56]

Members of the "Plowshares Eight" were convicted of burglary, conspiracy, and criminal mischief. They received sentences ranging from eighteen months to ten years. The courts imposed lengthy sentences to deter others from following their example. It didn't work. Within months, another action took place and a movement was born. Over the course of the next thirty-five years, over 200 activists participated in more than eighty campaigns, spreading to Australia and several European countries.[57]

Like the draft board raids, the Plowshares "disarmament acts" were controversial. Some Catholics were offended by the use of blood. One Plowshares activist clarified why they include it, stating, "War has been sanitized . . . because we mostly do it through technology and satellite surveillance. . . . So when we use blood, it has a very powerful effect. . . . It says, 'This is what we're talking about: human life. All this technology is made to destroy it, to spill human blood.'"[58] Many other peace activists were uncertain about property damage, questioning whether it is nonviolent. A movement participant explained:

We are often asked the question about whether property destruction is nonviolent and there are a number of ways of answering it. One is to analyze the term "property." Are nuclear weapons property? We say no; they are anti-property. They're about destroying what is human, what is proper, what is good, what is decent. . . . The proper thing to do is to disable them, to unmake them, to convert them into something that *is* property. We try to say this warship should be used to bring food to starving nations. We're trying to unmake their killing nature. We're not damaging property; we're improving a weapon that is designed to kill innocent people, civilians, children and therefore [this tactic] can in no way be considered violent because you are rendering a violent piece of machinery nonviolent. It's nonviolent because you have made it inoperable, incapable of hurting others.[59]

The US Bishops' *Challenge of Peace*

Catholic activism on the issue of nuclear weapons did not go unnoticed. While many members of the Catholic hierarchy rejected radical actions such as those taken by the Plowshares movement, they could not ignore the fact that many of their parishioners were concerned about the threats associated with the nuclear arms race and were questioning the morality of their government's security policies. In addition, the election of Ronald Reagan in the fall of 1980 brought new urgency to the situation, since the president-elect called for a massive arms buildup and opposed the SALT II arms limitation treaty that President Carter had negotiated. The US bishops were at a crossroads and needed to make a public statement. In November 1980, the National Conference of Catholic Bishops met (later renamed the US Conference of Catholic Bishops), and Auxiliary Bishop Tom Gumbleton, president of the US branch of Pax Christi, took the floor to plead with his colleagues:

> We've just elected a President who has stated his conviction that we can have superiority in nuclear weapons, an utter impossibility. We have a Vice-President who has clearly stated that one side could win a nuclear war and that we must be prepared to fight one and to win it. When we have that kind of thinking going on, it seems to me we are getting ever more closer [sic] to the day when we will wage that nuclear war and it will be the war that will end the world as we know it. We are at a point of urgent crisis. We have to face this question and face it very clearly.[60]

The bishops agreed with Auxiliary Bishop Gumbleton, appointing a committee to draft a pastoral letter on the nuclear arms race. Archbishop Joseph Bernardin of Cincinnati, who was well known for his diplomacy and consensus-building skills, headed the committee. He in turn appointed Gumbleton, along with Auxiliary Bishop John O'Connor of the Military Vicariate. Two more bishops were selected who represented the middle ground: Bishop Daniel Reilly of Norwich, Connecticut, and Auxiliary Bishop George Fulcher of Columbus, Ohio. In addition, representatives from men's and women's religious orders were appointed, including Father Richard Warner and Sister Juliana Casey.[61]

From the beginning, the process of creating an official pastoral statement on nuclear weapons was an open one. In contrast to the traditional closed methodology used by the Vatican to produce encyclicals, the US bishops invited in consultants, experts, and laypeople. This in itself may reflect the influence of movements, which pushed over the years to have input into the official social teachings of the church. The bishops began with a "listening phase" in which they met with a wide array of people. They began in May 1982 by talking with Reagan administration officials—including the defense secretary, the director of the Arms Control and Disarmament Agency, and the undersecretary for political affairs. The committee also collected testimonies from activists in peace organizations such as Pax Christi and Sojourners.[62] Based on this input, the bishops began writing their pastoral letter.

While the committee members were drafting the document, Pope John Paul II delivered a message in June 1982 to the general assembly of the United Nations for its special session on disarmament. In that message, the pope built upon the 1964 pastoral constitution *Gaudium et Spes*, which unequivocally condemned nuclear attacks on populated centers, based on the premise that such attacks violate just war principles of discrimination and proportionality. Yet John Paul II also recognized nations' desire for protection against aggressors, and he acknowledged the real threat that the Soviet Union posed. Hence, he stated that nuclear deterrence might be morally permissible but only as a step toward disarmament.[63]

One week after the pope's statement, the US bishops' committee released its first draft, entitled "God's Hope in a Time of Fear," which was distributed to the bishops' conference and was printed in the *National Catholic Reporter*. The draft began with an overview of the threats posed by nuclear weapons. It then highlighted the Christian legacy of pacifism, emphasizing the teachings and practices of Saint Francis of Assisi, Dorothy Day, and Martin Luther King Jr. While underscoring this pacifist tradition, the bishops' committee still recognized the right of states to defend their citizens. Yet the committee stated that the Catholic Church and its members must have "profound doubts" about the use of nuclear weapons in self-defense. The document condemned first-strike attacks and even the threat of a nuclear attack as morally unacceptable. It also incorporated the views of the nuclear freeze movement by calling for an immediate end to the production and deployment of nuclear armaments and negotiations to reduce existing stockpiles. Acknowledging that this would inevitably be a slow process, the committee stated that the possession of some nuclear weapons would be permissible, but not as a permanent solution.[64]

Once the draft was released, the committee moved into its second stage of public hearings. Comments came flooding in, including responses from seventy American bishops—most of which were favorable. Responses also came from Reagan administration officials, who did not have such favorable things to say about the document. Secretary of Defense Casper Weinberger justified the administration's deterrence policy as a source of safety and security and argued that the "burden of proof" fell on the bishops if they insisted on departing from this practice.[65] Lawrence Eagleburger, the undersecretary of state for political affairs, argued that a nuclear freeze would weaken the US government's bargaining power in negotiations with the Soviet Union. But these were minority views in the 700-plus pages of comments the committee received from bishops, clergy, laypeople, and security studies experts, most of whom strongly supported the statement; thus the concerns of the Reagan administration were sidelined as the committee began to revise the document.

Eventually, the committee released its final document, the pastoral letter *The Challenge of Peace*, which covered the biblical and ethical traditions of the just war position, pacifism, and nonviolence. The bishops affirmed that all are acceptable, and therefore they supported those Catholics who choose full conscientious objection or selective conscientious objection to war. The document also indicated that the American bishops were firmly committed to an agenda of disarmament and only begrudgingly tolerated deterrence as a realistic assessment of the global circumstances. Yet the bishops were firm in their insistence that first use of nuclear weapons was never morally justifiable. Moreover, they rejected the quest for nuclear superiority and underscored that deterrence was only an interim step toward disarmament.[66] The pastoral letter also included a "theology of peace," calling upon Catholics to engage in active nonviolence to obstruct acts of aggression. The final document stated:

The Christian has no choice but to defend peace, properly understood, against aggression. This is an inalienable obligation. It is the how of defending peace which offers moral options. . . . We see many deeply sincere individuals who, far from being indifferent or apathetic to world evils, believe strongly in conscience that they are best defending true peace by refusing to bear arms. In some cases they are motivated by their understanding of the gospel and the life and death of Jesus as forbidding all violence. In others, their motivation is simply to give personal example of Christian forbearance as a positive, constructive approach toward loving reconciliation with enemies. In still other cases, they propose or engage in "active non-violence" as programmed resistance to thwart aggression, or to render ineffective any oppression attempted by force of arms.[67]

Later in the document, the bishops once again underscored the value of nonviolence as an alternative:

Non-violent resistance, like war, can take many forms depending upon the demands of a given situation. There is, for instance, organized popular defense instituted by government as part of its contingency planning. Citizens would be trained in the techniques of peaceable non-compliance and non-cooperation as a means of hindering an invading force or non-democratic government from imposing its will. Effective non-violent resistance requires the united will of a people and may demand as much patience and sacrifice from those who practice it as is now demanded by war and preparation for war. It may not always succeed. Nevertheless, before the possibility is dismissed as impractical or unrealistic, we urge that it be measured against the almost certain effects of a major war.[68]

Conclusion

Even though some considered the final version of the pastoral letter to be a softer version of earlier drafts, *The Challenge of Peace* was widely hailed as a "watershed event in the history of the U.S. Catholic Church."[69] It marked a significant shift in the American Catholic Church, which for centuries had endorsed the ideas of the just war tradition. With the release of *The Challenge of Peace,* the church was now endorsing nonviolent alternatives. While this shift was partly a reflection of the rapidly expanding militarism of that time and the growing destructive capacity of nuclear weaponry, it also indicated that activist efforts were having an effect. Peace activists—such as those in PAX, the Catholic Worker, the Catholic Peace Fellowship, and the Plowshares movement— had made peace, war, and disarmament important topics for American Catholics to address.

3

Equality for Women and Catholic Feminism

While progressive Catholic activists challenged the church's just war position and support for escalating US militarism, others were challenging the church's belief in gender complementarity and exclusively male ordination. For centuries, the Vatican had stated that God had created men and women differently, and thus they have distinct roles within the church and home. Although various papal teachings underscored that men and women are of equal worth in the eyes of God, they had different attributes. Pope Pius XII stated, "[They] are not equal in every respect. Certain natural gifts, inclinations and dispositions, are proper only to the man, or only to the woman, according to the distinct fields of activity assigned them by nature."[1] These "natural" dispositions included female traits of sacrifice and service, and thus women's priority is to their families, according to traditional Catholic teachings.

Yet in the 1960s, secular and religious women alike were challenging such assumptions. In 1963, Betty Friedan published her influential book, *The Feminine Mystique.* In it, she wrote about the "problem that has no name"—that is, that completely devoting oneself to raising children and maintaining a household can leave one feeling unfulfilled, since women's other interests and abilities have no acceptable outlet:

> Each suburban wife struggles with it alone. As she made the beds, shopped for groceries, matched slipcover material, ate peanut butter sandwiches with her children, chauffeured Cub Scouts and Brownies, lay beside her husband at night—she was afraid to ask even of herself the silent question—"Is this all?" . . . The only way for a woman, as for a man, to find herself, to know herself as a person, is by creative work of her own.[2]

Additionally, numerous Catholic women had been active in the US civil rights movement during this period, promoting equality for African

Americans. Why, they asked, shouldn't women also be afforded equality in all spheres of life?

These influences helped promote the secular second-wave feminist movement in the United States. They also contributed to Catholic feminism. Yet, as historian Mary Henold argues, the Catholic feminist movement should not be considered merely an extension of its secular counterpart. In fact, some secular activists believed that feminism and Catholicism are incompatible, since they saw the Catholic Church as inherently patriarchal and sexist.[3] This was clear when Ti-Grace Atkinson spoke at Catholic University in 1971, shortly after she led the radical feminist departure from the liberal feminist National Organization for Women (NOW). She denounced the Roman Catholic Church for its "'conspiracy to imprison and enslave women,' after which she exclaimed, 'Motherfuckers! . . . The struggle between the liberation of women and the Catholic Church is a struggle to the death. So be it!'"[4]

While Catholic feminists share many beliefs, values, and goals with secular feminists, their movement had different roots. Moreover, those involved in the Catholic feminist movement took on different issues, such as the ordination of women and the transformation of exclusionary church practices and teachings. Their style of resistance was distinct, too. They often fought for women's rights through so-called unobtrusive tactics such as articulating egalitarian Catholic theologies and implementing gender-inclusive church practices.[5]

This chapter examines the origins, themes, and actions of the Catholic feminist movement in the United States. It begins with an overview of Catholic teachings on women, then looks at early voices and organizations that challenged these views and proposed biblical equality. Finally, the chapter focuses on several strategies of resistance, including movements for women's ordination, the creation of alternative "Women-Church" groups, and the promotion of diverse perspectives on contraception and reproductive rights.

Church Teachings on Gender Complementarity and Male Clerics

In the first seventy years of Catholic social teachings, women's concerns were rarely addressed. In fact, women were largely invisible, mentioned only in minor passing references. For instance, in *Rerum Novarum*, Pope

Leo XIII was primarily concerned about the dignity of workers in the height of the industrial era. His teachings were directed toward men, even though women also toiled in factories. When Leo did reference women, he held that their nature dictated their role within the home and that working outside the home constituted an aberration from natural law. This belief set the tone for all subsequent teachings, including Pope Pius XI's comments forty years later in *Quadragesimo Anno*. Pius XI stated, "Mothers, concentrating on household duties, should work primarily in the home or in its immediate vicinity. It is an intolerable abuse, and to be abolished at all cost, for mothers on account of the father's low wage to be forced to engage in gainful occupations outside the home to the neglect of their proper cares and duties, especially the training of the children."[6] The Vatican continued this line of thought in the encyclicals *Pacem in Terris* (1963) and *Octogesima Adveniens* (1971), affirming that men and women have equal worth in God's eyes, but that they have divergent roles.

Influences on Catholic Feminism

These teachings on gender were largely accepted for many decades. Yet by the mid-twentieth century, some US Catholics questioned the assumption that all females had similar natures that inherently predisposed them toward work in the home. Many also challenged the legitimacy of church teachings on contraception. These trends eventually culminated in formal Catholic feminist organizations in the 1970s, but important groundwork was laid much earlier. I begin this section with a review of various groups that contributed to an emergent feminist consciousness through their training of Catholic women and through social justice activism that instilled a critical mind-set. I then turn to the influence of the Vatican II Council, which both inspired and infuriated incipient Catholic feminists.

The Grail

One of the early contributors to Catholic feminism was the Grail movement. Established in 1921 by a Dutch Jesuit, Jacques van Ginneken, this movement trained women to serve as lay apostles and to promote

Christian humanism on a number of issues, including racism and poverty. After spreading through Europe, the Grail was introduced in the United States in 1940, with training centers established in six cities. Although the number of participants was relatively small, this training provided women with leadership skills and a new role within the Catholic Church. It also underscored that faith required a commitment to equality and social justice. As historian Jay Dolan stated, "The Grail reached relatively few people in the United States; an estimated fourteen thousand had participated in Grail programs by 1962. But . . . it was preparing these women for the church of the future. When the time came, Grail-trained women would emerge as advocates of a new Catholicism."[7]

Christian Family Movement

The Christian Family Movement (CFM) was another important influence on the development of Catholic feminism. This group emerged out of the Catholic Action trend, which called laypeople to transform society through the process of observing injustices, judging the situation in light of scripture, and then taking action (see-judge-act). CFM was officially launched in Chicago in 1949, headed by Pat and Patty Crowley. Under their leadership, the movement expanded to 30,000 couples, who focused primarily on issues of racial inequality and poverty. This movement was significant, since it prioritized the ideas of laypeople; priests were allowed to attend group meetings but primarily for the purpose of listening. To emphasize this point, priests were not allowed to speak until the end of the meeting to ensure that laypeople were at the front and center of the movement.[8] CFM also expanded the consciousness of many participants, who began to see social inequalities as contrary to God's will. As Patty Crowley put it, "For the first time in our experience of the church, our ideas were being respected. We were becoming independent, thinking for ourselves."[9]

Because of their leadership, the Crowleys in 1966 were invited to participate in the Papal Birth Control Commission, which strongly recommended that the Vatican lift the ban on contraception. They were disappointed when the Vatican ignored the commission's recommendation. For Patty Crowley and other Catholic laypeople, this ban led to critical questioning of gender issues more broadly. In fact, Patty Crowley decided to devote the latter part of her life to women's causes, establishing housing for homeless women and working with incarcerated women.[10]

While the Grail and CFM were part of the broader Catholic Action movement of that era, these two organizations stood out from others for three reasons. First, they were willing to take more radical stances on various social issues. Second, they were largely led by women. Third, they chose to be autonomous from other Catholic Action groups in order to retain their independence. Even though the Grail and CFM cannot be characterized as feminist in the beginning, they contributed to the critical thinking and engagement of women within the Catholic Church.

The "New Nuns"

A third influence on Catholic feminism came from the "new nuns," a term that refers to members of religious orders that engaged in nursing, teaching, and social work. Starting in the 1950s, these professions required more education and training. Because most Sisters entered religious life straight out of high school, few had the required credentials, and thus they began enrolling in universities. To promote education and greater professionalization among women religious, the group known as the Sister Formation Conference was formed in 1954. Two years later, the Conference of Major Superiors of Women (CMSW) was created and began discussing ways to modernize their religious orders. As Henold noted:

> The Vatican supported their goal of training, but the hierarchy did not foresee the consequences of encouraging women religious to seek higher education or of gatherings in one place. Women religious began to be influenced by the works of the Catholic revival, bringing the spirit of change in the American church of the fifties to the sisterhoods. Discussions of teaching credentials and training gradually led to talk about anachronistic dress, the desire for new apostolates, and how to modernize the sisterhoods, all happening well before the Second Vatican Council.[11]

By the 1960s, these new nuns were involved in other contemporary issues as well, including the civil rights and peace movements.

Vatican II Council

The Vatican II Council, held from 1962 to 1965, was another stimulus to Catholic feminism. Although women were not included in the deliberations, the council did encourage openness and an engagement with the modern world, which included an expanding feminist movement. It generated an atmosphere in which discussion of women's rights was possible.[12] Vatican II also created space for dissent as Catholics throughout the world witnessed bishops debating and disagreeing with one another. This revealed that the church was not homogeneous or monolithic but entailed a variety of viewpoints.

Yet Vatican II had mixed effects. On the one hand, it outraged many feminists, since it was clear during the meeting that sexism and patriarchy were firmly intact. For example, during council meetings, a female reporter was asked to leave the main floor during a session and sit in the balcony. Another woman, a British economist, planned to address the council fathers on the issue of global poverty; she was denied permission to speak, and her speech had to be delivered by a man. To many, this was clear evidence that institutional Catholicism discriminated against women. In response to these criticisms, the Vatican Council invited twenty-three female auditors to the third session. Even then, those twenty-three women were forced to eat at a separate café.[13] On the other hand, however, the Vatican II Council inspired others to challenge outdated Catholic notions about women in the modern world. The executive director of the National Council of Catholic Women, Margaret Mealey, commented:

> By the action and pronouncements of Vatican II, women have been given their wings. But too may pastors and bishops are reluctant to let them fly. If the church is to be relevant in the world, it must pay serious attention to the status of its women. Catholic women are growing tired of being ignored in this most important area of their lives, but they are ready to step forward and assume an adult role in the Church with intelligence and grace when it is offered. It is not yet too late—but it is surely high time.[14]

In this spirit, members of the Grail movement decided to embrace feminism. They saw it as a natural extension of the Vatican II emphasis on social justice and the dignity of all people—which, they argued, included women.[15]

Forms of Catholic Feminist Activism

While all these influences spurred American Catholic women to action, many of their tactics were different from those of other progressive movements. Instead of demonstrations, boycotts, or civil disobedience, their activism primarily took four forms. First, it challenged traditional church teachings, particularly beliefs in the "essential woman" and gender complementarity. This was done through the development of feminist theologies that emphasized scriptural egalitarianism. Second, Catholic feminists engaged in "discursive politics," a term used by Mary Katzenstein to denote the "politics of reflection and reformulation" and the process of meaning making.[16] She stated, "Discursive politics is intended to challenge deeply held beliefs, but it directly challenges the way people *write* and *talk* about these beliefs."[17] Third, Catholic feminists pushed for changes in church practices, including women's ordination and inclusive liturgical practices. Fourth, feminists challenged the church's stance on contraception. We now turn to a more in-depth examination of these various forms of activism.

Feminist Theology

While the Vatican II Council was under way, a number of feminists began publishing critical views of traditional Catholic teachings about women. One of the earliest was Rosemary Lauer's article "Women and the Church" (1963), published in *Commonweal*, a Catholic periodical for laypeople. Lauer described the various forms of discrimination that women experience and critiqued the institution's patriarchal history, citing the most misogynistic quotations from early Christian fathers. She also noted the contradictions between the social justice rhetoric of Vatican II and the reality of Catholic women's experiences. She concluded her article by calling for wide-scale changes in the church, including female ordination.[18]

Lauer's article inspired a young theologian, Mary Daly, who was finishing her doctoral studies in Switzerland. Daly immediately wrote a letter to the editor at *Commonweal*, praising the article and predicting that many more would follow. Daly wrote, "This much I know: the beginnings of these articles and these books (how badly we need these books, especially!) are already in the minds and on the lips of many of us. And—this is both prophecy and a promise—they will come."[19] She was right. According to historian Mary Henold, there were forty articles printed between 1954 and 1970 that were written by thirty-seven Catholic feminists (two-thirds of whom were laywomen) and published in sixteen different Catholic periodicals.[20]

I can only briefly highlight here several works that were influential during this early period. These include Sidney Callahan's *The Illusion of Eve: Modern Woman's Quest for Identity* (1965), Mary Daly's book *The Church and the Second Sex* (1968), and the various writings of Rosemary Radford Ruether. In these publications, the authors proposed ways that the church could open itself to a new generation, fulfilling the intentions of the Vatican Council. For the Catholic Church to modernize, these writers argued, it would first need to relinquish its archaic myths regarding women. Toward that goal, the theologians took a dual approach. First, they bluntly criticized the sexism present in Catholic traditions, theology, and clerical culture. Second, they offered a new conception of Catholic women's identity and an alternative interpretation of scripture. As Henold observed, "Such an approach resulted in a distinct faith-based feminism coupled with a complex, often ambivalent relationship to the church. . . . In their first phase, Catholic feminists were generally optimistic about the church's future and their relationship to it."[21]

To delve into the themes of these early writings, I begin with Sidney Callahan's work. Callahan, a convert to Catholicism, had been inspired by the work of the Grail, Dorothy Day, and the new reformist liturgies. When a publisher at Sheed and Ward Press asked Callahan to write a book about Catholic women, she agreed. Initially, she intended to emphasize the legitimacy of the church's "eternal woman" teachings, which held that females are predisposed to sacrifice and suffering, making them uniquely equipped to focus on family life and the home. In the course of writing the book, however, she was transformed. She ended up criticizing this teaching and articulating a Catholic version of Friedan's *Feminine Mystique*. Yet Callahan's book was not heavily theological. Instead, she practically promoted the idea that Catholic women could pursue their careers while simultaneously fulfilling their marriage and family commitments and addressing social issues. Yet this book was important, offering an early challenge to the church's view that women's divinely ordained role was to serve their spouses and children.

A few years later, Mary Daly confronted the Catholic Church's legacy of patriarchy and inequality in her book *The Church and the Second Sex* (1968). Although Daly was critical of the church's treatment of women, she maintained that the church was redeemable. To redeem itself, Daly argued, the church had to break away from its limiting and contradictory views of women and its exclusionary practices. In a 1968 interview in the periodical *U.S. Catholic*, Daly explained:

> The church and the history of the church's attitude toward women has been a record of contradictions. On one hand, the church has put women on a pedestal; you see this in the scriptures, in the Fathers, the theologians, in the popes—particularly Leo XIII, Pius XI, Pius XII. On the other hand, in point of fact, the church has actually humiliated and degraded women. When I say women have been put on a pedestal, I mean in the figure of one woman—Mary, the ideal, the model. This has served as a compensation process, because women in the concrete as individuals are not treated as human beings of equal stature with men in the church. . . .
>
> Now you ask me what are the signs of the secondary status of women in the church. The most obvious sign and crystallization of the whole problem, to me, is the exclusion of women from the priesthood. Here you have a clear-cut case. By the very fact that women are excluded, you are saying that no matter what the personal qualifications of the individual, no matter what the educational stature or virtue, by reason of sex alone a whole mass of persons are excluded from functions, which obviously they are capable of performing. But I take this merely as symbol and sign of the problem. I don't think it will be any panacea to go out and ordain women. . . . [S]tart with the liturgical functions. Consider the experience of a young girl going to Mass in the ordinary parish church. She sees that, first of all, the Mass is being said by a priest and the servers are all boys. When she goes to confession, she confesses her sins to a man. When she receives Confirmation, a man does this. The Pope is a man. And the angels are called he. Christ is male. God is called He. I think you have to

consider the very subtle conditioning that comes through. She is conditioned to think in terms of specific inferiority because of this.[22]

Daly also made an important contribution by providing an alternative explanation for church teachings that have been used to justify differential treatment of men and women. She argued that these teachings had to be understood as a reflection of a particular culture and time period:

In my book, I analyze biblical texts—scripture, Genesis, St. Paul. The New Testament statements reflecting the antifeminism of those times were never those of Christ. The most striking antifeminist passages are, of course, in the Pauline texts and they are the ones most frequently cited by clerics who were brought up in the old school. There is a fundamental answer to this: We have to see these texts in their historical context. For example, St. Paul wanted women to have their heads covered because in Corinth to go out with your head uncovered was to behave like a prostitute in that society. But to take that statement out of context and now tell women that they should have hats on in church is rather absurd. So a fundamental principle is to see statements always within the context of evolving consciousness and cultural revolution. To take biblical statements as dicta for what must be done now, abstracting from time and space and abstracting from history, is, I think, a perversity.[23]

At that time, Daly was still optimistic about the church's capacity to change. In recognizing that scriptural teachings on women's behavior were primarily a reflection of that era's cultural practices, the Catholic Church could dispense with these gender-based practices and move toward egalitarianism. Daly stated:

Now hopefully we can still discover within Christianity the seeds of liberation. You can find within Christianity the message of the dignity of the human person. It's there. . . . Essentially, all of us are made in the image of God. This is what we have to consider. If there is value in Christianity, it is in this: That it has given the message that we are all born to develop ourselves in creative, self-transcendent activities, to move more and more in the image of God. Any teaching and any practice that hampers this would be harmful and would really be anti-

Christian. . . . I would say that Vatican II has opened the way and things are moving forward.[24]

Within a few years, however, Daly changed her opinion. She concluded that the Catholic Church was irredeemably oppressive, and she rejected Christianity.

Another influential feminist theologian of the post–Vatican II era is Rosemary Radford Ruether. Ruether has written numerous works, including dozens of books and hundreds of articles. Her early groundbreaking work included the article, "Male Chauvinist Theology and the Anger of Women" (1971) and the books *Religion and Sexism: Images of Women in the Jewish and Christian Traditions* (1998), *Sexism and God-Talk: Toward a Feminist Theology* (1983), and *Women-Church: Theology and Practice of Feminist Liturgical Communities* (1985), among others. In these works, Ruether's primary emphasis is on the need to end the church's patriarchy and sexism. For centuries, church leaders had depicted women in unfavorable and inferior terms. For example, Tertullian described women as "the devil's gateway," while Augustine argued that "the good Christian likes what is human, loathes what is feminine."[25] Centuries later, Thomas Aquinas continued the legacy, stating that "woman is defective and misbegotten" and "in a [natural] state of subjection."[26] Ruether stressed that theology had been written by men, who assumed themselves to be normative human beings and women to be secondary. Such patriarchy distorts the message of the gospel. Ruether wrote:

> Women have been defined as possessing an inferior and non-normative humanity, to be more responsible for the origins of evil than males, to be more prone to sin than males, to be in a state of subjugation, both as an expression of their lesser nature and as punishment for their role in original sin, to lack the image of God and to be unable to represent Christ and to be unordainable.[27]

Ruether called upon the church to adopt new beliefs and traditions that uphold and affirm the humanity of both women and men.[28]

In summary, the writings of Callahan, Daly, Ruether, and other Catholic feminists included four key themes. The first theme is a critique of the history of patriarchy and sexism within the church. Specifically, these feminists took aim at the "essential woman" idea within Catholicism that glorified the traits of passivity, receptivity, sacrifice, and suffering. Such glorification is most clearly visible in the veneration of the Virgin Mary. These feminists argued that such traits were not exclusively female and that the church overemphasized differences between men and women, which inevitably led to discrimination.

A second theme within Catholic feminism is that patriarchal and discriminatory behaviors are incompatible with the life and teachings of Christ. As Sidney Callahan put it, "Christ treated women with revolutionary equality. . . . He taught women, healed women, forgave them, and cherished them as friends. . . . Christianity is a revolutionary religion; its view of women is part of that revolution."[29] Catholic feminists noted that Christ's female followers were the only ones who accompanied him during his crucifixion and were the first to be given the mandate to spread the word of his resurrection. If the church is to model Christ's behavior, it must welcome women fully.

Third, Catholic feminist theologians criticized the sexism present in liturgical practice, including the ban on women in holy orders, the priesthood, and the hierarchy. They sought to open all liturgical positions to women, including the roles of lector, altar server, sacristan, and priest. As Lauer put it, "Woman's soul does not differ from man's and therefore can receive the sacramental character of ordination as well as his."[30] An exclusively male priesthood is, she maintained, an anachronism.

The fourth theme of Catholic feminism is the denunciation of the church's teachings on birth control and its stance that sex is only about procreation. Ruether was a particularly vocal critic of these policies. She argued that most spouses had sex for the intimacy and bond that it forges between two partners. She also pointed out the contradiction in the church's acceptance of the rhythm method: it divorced sex from procreation, but it was deemed acceptable by the clergy. So why weren't other forms of contraception accepted? Ruether further addressed the problems that resulted from multiple pregnancies and the burdens they placed on marriages and families. Under these conditions, she argued, "sex comes to mean fear, not love. . . . The more happily two people are married, the more deeply they know that sexual intercourse has a validity and meaning of its own. . . . this union of man and woman is an end in itself, and its fruits are just as real in the sterile marriage as in the fruitful one." She argued that men and women want control over their lives: "I see very clearly that I cannot entrust my destiny just to biological chance. . . . A woman who cannot control her own fertility, who must remain vulnerable to chance conception, is a woman who cannot hope to be much more than a baby-machine."[31]

The Call for Women's Ordination

Inspired by these new theological teachings, a number of feminist organizations formed in the 1970s with the intent to open the Catholic Church to women's participation. The impetus for this came from two sources. First, in 1972, Pope Paul VI issued an apostolic letter, *Ministerium Quaedem*, which reaffirmed the church's exclusion of women from the priesthood and from other lay ministries. Second, the United Nations declared that 1975 would be designated the International Women's Year.

Catholic women felt that the time was right to challenge their church. At the 1974 annual meeting of the Leadership Conference of Women Religious, the organization passed a resolution to push for the opening of all ministries and decision-making bodies within the church to women. Separately, a laywoman, Mary Lynch, brought together 31 people in December 1974 for a strategy and discussion session. This group organized the first national women's ordination conference, held in Detroit in 1975, and was amazed when 1,200 people showed up and another 500 had to be turned away.[32] To create an organizational base to ensure continuity in the struggle, the group formed the Women's Ordination Conference.

The Vatican became concerned about the growing feminist demand for women's ordination. In response, the experts of the Pontifical Biblical Commission—a group within the Roman Curia whose task is to ensure appropriate interpretation of scripture—met in 1976. After deliberations, the commission issued an announcement that there was no scriptural basis for denying women access to the priesthood. This led the Vatican's Congregation for the Doctrine of Faith to release its own document, "Declaration on the Question of the Admission of Women to the Ministerial Priesthood," in January 1977. In this declaration, Vatican leaders stated that women cannot become priests for three reasons: (1) none of Christ's disciples were women, (2) the Catholic Church's apostolic and infallible tradition has always had an exclusively male priesthood, and (3) women do not reflect the image of Jesus.[33] The document stated: "The Incarnation of the Word took place according to the male sex: this is indeed a question of fact, and this fact, while not implying an alleged natural superiority of man over woman, cannot be disassociated from the economy of salvation."[34]

Rather than putting an end to the issue, the Vatican document had the opposite effect. Polls indicated that the proportion of US Catholics who supported female ordination actually expanded after the declaration to more than 60 percent.[35] So when the Women's Ordination Conference met again in Baltimore in 1978, feminists such as Elisabeth Schüssler Fiorenza argued that their response should be to challenge the church, not accept its decree. Their resistance took two forms: (1) continuing the dialogue with the church about women's ordination, using biblical scholars' work to offer another interpretation of women's roles; and (2) initiating public protest. One month after the declaration's release, feminists gathered for prayer vigils at cathedrals throughout the nation. Many of them were denied entrance, and thus they vigiled on the front steps, garnering even more media attention. National protests were held in Washington, DC, and Chicago, while feminists invited bishops to discuss the issue.

Catholic feminists found another opportunity to press for women's ordination in 1979, when Pope John Paul II visited the United States. During his stop in Washington, DC, Sister Theresa Kane, president of the Leadership Conference of Women Religious, urged the pope to open up the priesthood and all ministries to women. He ignored her comments, delivering his prepared speech without any reference to the ordination issue.[36]

Eventually, some Catholic feminists concluded that they should not wait for the Vatican to change its position. Some considered ordination in other denominations, such as the Episcopalian Church. Fiorenza spoke out against this idea, arguing that "to move out of the church rather than continue the struggle within it would mean giving up our birthright and abandoning our people who are Catholic wo/men."[37] Womenpriest Bishop Bridget Mary Meehan put it similarly, "Does that mean that they can take our faith away? My faith is in my DNA. I'm an Irish Catholic woman and I'm passionate about my faith. I'm as much a Catholic as the pope is. We're not leaving the church, we're leading the church."[38]

This was the sentiment behind a movement called Roman Catholic Womenpriests, which in 2002 began to illicitly ordain women. To date, nearly 150 womenpriests have been ordained, and they celebrate the Eucharist in their homes or in small communities. They follow the "worker priest" tradition in which they are employed in other fields and conduct pastoral duties without salary, for the most part. These womenpriests see themselves as part of the apostolic tradition of being ordained by bishops and thus part of the succession of priests from the early church. However, they reject numerous parts of the traditional priesthood. They reject celibacy; many are married. They reject the tradition of hierarchy; instead, they have an elected group from the community that makes administrative decisions. They reject the idea of obedience to bishops; they choose instead to be obedient to the Holy Spirit.[39] In short, they are engaged in a type of activism called prefigurative politics: living today as you want the future to be. As one womanpriest put it, "We live inside the not yet, right now."[40]

Roman Catholic leaders, including the pope, have condemned this practice, and the womenpriests have been excommunicated. Yet the movement shows no signs of disappearing as the womenpriests work to transform the church by deconstructing "the pathology of the male priesthood, its myths, its exclusivity, its misogyny."[41] They do not see themselves as disobedient to the church; they argue that their obedience is to God, not to the Catholic hierarchy.

The Emergence of Women-Church and Discursive Politics

In this initial period of Catholic feminism, two trends emerged in the 1970s. Some women, like Mary Daly, abandoned the church, believing that it was irredeemable and intrinsically oppressive for women. Others remained but concentrated on changing the church by pushing for women's ordination. Yet during this time, numerous Catholic feminists—women religious and laywomen alike—realized that female ordination was not the only issue. In fact, some wanted to do away with the notion of priesthood altogether and create egalitarian worship communities.

By the 1980s, another group of feminists embraced Elizabeth Schüssler Fiorenza's concept of a "discipleship of equals."[42] Building on this concept, they created the Women-Church movement, which expressed feminist spirituality through the creation of its own liturgy. Moreover, in response to criticisms that the Womenpriest movement was a white elitist movement, they envisioned themselves as church from the margins. From its beginnings in 1983, the Women-Church movement was bilingual—in English and Spanish—and approximately 10 percent of those who participated were Latinas.[43] The purpose of this movement was not only to move away from a priesthood but also to transform the language and practices of worship to be gender inclusive. Feminist theologian Rosemary Radford Ruether articulated the rationale behind the movement:

> We must do more than protest the old. We must begin to live the new humanity now. *We must begin to incarnate the community of faith in the liberation of humanity from patriarchy in words and deed, in new words, new prayers, new symbols, and new praxis.* This means that we need to form gathered communities to support us as we set out on our exodus from patriarchy. . . . [W]e often cannot even continue to communicate within these traditional church institutions unless we have an alternative community of reference that nurtures and supports our beings.[44]

These new Women-Church groups operated like base communities or house churches. Groups of women would gather regularly for potlucks, to share stories, and to celebrate liturgy. The liturgical experience typically includes rituals that help women heal from the wounds that many have experienced: domestic violence, rape, and shaming of their sexuality or sexual orientation. They read passages that call upon participants to remember their foremothers. There is no hierarchical leadership, and participants reject the division between laypeople and clergy.[45] Rather, members take turns planning, hosting, and leading the liturgy. It is a reversal of the Vatican's hierarchical system.

Although one could view this as women breaking away from Roman Catholicism to start their own church, these Catholic feminists insist that is not what they are doing. They are still within the church and committed to it; they just are building an "alternative institution" that embodies the ideals of feminism and rejects, in word and action, all forms of patriarchy. By practicing differently, they are transforming Roman Catholicism. As one participant put it: "Every institution in this country is patriarchal. . . . Am I going to tell women not to run for Congress, not to take tenured positions in universities? No, I'm going to tell them to take that chisel and chisel from inside."[46]

But can we really call this activism? Women-Church activism takes the form of building alternative institutions and reclaiming power. As John Gaventa has argued, there are three dimensions of power: (1) the power to make decisions; (2) the power to determine policy and public debates; and (3) the power to control "social myths, language, and symbols" that influence people's options.[47] While Catholic feminist activists had no power to make decisions regarding ordination or opening up lay ministries to women, they do have the capacity to shape public debates about women within the church, and they do have the capacity to change language and symbols, which they do through the Women-Church practices.[48]

The Women-Church and Womenpriest movements can be viewed as complementary, as Ruether has stated. The former is more of an informal community, like a circle of friends who meet regularly to discuss books and ideas; the latter is a formalized ministry that is comparable to a class with credentialed instructors. From Ruether's perspective, one provides a vision of a renewed church while the other provides a vision of a renewed priesthood.[49] Both are acts of resistance that aim to transform the Catholic Church.

Challenging the Church's View of Birth Control and Family Planning

Another major issue for Catholic feminists is contraception and family planning. In fact, numerous scholars have argued that the controversy over birth control propelled many Catholic laywomen toward activism.[50] The opposition began as early as 1930, when Pope Pius XI released his encyclical *Casti Connubii*. In this document, the pope unequivocally condemned birth control, stating, "Any use whatsoever of marriage, in the exercise of which the act by human effort is deprived of its natural power of procreating life, violates the law of God and nature, and those who do such a thing are stained by a grave and mortal flaw."[51] But from the beginning, some families used birth control despite the Vatican's prohibition. And, as priests saw the burden that resulted from having large families, particularly for working-class parents, many felt conflicted themselves. A few years after *Casti Connubii* was released, the Catholic Church proposed the rhythm method of birth control, which entails abstaining from sex when a woman is ovulating.

By the 1960s, however, many US Catholics rejected the rhythm method for several reasons. First, the method was not particularly reliable, and using it often resulted in unplanned pregnancies. Second, many women found the required practice of taking their rectal temperature each morning (to discern if they were ovulating) to be unpleasant or downright repulsive. One woman stated, "It is our view that if clergy took rectal temperatures that Catholic marrieds would not still be waiting for an answer on contraception."[52] Third, more laypeople opposed the rhythm method because they increasingly saw sex as an inherently valuable part of marriage and not merely for the purpose of procreation. Abstinence, therefore, put a strain on a very important part of marital life. Not surprisingly, then, one national survey found that 38 percent of American Catholics were using contraception by 1960.[53]

Dissent over the church's teachings became more overt in 1963, when the lay-edited Catholic magazine *Jubilee* published two articles that challenged the ban on contraception. The magazine subsequently received a deluge of letters from readers, who heartily agreed with the articles. Many laypeople were questioning the morality and logic of the church's stance. Leslie Woodcock Tentler summarized the sentiments of many Catholics in this era:

> Cannot one sin by *having a child*, in the telling words of one father of a family of five—a child for whom the parents were not physically, emotionally, or financially prepared? Was it not gravely wrong to risk one's marriage in dogged obedience to a teaching that no longer made moral sense? . . . Was it right to consign every married woman to a life wholly centered on childbearing, no matter what her talents and aspirations?[54]

Increasingly, laypeople were making up their own minds. Consequently, the proportion of Catholics who used birth control increased steadily, to 53 percent in 1965 and then to 68 percent in 1970.[55]

Yet as a growing number of laypeople were discussing birth control, the Vatican reinforced its stance on contraception. The papal encyclical *Humanae Vitae* was published in 1968, reiterating that the use of birth control was a sin. Many laypeople were stunned, especially since the appointed papal commission had recommended revising the teaching.

How did American Catholics respond to *Humanae Vitae*? Most simply ignored the teaching.[56] In essence, they practiced the tactic of noncooperation. Others overtly challenged the church's ban on contraception and family planning. In 1970s, a lobby group was formed called Catholics for the Elimination of All Restrictive Contraception and Abortion Laws. A few years later, in 1973, this lobby group contributed to the emergence of a new organization called Catholics for a Free Choice, which was later renamed Catholics for Choice.[57] This organization worked for reproductive rights, but it also aimed to legitimate the role of individual conscience as the basis for moral decision making. The organization's tasks included providing educational materials and research to Catholic members of Congress, emphasizing that the majority of American Catholics did not agree with Vatican teachings on contraception, abortion, and sexuality.

Catholics for Choice captured international attention during the US presidential election of 1984. Walter Mondale won the Democratic primary race and selected Geraldine Ferraro as his vice presidential running mate. Cardinal John Joseph O'Connor, archbishop of New York, warned that Catholics should not vote for Ferraro because of her prochoice position. The president of Catholics for Choice, Frances Kissling, decided that it was time to respond. In October 1984, the organization took out a paid advertisement in the *New York Times*, with the headline "A Diversity of Opinions on Abortion Exists among Committed Catholics." The ad, signed by more than eighty priests, nuns, and lay theologians, stated that there was more than one ethically legitimate position on abortion within the Catholic tradition and called for a dialogue on the topic.[58]

The Vatican responded quickly, sending notices to the bishops and religious superiors of those who had signed. The letter, from Cardinal

Jean Jerome Hamer, head of the Vatican's Sacred Congregation for Religious and Secular Institutes, warned that the ad contradicted church teachings, which stated that abortion is a sin and that anyone who has an abortion incurs automatic excommunication. The letter required a public retraction from all those who signed the ad; those who refused to do so would face repercussions, including the possibility of being dismissed from their religious orders. The laypeople who signed the ad also faced punitive measures. Several academics found that nearly all their speaking engagements at Catholic universities were canceled. Yet the repressive measures were not effective. While two priests and two brothers did issue retractions, the others did not, and their religious superiors refused to punish them. And a year after the initial ad was published, another group called the Committee of Concerned Catholics issued a letter of solidarity and support for the signers, upholding their right to dissent.[59] In the end, most of those who signed were involved in a two-year negotiation with the Vatican, which resulted in a compromise. Some Catholic feminists saw this as an important victory in which the heads of religious orders refused to dismiss those who had signed, thereby upholding the right of Catholics to hold differing views on this issue.

In bringing this chapter to a close, it is important to emphasize that not all Catholic feminists are pro-choice. Many are pro-life. Whatever their position, these feminist activists have called upon church leadership to listen to the experiences of laypeople, since church leaders, as celibate men, do not always understand the challenges of family planning and marital sexuality. Particularly on the issue of birth control, Catholic feminists challenged the policy, stimulated debate, and encouraged people to follow their own moral conscience.

Conclusion

For decades, American Catholic feminists have been active, calling upon the church to fulfill the vision of the Vatican II Council to open itself to the modern world. Part of that entailed addressing the needs of modern women, who found themselves limited and constrained by Catholic beliefs about women's nature. It also entailed the denunciation of the church's history of excluding women from many aspects of religious life and ministry. These feminists have called for egalitarian and inclusive forms of worship. They have demanded that the Catholic hierarchy take into account the effects that its contraceptive ban has had on the daily lives of married men and women. They have underscored the right to dissent with church leaders. For the most part, this was activism within the church, aiming to transform the institution as well as the men and women who viewed themselves as loyal Catholics. Although the movement has not instigated any official change within Vatican policy, it has influenced many laypeople, who have increasingly chosen to follow their own conscience on such matters, even when it contradicts official church positions.

4

Liberation Theology and the Central America Solidarity Movement

I was a priest before I joined the underground [guerrillas]. . . . It was as a priest, a very young and idealistic priest, that I first moved out to the jungles to work with the people. And of course it was the people who ended up educating and working with me. . . . You would not believe how the first project went. They knew I was coming to teach reading and writing, and when I arrived the village had already organized itself. Ten members of the community had been selected to learn first and were excused from community work for the time they were to study. The others carried their workload for them. In return, they studied. I mean they really studied. After ten days they could read and write. Not well, not quickly, but they could read and write. I was dumbfounded. And the villagers had already arranged for how these ten were now to teach another group of ten each, and so on, until the community was educated. I had come with so many ideas about community organizing, community spirit, but these people were far ahead of me. . . .

I would never have left if the army had not arrived. I would have stayed forever as a jungle priest . . . but there was trouble over land. The villagers had been there for generations, sweating and laboring to change the land from the malarial swamp it was, into decent farmable lands. They had built up their village, organized some medical care, and communally purchased equipment and machinery. It was working. Out of nothing they had created a decent life, poor but decent. And now wealthy families nearby began to claim that the land was theirs, and the army came to support those claims. People began to be threatened. Some were killed, some houses were burned. . . . We tried legal channels but the people were cheated. The courts mistranslated their documents to state that they were relinquishing their lands instead of claiming them as their own. . . .

[T]he repression grew worse. Throughout our whole region there was death. I was working wildly, near despair. It was then that I received word that the army decided to kill me. I would not be the first priest to die in Guatemala—several others, even foreigners, had already died here, assassinated. A woman came to tell me, the wife of a soldier involved in the plans. She had heard them plotting in her back room, and being a religious woman, had come to warn me. . . . And so I left, fleeing underground to the capital to the homes of some old friends. I had heard of a new resistance movement starting up, one that focused heavily on recognition of Indian rights and that was composed mostly of Mayan villagers. I asked my friends about this . . . determined to find these people. They laughed gently at me, embracing me and shaking their heads. . . . [T]hey told me, "Those people you are looking for are back there, right back up there where you have been all these years." . . . And so now, fifteen years later, I am still with the guerrillas, still with the people I have always loved. They are no longer tilling their lands, and I am no longer saying Mass, but we are still together, struggling for our community, struggling for a better future.[1]

This is the brief account of a priest who joined Guatemala's revolutionary movement in the 1980s. During this period, religion and politics were mixing in powerful and controversial ways throughout Latin America as a result of liberation theology. To understand why this unique religious belief system emerged, one must understand the history of the region, where centuries of colonialism established a strong Roman Catholic tradition as well as economic and political systems that concentrated power and wealth in the hands of a small minority. This minority became increasingly affluent while most of the population was impoverished. As the gap between the rich and the poor expanded, indigent Latin Americans began to mobilize. Many joined unions and organizations that were working to redistribute land and promote access to education and health care services. They quickly found that the nation's elites were not supportive; on the contrary, the upper class and the government actively resisted any efforts at change. The elite-backed government cracked down brutally. Yet as the state became more repressive, the poor became more revolutionary.

With revolutionary impulses expanding, leaders of the Latin American Catholic Church concluded that they could not remain neutral. Influenced by the Vatican II Council's emphasis on engaging with the modern world, many priests and nuns questioned how Catholics should respond to this suffering and inequality. Out of this reflection process, liberation theology was born.

This chapter examines the conditions that fostered liberation theology, providing a brief overview of this theology's central themes and how it fueled revolutionary movements, particularly in Nicaragua, El Salvador, and Guatemala. The chapter also summarizes the Catholic hierarchy's responses, ranging from sympathy to condemnation, and highlights several US movements that expressed solidarity with Central American Catholics who were fighting for social justice.

Background

Colonization

When the Spanish and Portuguese set out for the "new world," they were driven by a variety of motives. They were compelled by the desire to acquire wealth, to expand the territory and influence of their homelands, and to save the souls of the indigenous people. The impact of colonization was devastating to the Mayan, Aztec, and Incan civilizations, which once numbered between 90 and 112 million.[2] These groups were decimated by new diseases brought by the Europeans, as well as by the military might of the Spanish, who used their power to enslave many, to confiscate land, and to execute those who resisted.

The Catholic Church often sanctioned these actions as necessary for spreading the gospel. Some Catholic leaders even expressed doubts about whether the indigenous had souls.[3] But not all Catholic leaders shared these views. In the sixteenth century, several individuals spoke passionately against the brutalization of indigenous peoples. For example, Antonio de Montesinos preached to the settlers of Española:

> Tell me by what right and under what law do you hold these Indians in such cruel and horrible servitude? By what authority do you make such detestable war against these people who were dwelling gently and peacefully in their lands? . . . You kill them every day to gain wealth! . . . Are they not men? Do they not have souls? Are you not commanded to love them as yourselves?[4]

By the nineteenth century, most Latin American nations had gained independence. Those who had pushed for independence were primarily elites with a liberal orientation who wished to minimize the Catholic Church's role in national affairs. Feeling threatened, the Catholic hierarchy in most Latin America countries aligned themselves with the conservative parties, large landowners, and the old aristocracy that embraced traditional church-state alliances. It increasingly devoted itself to serving these elites, primarily through teaching in private Catholic schools and serving wealthy parishes. Over time, this focus on elites, combined with a shortage of clergy, meant that the Catholic Church had diminishing ties to and influence on the impoverished populations in Latin America.

Decline of Modernization Theory and the Rise of Dependency Theory

Moving into the twentieth century, Latin Americans turned their attention to methods of modernization. By midcentury, economists in wealthy nations were formulating policies to stimulate prosperity globally. In the 1950s and 1960s, the dominant approach to development was rooted in modernization theory, promoted by US economist Walter Rostow, who served as an adviser to President Dwight Eisenhower. The basic premise of Rostow's approach is that underdeveloped nations need to adopt the values, institutions, and practices of the United States and Western European countries. Specifically, modernization theory holds that most undeveloped nations, such as those in Central America, were in a traditional stage in which agriculture was the primary form of production and societies were dominated by family and clan affiliation. In order to advance, such nations need to open themselves to Western values, technology, and aid. Once this occurs, the nation moves toward the "take-off stage," whereby the influence of traditional institutions (such as tribes and extended families) declines and people move from a subsistence existence toward economic specialization, which stimulates local trade. As trade expands, people develop a profit motive, which in turn promotes industrialization and efficiency. Eventually, the country will move into the next stage of development, called the "drive to technological maturity," in which countries begin exporting goods and participating in international trade. Eventually, as the economy expands and incomes rise, a nation can reach the "high mass consumption" stage whereby citizens primarily reside in urban centers, have a wide array of goods and services available, and have access to education and health care.[5]

Modernization theory had a strong influence on international development policy, but there were growing criticisms. One of the main critiques was that this is a Eurocentric approach that compels societies to abandon their own culture and adopt the culture of industrialized nations. This approach, according to critics, has contributed to the devastation of indigenous cultures. Moreover, it assumes that market capitalism is unequivocally good without recognizing the problems that high mass consumption societies create, including environmental devastation and predatory labor policies. Finally, it suggests that undeveloped nations are to blame for their plight, choosing traditional and backward practices rather than technological and industrial advancement.

An alternative view, known as "dependency theory," was proposed in reaction to modernization theory. Dependency theorists, such as Andre Gunder Frank, argued that undeveloped nations are not to blame for their poverty. Rather, these countries are impoverished because Western nations have intentionally underdeveloped them. These theorists posit that the international capitalist system relies on a division of labor between rich "core" societies and poor "peripheral" nations. Core nations exploit peripheral ones in a variety of ways, using their land, labor, and resources for their own profit and to have access to inexpensive goods.[6]

This type of global exploitation can occur because of the colonial legacy of many underdeveloped nations, including those in Central America. When nations gained political independence from their colonizers, they often did not gain economic independence. Instead, the newly autonomous government typically inherited a highly stratified system in which a small minority held a disproportionate share of wealth and political power while the formerly colonized often were landless, lacked resources, and had little political representation. These postcolonial circumstances made it difficult to bring about change within the political system, which was dominated by elite interests.

A second concern is that underdeveloped nations often have narrow, export-oriented economies. During colonization, the conquering countries confiscated land from indigenous groups and set up large plantations to grow crops for export—such as coffee, sugar, and bananas—that could not be cultivated in European climates. This meant that local people had little or no land to grow food, increasing their hunger and malnutrition rates. Another problem with these narrow, export-oriented economies is that they put nations in a highly precarious situation: if a freeze or pest infestation destroyed crops, the entire economy would be adversely affected. This is in marked contrast to nations with diversified economies, which are able to weather a downturn in one export since they have numerous other products and services to sell.

Finally, there is the effect of multinational corporations. Global companies began moving into underdeveloped countries in the twentieth century precisely because there were few regulations, and companies could pay wages that were well below standards in the industrialized north. The elite classes welcomed multinational corporations into their countries as a way to curry favor with wealthy nations. Moreover, in the event that the poor would rebel, the local elites believed that multinational corporations would appeal to their home governments to stop the uprising to ensure that their profitable businesses could continue. In short, these arrangements were highly lucrative for local elites as well as multinational corporations, and thus the two groups collaborated with and supported one another.

Guatemala's history illustrates dependency theory and the difficulty of breaking free from neocolonial structures. Colonization of the region began in 1524, when Spanish conquistadors came in search of gold and silver. What they quickly realized, however, was that the real wealth was in Guatemala's fertile soil, and they seized the most arable land. Then they outlawed indigenous communal lands and passed legislation that required all Maya to work for the colonizer-owned farms for an established number of hours per week. Over time, this enabled colonizers to develop plantations that grew cacao, tobacco, sugarcane, and bananas for export. As demand for these crops increased, colonists confiscated more land, expanding their estates while diminishing the amount of land available to the Maya. Because many of the poor no longer had sufficient land to feed their families, they were forced to work on the plantations, typically for substandard wages.

These practices increased the gap between the rich and the poor. By the start of the twentieth century, 2 percent of Guatemalans owned 70 percent of the land, and Guatemala had become the most impoverished nation in the Western Hemisphere. By the mid-1980s, 80 percent of peasants lived in destitution, the illiteracy rate was more than 70 percent, and unemployment or underemployment affected 45 percent of the population.[7]

Multinational corporations compounded Guatemala's social ills. One company in particular, the United Fruit Company (also known as Dole), played an influential role. The corporation had purchased large tracts of land for banana production, making it the single largest landowner in the country. The Guatemalan government provided numerous benefits to the company, including exemption from import duties, minimal export taxes, and freedom from government regulations.[8] The United Fruit Company's interests were protected by a series of dictators. One of the most notorious of these was General Jorge Ubico, who took office in 1931. Ubico legalized the killing of Maya by landlords, undermined labor practices, and strengthened the repressive capacity of the military. His policies were so extreme that a broad-based opposition coalition emerged that included unions, university students, and disillusioned military officers. Together, they launched a series of general strikes that deposed Ubico in 1944.

Empowered by its success, the coalition pressed for more change, calling for a national election and the implementation of democracy. When the election was held, opposition candidate Juan Jose Arévalo won with 85 percent of the vote. Once in office, he introduced a series of progressive policies, including lawful unionization of workers, voting rights for women and the illiterate, and modest land reform.

More comprehensive change came in 1951, when Jacobo Arbenz was elected president. Arbenz promoted diversification of the economy and an end to special privileges for foreign companies. He also facilitated land redistribution by decreeing that any estate larger than 233 acres that had not been cultivated in three years would be purchased by the government and sold to peasant families. The landowners would be compensated for the full value of the land. By 1954, the state had purchased 2.7 million acres, which were sold to roughly 100,000 peasants.

A portion of the United Fruit Company's land was designated for purchase, since the company was cultivating only 15 percent of the 550,000 acres it owned. Company executives were outraged by the policy and turned to the US government for assistance. In particular, the company appealed to John Foster Dulles, secretary of state, and Allen Dulles, deputy director of the Central Intelligence Agency (CIA), both of whom had done legal work for the United Fruit Company and received large stock packages from the corporation. The Dulles brothers persuaded President Eisenhower that Arbenz was a communist threat who needed to be removed from power.

Eisenhower gave the CIA permission to undertake a destabilization effort in Guatemala in 1954. Those plans culminated in a feigned coup, with the CIA sending planes to bomb Guatemala City while airing reports that attacking forces had arrived. Believing that the attacking troops had won, Arbenz resigned, and Colonel Carlos Castillo Armas was appointed president.[9] The Castillo Armas regime quickly arrested activists, particularly targeting United Fruit Company union organizers as well as indigenous leaders. It is estimated that 8,000 peasants were killed in the first two months of the new regime. Moreover, the new president reversed many of Arbenz's social programs, cutting literacy programs, canceling the registration of 533 unions, and returning 99 percent of the land that had been redistributed under earlier land reform measures. The US government declared this a victory for democracy and sent $80 million to the new regime.[10]

As progressive Guatemalan activists reflected on the events of 1954, they concluded that there was no way to bring about change by working within the system. When they tried that route, electing Arévalo and Arbenz, a powerful multinational corporation and the US government quickly overturned their efforts. Like dependency theorists, they concluded that the industrialized "core" countries wanted to keep Guatemala and other Latin American countries from developing because they wished to continue exploiting these "peripheral" nations' resources and labor. What other options did the poor have? Many Guatemalans concluded that they needed a revolution. Through armed struggle, the oppressed could overthrow the existing political and economic systems and finally bring power to the exploited majority.[11]

Vatican II

Guatemalans were not the only ones who pursued revolutionary struggles. Parallel developments occurred throughout Latin America during the 1950s and 1960s. The outbreak of such liberation wars, the growth of the nuclear arms race, and the rapid expansion of capitalism and economic inequality compelled the Roman Catholic Church to open itself to the world and its troubles. Pope John XXIII instigated the Vatican II Council (1962–1965) to discuss how the church should respond to these issues. The council altered the responsibilities and practices of clergy, promoting new worship practices and ministries. It also addressed the pressing needs of the Latin American church—especially the severe shortage of priests. Because the Catholic Church had historically served the upper classes, it had lost touch with the poorest Latin Americans, and hence fewer people were entering the priesthood and the convents. In response to this shortage of clergy, the pope decided to send 10 percent of US nuns and priests to the region as missionaries, and most were assigned to work in impoverished communities. North American missionaries moved into Latin America's urban barrios and the underdeveloped countryside with the task of developing outreach programs that would bring the poor back into the church.[12]

It did not take long for these missionaries to become acutely aware of the injustices that the poor routinely faced. And the more suffering they encountered, the more they questioned how they should respond. Due to Vatican II, they no longer saw themselves as attending only to their parishioners' spiritual concerns; they had to address parishioners' material, social, and political concerns as well.

Some Catholic leaders were already speaking out on these issues. Dom Hélder Câmara, bishop of Rio de Janeiro, had long criticized the devastating effects of capitalism in Latin America.[13] Câmara had been an important influence in the Basic Education Movement (1961–1967) that promoted "consciousness-raising" and literacy among the poor. At the conclusion of the Vatican II Council, he organized a group of bishops, who collectively wrote *A Message to the People of the Third World*. In this document, Hélder Câmara and the others stated that "the gospel demands the first, radical revolution" and that "wealth must be shared by all." The document, which charged the wealthy with waging class warfare against the poor, stated that "true socialism is Christianity integrally lived."[14]

Other Catholics joined revolutionary movements. Particularly influential was Camilo Torres, a priest and sociologist who had collected data on poverty in Colombia. In 1965, Father Torres organized a coalition of peasants, shantytown residents, blue-collar workers, and professionals who wanted change. When his religious superiors denounced his work, Torres renounced the priesthood and joined the Army of National Liberation. He declared, "I took off my cassock to be more truly a priest. . . . The duty of every Catholic is to be a revolutionary, the duty of every revolutionary is to make revolution."[15] Torres's decision was highly controversial, generating significant debate about the limited effects of reformist approaches and the legitimacy of armed revolution.

Popularum Progressio

Catholic leaders in Rome were also addressing these issues of poverty, inequality, and social change. Pope John XXIII, who initiated the Vatican II Council, did not live to see its completion. He died on June 3, 1963, and was succeeded by Pope Paul VI. In 1967, Paul VI released the encyclical *Popularum Progressio* ("On the Progress of Peoples"), which had an important influence on Latin American Catholics. The main emphasis of the encyclical was on international poverty, structural injustices, and development. Pope Paul VI's comments reflect the premises of dependency theory and the emerging ideas of liberation theology:

> Colonizing powers have often furthered their own interests, power, or glory and . . . their departure has sometimes left a precarious economy, bound up for instance with the production of one kind of crop whose market prices are subject to sudden and considerable variation. . . . [T]he poor nations remain ever poor while the rich ones become richer.[16]

In this encyclical, the pope condemned the abuses of unbridled capitalism. He argued that this economic system is flawed because it is driven by a profit motive and emphasizes competition rather than justice. Moreover, it underscores the individual's right to private ownership but fails to emphasize the common good or a person's social obligations. This has created a system of exploitation in which the wealthy focus on their own enrichment without concern for the well-being of the poor, resulting in severe inequalities that generate conflict and revolutionary impulses. Paul VI acknowledged and legitimized such revolutionary sentiments but insisted it was not the solution. He wrote:

> There are certainly situations whose injustice cries to heaven. When whole populations destitute of necessities live in a state of dependence barring them from all initiative and responsibility, and all opportunity to advance culturally and share in social and political life. Recourse to violence, as a means to right these wrongs to human dignity, is a grave temptation. . . . We know, however, that a revolutionary uprising—save where there is manifest, long-standing tyranny which would do great damage to fundamental personal rights and dangerous harm to the common good of the country—produces new injustices, throws more elements out of balance and brings on new disasters. A real evil should not be fought against at the cost of greater misery.[17]

In light of these serious problems, Pope Paul VI proposed "authentic development" that promotes the good of every person. In addition to economic growth, this entails "the transition from less human conditions to those which are more human" in social, spiritual, and political realms.[18] Specifically, the pope called for three strategies to address the problem of unequal development. First, wealthy industrialized nations need to *offer solidarity and aid* to the poorer ones. Second, *fair trade relations* must be established to end the exploitation of undeveloped countries. Third, *universal charity* is needed. Within underdeveloped nations, the pope emphasized that the poor should initiate and direct social transformations: "The people themselves have the prime responsibility to work for their own development . . . to become the artisans of their destiny."[19] For Latin American progressive Catholics, *Popularum Progressio* confirmed their right to transform their economic and political systems.

Medellín Meeting of the Latin America Bishops Conference

Inspired by the Vatican II Council and *Popularum Progressio*, the Latin American Episcopal Conference—the organization that brings together the region's bishops—met in Medellín, Colombia, in 1968 to discuss how to implement these ideas. The resulting document was a bold new mission for the Latin American Church.

The Medellín document begins with an analysis of Latin Americans' suffering. The bishops stated that the roots of the troubles are found in the region's neocolonial system and strong biclassism. These exploitive systems constitute structural violence, which has undermined peaceful relations. The bishops attributed blame for these conditions to the upper classes, writing: "Those who have the greater share of wealth, culture, and power are responsible to history for provoking explosive revolutions of despair."[20] In another part of the document, they challenged Catholic laypeople to construct a new social order, calling this "an eminently Christian task."[21]

What would this new social order look like? The bishops condemned both liberal capitalism and Marxism as undermining human dignity. Instead, they called for social education and "conscientization" so the downtrodden would know their rights, exercise them, and create their own future. In addition, they encouraged the formation of popular organizations, such as peasant and workers' unions, to empower the poorest segment of society. Finally, the bishops called for a transformation of Latin America's economic and political structures. They wrote:

> [Improving the situation for indigenous populations] will not be viable without an authentic and urgent reform of agrarian structures and policies. This structural change and its political implications go beyond a simple distribution of land. . . . This will entail . . . the organization of peasants into effective intermediate structures, principally in the form of cooperatives.[22]

To start the process of conscientization and liberation, the bishops called for the development of "base ecclesial communities" (BECs), which are small neighborhood church groups that meet in community centers or members' homes for Bible study, discussion, and political engagement. Heading these communities were laypeople who had been trained to facilitate discussions of scripture using the Socratic method of dialogue, which was initiated to address the lack of clergy, but it also cultivated participants' analytic skills and social awareness.[23] As soon as these BECs were introduced, Latin Americans embraced the practice wholeheartedly. Within a decade, there were between 150,000 and 200,000 BECs throughout the region.[24]

The Medellín document had a powerful impact. It demonstrated that the Roman Catholic Church was no longer supporting the social and political status quo. After centuries of alliances with the government and elite classes, the church had shifted its allegiance to the poor. Moreover, the document indicated that Latin America's bishops were focusing their efforts on building a horizontal, community-grounded church instead of reinforcing the traditional vertical hierarchy.[25]

Liberation Theology

Throughout the 1960s, Catholics wrestled with the problems of global poverty and underdevelopment. *Popularum Progressio*, the Vatican II Council, and the Medellín document condemned the existing global economic system as unfair and sinful, enriching a small portion of the population at the expense of others. These conditions had created such egregious inequalities that comprehensive social transformation was needed. Out of these circumstances emerged a new theology—a theology of liberation.

In his book *A Theology of Liberation* (1971), Gustavo Gutierrez of Peru offered the first systematic presentation of ideas that had been percolating among Latin American Catholics over many years. Soon several others—such as Juan Luis Segundo, José Míguez Bonino, and Leonardo and Clodovis Boff—were also contributing to this work. In this section, I summarize the main themes of liberation theologians.

The first theme is a redefinition of theology as *critical reflection on praxis*. Traditionally, theology begins with the determination of "correct thinking" (orthodoxy). From these beliefs, one can discern appropriate pastoral activities. Gustavo Gutierrez turned this practice on its head, introducing a new method that begins with praxis—a concept associated with philosopher Georg Wilhelm Friedrich Hegel, who used the term to denote socially transformative actions. For liberation theologians, praxis means that Christians should start with acts of service for social justice, rather than a purely intellectual search for the truth. As Gutierrez put it, "First is the commitment of charity, of service. Theology comes afterwards, it is the second act. . . . The pastoral activity of the Church does not flow as a conclusion from theological premises. Theology does not produce pastoral activity; rather, it reflects upon it."[26]

A second assertion of liberation theology is that *poverty and oppression are the result of structural sin.* Liberation theologians move beyond the conception of sin as an individual-level act of wrongdoing. They posit that exploitive social and economic structures are sinful. Juan Luis Segundo wrote, "[Structural] 'sin' is different from the 'sins' that come from freely made choices. [Structural] sin is a condition that subdues and enslaves me against my own will."[27] Similarly, Gutierrez stated, "Sin is evident in oppressive structures, in the exploitation of human by human, in the domination and slavery of peoples, races, and social classes."[28]

A third theme is the idea that *Christ is a liberator.* Jesus condemned tax collectors who were exploiting the poor and drove them out of the Temple to disrupt their unjust practices. He spoke out against the Pharisees, who were more concerned about complying with rules than helping those in need. He did not preach obedience to Roman rule, an oppressive political system that subordinated Jews. Rather, he told his followers to "give onto Caesar what is Caesar's and give unto God what is God's." Consequently, when Roman authorities arrested Jesus, he was charged with political crimes: he was accused of "declaring himself a king" (i.e., political sedition) and "stirring up people for revolt."[29] Gutierrez noted, "Jesus *died at the hands of the political authorities,* the oppressors of the Jewish people. According to Roman custom, the title on the cross indicated the reason for the sentence; in the case of Jesus, this title denoted political guilt: King of the Jews. . . . We see clearly that the trial of Jesus was a political trial and that he was condemned for being a zealot."[30] In short, liberation theologians maintain that social and political justice is central to Christ's message.

A fourth premise of liberation theology is the *preferential option for the poor.* Historically, the Roman Catholic Church has been "closely linked to the established order."[31] However, this established order has exploited the vulnerable. Hence the church must proclaim its solidarity with the oppressed and become a church of the poor. Ronaldo Muñoz wrote:

> The church must incarnate itself among the common people, among the poor and marginalized of the earth; for that is where Jesus Christ himself once became incarnate and fulfilled his ministry. . . . Today the church is being summoned to undergo a conversion to the poor of the land. . . . This means that the church must thoroughly revise its structures, its viewpoints, its practices, and the concrete life of its members. . . . The aim of all this is to ensure that the poor will be able to find in the church their own true home as an oppressed, believing people, the expression of their own faith and hope, and the anticipation of their own yearnings for liberty, community, and participation.[32]

A fifth point is that liberation theologians insist on the *unity of history*. For centuries, theologians have grappled with the relationship between world history (the profane) and salvation history (the sacred). The traditional view, known as "historical dualism," holds that these are two distinct histories that unfold on separate but intersecting planes, eventually culminating in the establishment of the kingdom of heaven.[33] Liberation theologians reject this view, since the poor have been told for so long that their suffering would end when they reached heaven. Instead, liberation theologians assert that there is no salvation apart from human history; the Kingdom of God is created in this world. Leonardo Boff stated:

> There are not two histories and two realities. . . . The kingdom takes flesh in justice. . . . This [salvation] process . . . can be understood as a process of liberation *from* situations that contradict God's salvific design, *for* situations that gradually conform to that design. . . . In a nutshell, we could say: Liberation in Jesus Christ is not identified *with* political, economic, and social liberation, but it is historically identified *in* political, economic, and social liberation.[34]

Gutierrez also underscored this point, writing: "The struggle for a just world in which there is no oppression, servitude, or alienated work will signify the coming of the Kingdom."[35]

Sixth, liberation theologians posit that the ultimate goal of their work is the *creation of a new society and a new humanity*. They call for more than reformist measures; they want to abolish the oppressive status quo and establish a qualitatively new society. This is referred to as the "historical project" of liberation theology. In this project, capitalist "developmentalism" (as embodied in modernization theory) is rejected and replaced with socialism. Leonardo and Clodovis Boff argued, "The Christian ideal is closer to socialism than to capitalism. It is not a matter of creating a Christian socialism. It is a matter of being able to say that the social system, when actually carried out in reality, enables Christians better to live the humanitarian and divine ideals of their faith."[36] However, they were not advocating for Soviet-style socialism. Jose Bonino wrote, "The socialist system which will finally emerge in the Latin American countries will not be a copy of existing ones, but a creation related to our reality. . . . There is a strong sense of freedom to find an authentic Latin American socialism, forged in a realistic understanding of our situation, true to our own history and to the characteristics of the Latin American people."[37] Local people will create this new society; they will fight as "agents of their own destiny" and "protagonists of their own liberation."[38] This new society will promote egalitarianism and freedom, where power and wealth are shared equitably and racial and class divisions are eliminated.

Reflecting on these theological premises, some may feel that this is little more than a religious promotion of Marxism. Liberation theologians concede that they use Marxist analysis, but only as an analytical tool that helps them understand the sources of poverty in Latin America— not as a comprehensive worldview. Clodovis Boff wrote, "By no means is Marxism the moving force, basis, or inspiration of the theology of liberation. Christian faith is. . . . When Marxism is used at all, it is used only partially and instrumentally."[39] Liberation theologians' limited acceptance of Marxism is merely an acknowledgment that class struggle is a reality, a brutal one, which must be addressed. Their quest for social justice is always grounded in biblical teachings, and they reject Marxist beliefs that are incompatible with their faith. In fact, because of Marx's condemnation of religion, liberation theologians have stated publicly that a "rigid Marxist orthodoxy or dogmatism is immediately rejected" and collaboration with orthodox Marxists is untenable.[40]

Liberation Theology and Central American Revolutions

Throughout Latin America, Catholics were putting liberation theology into practice. Within base ecclesial communities, many laypeople decided to get involved in organizations that demanded land reform, livable wages, more humane working conditions, and a political voice. Yet the more they organized, the more the state repressed them. Eventually, some joined revolutionary movements, believing that it was not possible to work for change within the system. They needed to overthrow the existing system in order to build a more just society.

The first successful revolution inspired by liberation theology was won in July 1979, when the Sandinista National Liberation Front (FSLN) overthrew the Somoza dictatorship in Nicaragua. When the revolutionaries assumed power, the FSLN issued a communiqué that thanked the many Christians who had aided the revolution. In the beginning, most citizens were supportive of the new Sandinista government, since Nicaraguans from all socioeconomic backgrounds were glad to be free of Somoza's oppressive rule. They also felt a sense of pride when the Sandinistas made notable gains, such as dramatically increasing literacy rates, which won praise from the United Nations. Yet this national unity rapidly disintegrated as the upper classes saw their privileges erode and they realized that the revolution wanted to reconstruct the social order, not merely remove a corrupt dictator. Elite Nicaraguans turned to the United States for help in opposing the revolutionary government. President Reagan responded by cutting off $15 million in economic aid to Nicaragua, which included food shipments. He also imposed an economic embargo that obstructed loans and blocked trade. Additionally, he ordered the CIA to spend $19.5 million to train and arm a counter-revolutionary group known as the Contras.[41]

The Contras' initial strategy was to directly combat the FSLN forces. It quickly became apparent that this would not work, since much of the population supported the new state. With CIA guidance, the Contras shifted their focus to attacking the human and material infrastructure of the country. Their plan was to disrupt the economy and social services, and damage the infrastructure to inflict economic and psychological hardship on Nicaraguans, thereby making everyday life difficult. They hoped this would foster popular discontent with the Sandinistas, who would have difficulty delivering the promises made during the revolution. Hence the Contras attacked schools and day care centers, health clinics, food storage facilities, bridges, electrical power lines, agricultural cooperatives, state farms, grassroots organizations, and any individuals associated with these targets.[42]

These Contra attacks were devastating. Approximately 80 percent of the country's basic foods were grown in regions that were regularly attacked, causing billions of dollars in losses that crippled the national economy. Moreover, the attacks forced the FSLN government to increase its defense costs, which directed funds away from social programs and contributed to inflation. Finally, the human costs of the Contra War were demoralizing. Roughly 30,000 Nicaraguans lost their lives; many of them were doctors, teachers, engineers, farmers, and those working in social services.[43] In the United States, a growing number of Americans were concerned that their tax dollars were funding a counterrevolutionary force that was assassinating civilians and deliberately destroying schools, health clinics, and farms.

Despite the challenges that the FSLN government faced, the Sandinista revolution inspired liberation movements in neighboring Guatemala and El Salvador. In El Salvador in the 1970s, citizen organizing had resulted in escalating levels of state-sponsored repression. During this period, the government killed between 500 and 800 civilians each month, eliminating the possibility of working for change within the political system. As a result, many Salvadorans joined the Farabundo Marti National Liberation Front (FMLN).

As the FMLN guerrilla movement gained momentum, the Salvadoran military targeted clergy and laity in the base ecclesial communities, since they considered them seditious for teaching liberation theology. The political targeting of church leaders started in 1970, when Father José Alas was kidnapped and beaten after publicly calling for agrarian reform. Over the next years, other priests were exiled, abducted, tortured, and killed by the Salvadoran National Guard. By 1977, a notorious death squad known as the White Warriors announced that the Jesuits, whom they considered particularly subversive, had thirty days to leave the country or they would be assassinated. When they refused to leave, the military bombed the Jesuit university in El Salvador and circulated anonymous pamphlets stating, "Be a patriot! Kill a priest!"[44]

The persecution of Catholic clergy gained worldwide attention in 1980, when El Salvador's archbishop, Oscar Romero, was killed. Romero was initially critical of liberation theology; he was concerned that the emphasis on social justice would detract from spiritual matters. Romero's views changed rapidly, however, when he encountered the poverty and repression that many Salvadorans experienced. He was particularly shocked when Father Rutilio Grande, his friend and a human rights advocate, was murdered. Romero stated, "[Father Grande's assassination] gave me the impetus to put into practice the principles of Vatican II and Medellín, which call for solidarity with the suffering masses and the poor and encourage priests to live independent of the powers that be."[45] Romero became an outspoken critic of the military regime's abuses. He also called for wide-scale economic reform, stating, "The situation of injustice is so bad that the faith itself has been perverted; the faith is being used to defend the financial interests of the oligarchy."[46] But being outspoken came with a price, as he received numerous death threats. The archbishop knew that he was risking his life, but he continued to push for an end to the violence and economic exploitation. In one of his last interviews, he stated:

> I have frequently been threatened with death. I must say that, as a Christian, I do not believe in death but in the resurrection. If they kill me, I shall rise again in the Salvadoran people. . . . If they manage to carry out their threats, I shall be offering my blood for the redemption and resurrection of El Salvador. Martyrdom is a grace from God that I do not believe that I have earned. But if God accepts the sacrifice of my life, then may my blood be the seed of liberty, and a sign of the hope that will soon become a reality. May my death . . . be for the liberation of my people.[47]

Romero's words were prophetic. On March 24, 1980, he was shot while celebrating Mass.

Romero's death ignited liberation-oriented churches in El Salvador. Five thousand people joined in his funeral processional, even under bombing and sniping threats. When Romero's casket was brought to the main cathedral for viewing, priests, nuns, and missionaries kept vigil day and night. Among them were two North American missionaries from Cleveland, Sister Dorothy Kazel and Jean Donovan. Dorothy Kazel was a member of the Ursuline order and had been in El Salvador since 1974. Jean Donovan, a layperson, joined the mission in 1979. The two women were fully aware of the repression in El Salvador, but they had been somewhat isolated from it, since they were located in a remote region. Shortly after Romero's assassination, however, death squads visited their area, killing six young men and decapitating a twenty-four-year-old lay leader. The victims had been tortured, and their bodies were so mutilated that they were almost unrecognizable. A few weeks later, more Catholic lay leaders were murdered.

Around this time, Maryknoll Sisters Ita Ford and Carla Piette arrived in El Salvador. They began working in the war-torn region of Chalatenango, where a recent massacre had left hundreds dead and the Salvadoran army's scorched-earth land sweep campaigns had forced many others to flee. Ford and Piette's work entailed transporting refugees; delivering food, clothing, and medicine; and reuniting separated family members. Several months into this work, the Maryknoll Sisters were caught in a flash flood that took the life of Carla Piette. To help continue the work, Maura Clarke—a Maryknoll nun who had spent fifteen years in Nicaragua—joined Ita Ford.

All four women knew that their decision to work in El Salvador was a dangerous one. The threats against them became more direct when, in the fall of 1980, they found a sign on the parish door. It had a picture of a severed head and a bloody knife, accompanied by text that read, "Everyone working here is a communist and anyone entering here will be killed." In December 1980, a few months after Romero's assassination, the four churchwomen were driving when they were pulled over by security forces. The women were forced out of their car, raped, and murdered. Their bodies were found at the side of the road.[48]

The deaths of Romero and the four North American churchwomen sent a shock wave from El Salvador to the Vatican to the United States. Many US Catholics wondered why their government was sending massive amounts of financial and military aid to a regime that was targeting, torturing, and killing priests, nuns, and an archbishop. Increasingly, the official Vatican stance and the views of US Catholic laypeople diverged. The Vatican condemned liberation theology and the movements it inspired, while North American Catholics began mobilizing campaigns in solidarity with Salvadorans, Nicaraguans, and Guatemalans.

John Paul II and the Vatican's Response

Just as liberation theology was turning Latin America into a revolutionary hotbed, the Vatican was turning more conservative. John Paul II was appointed pope in October 1978, less than year before the Sandinistas won the Nicaraguan revolution. The new pope was born and raised in communist Poland, and he knew firsthand the problems associated with Soviet-style socialism. Once he assumed the papacy, John Paul II appointed Cardinal Joseph Ratzinger to head the Vatican's Congregation for the Doctrine of the Faith. Together, Ratzinger and the pope openly criticized liberation theology and tried to suppress it by appointing conservative bishops throughout Latin America. The Vatican also censured and silenced liberation theologians. In 1983, Ratzinger sent a letter to Gustavo Gutierrez, detailing the Vatican's objections to his theology and summoning him to Rome for a private consultation.[49] In 1984, Ratzinger released a document entitled *Instruction on Certain Aspects of the Theology of Liberation*, in which he raised two main concerns: "first, that it takes over the Marxist analysis of society, thus running the risk of turning Christian faith into an ideology; second, that it favors the formation of a parallel church, the *Iglesia Popular* [popular church], in opposition to the official church represented by the bishops."[50] According to Ratzinger, these errors made liberation theology a "fundamental threat to the faith of the Church."[51] Around this same time, the Vatican officially silenced theologian Leonardo Boff for ten months.[52] The silencing backfired. Instead of thwarting liberation theology, it helped spread it as the Vatican's condemnation spotlighted this new religious belief system.

John Paul II also condemned liberation theology during his travels to Central America. One of the most contentious encounters happened in 1983, when the pope visited Nicaragua and expressed concerns that Catholics were too closely aligned with the revolutionary Sandinista government. Margaret Randall described the encounter:

> We knew that the pope was coming to give the Nicaraguan bishops a shot in the arm, to criticize the "priests in [the revolutionary] government" and to bolster the counter-revolution. But we had no idea it would be as bad as it was. Everything was compounded by the fact that the day before the pope's visit there was a mass burial of seventeen young Sand-

inistas. . . . The next day, beginning with the pope's initial address to the government and the people at the airport, it was clear that he had come to lecture and not to listen. . . . Father Ernesto Cardenal, poet and Minister of Culture, was on the reception line with his cabinet colleagues. When John Paul came to where he stood, a short exchange took place. . . . Ernesto fell to his knees and tried to kiss the pope's hand. What the head of the Catholic faith had said was, "You'd better put your relationship with the church in order. . . ." The day culminated in Managua with an outdoor mass in the July 19 Plaza, an event attended by an estimated 800,000 people (one-fifth of the country's population). The day before 10,000 had gathered in the same square to pay tribute to the young Sandinistas who had died. Friends wanted the pope to understand what was happening in Nicaragua, to feel their pain, to sympathize with their desire for a principled peace. But he refused. The mothers of the most recent victims [of the Contra War], standing up front, held photos of their sons for the pope to see. But all they received was his angry cry "Silence". . . . His inappropriate sermon was then increasingly interrupted by the people shouting, "People Power, People Power, People Power."[53]

US Solidarity Movements

While the Vatican increasingly opposed liberation theology and its correlated movements, many Catholic laypeople in the United States were inspired by it. Embracing the "preferential option for the poor," they explored ways to express solidarity with their Central American counterparts who were working for social justice. As the Contra War raged on and the United States aided the military regimes in El Salvador and Guatemala, these North American Catholics felt compelled to act.

Witness for Peace

One of the first solidarity movements emerged in 1983, when a former nun named Gail Phares led a delegation of religious leaders to Nicaragua. Phares had served as a Maryknoll missionary in Nicaragua and Guatemala in the 1960s, as part of the Vatican II mandate. That experience radicalized her, as she explained:

In the past, the church had really blessed the status quo and it was beginning, because of Vatican II, to question everything. . . . In the past, the gospel was preached basically as "God loves everybody but some were born to be rich and some were born to be poor. Just be patient. In heaven, it will be better." But after Vatican II, we began to listen more and ask more questions. We began to see that Christianity is not just a vertical relationship or that you simply do good works and do what you're told. . . . We began to read the scriptures with the poor, the people we worked with, and we applied it to what we saw. We saw people dying of hunger, people without medical care, education, people not being allowed to organize or being in danger if they did organize. We began to say, it is not God's will that people live this way. In a situation where a few people own most of the land and wealth, it is sinful—it is *not* God's will.[54]

Eventually, Phares realized that the most productive thing she could do was to change US foreign policies and the business practices that were contributing to injustice in Central America. She stated:

When I was a missionary in Guatemala, I worked with university students. We took upper class kids from law school, medical school, teacher training school and took them out into the countryside to live with peasants, the campesinos, who were Mayan. We used the methodology of Paulo Freire's *concientización* and it radicalized all of us because the elites in the city really didn't know much about the countryside and didn't have much contact with Mayans except as servants in their homes. . . . But in 1968, I was thrown out of Guatemala, along with a number of other Maryknolls, and I ended up in the States. I did not want to be here and fought real hard to go back. . . . But I realized I had to stay. Latin Americans will tell you, "We love you, but go home and work to change your country because we can't do anything until you change your country." I'd never worked in the United States and I didn't have a clue what to do. So once I decided to stay here, I began to develop a kind of *concientización*, a consciousness-raising methodology, with urban parishes in the United States. I ended up organizing NISGUA, the National Guatemalan Network.[55]

Phares later left her religious order, married, had children, and became the director of the Carolina Interfaith Task Force. When the Contra War was heating up, she applied the same organizing skills to raise awareness within the broader ecumenical community about US policy in Central America. Phares recruited high-profile religious leaders who traveled to Nicaragua to see firsthand the effects of the war. When they arrived in Managua in April 1983, they heard reports that Contras had just attacked villages near the Honduran border. They boarded a bus the next day, headed straight for the war zone. They eventually arrived at a village that had been under attack just hours earlier. The religious leaders spoke with the survivors, observed the damage and the blood-spattered walls, and picked up shrapnel, which they discovered had been manufactured in the United States. When one of the delegates pulled out his binoculars, he observed that the Contra forces were just over the border so he asked the villagers why they had stopped shooting. The villagers replied that they would not shoot when North Americans were present, since the Contras would not jeopardize the funding they received from the United States by killing or injuring US citizens. As the delegates rode back to Managua, one of them had an idea: if the presence of North Americans deterred Contra attacks, why not organize a permanent group of US volunteers to live and work in the villages?[56]

The idea took root, and the delegates began planning "Project Witness," which had two components. First, there would be long-term delegates who would live in the war zones to deter Contra attacks. Second, there would be short-term delegates who would travel to Nicaragua, learn about the political situation, visit war zone villages, and then return to their home communities to report to the media, their religious congregations, and their local political representatives.[57] During the summer of 1983, a proposal was circulated to various religious organizations, asking for support. Many responded, including Clergy and Laity Concerned, the American Friends Service Committee, the Fellowship of Reconciliation, the Presbyterian Church (U.S.A.), the United Methodist Church, the Catholic Worker, and the Religious Task Force on Central America, which was based in Washington, DC.[58] By October 1983, a national steering committee had developed a statement of purpose, created an organizational structure, and released a statement about this new organization, called Witness for Peace, describing it as "prayerful, biblically-based, nonviolent, and politically independent."[59]

Within a year, the organization had several regional offices, twenty-seven local support groups, and fund-raising and recruitment campaigns, and it had commissioned its first long-term volunteers. By December 1984, the progressive evangelical magazine *Sojourners* had hired a media specialist to cover the movement, depicting it as a "shield of love" for the Nicaraguan people. Every major national newspaper and several television networks picked up the story. But the media coverage didn't end there. A key strategy for the short-term delegation program was to teach participants how to publicize their experience locally. One Witness for Peace organizer summarized the effect:

> The strategy was to send people from all over the country with the mission to go to learn, and come back and be part of the resistance to U.S. policy. . . . People from the United States would go down [to Nicaragua] for short periods, were shown around, and lived with the poor. These were the people who were actually suffering the consequences of the U.S.–Contra War. And then they went back and worked as advocates. . . . There were three things we asked them [short-term delegates] to do. First, speak to your community, your church. Show them slides, tell them about your experiences, write a letter to your friends and family, tell everybody you know. Second, do media work. You could write a letter to the editor, but also let your local newspaper know what you're doing. Third, we asked them to do congressional work to change U.S. policy. . . . And to multiply that news story hundreds and thousands of times in towns and cities around the country, it began to have an effect. It counteracted the *New York Times* and the *Washington Post* that ran stories favorable to the Contras.[60]

Over the span of ten years, 4,200 US citizens traveled to Nicaragua with Witness for Peace, forging a sizable grassroots movement in opposition to US foreign policy. To complement the local work of returning delegates, the Witness for Peace office began coordinating national-level political campaigns. For instance, Witness for Peace organized the "End Contra Aid!" campaign in 1988 that generated 11,000 calls to various congressional offices.[61] In short, its strategy was three-pronged: provide some deterrence to Contra attacks by living and working in Nicaragua war zones, provide alternative views to contradict mainstream news accounts of the Contra War, and mobilize political forces to end Contra aid.

Pledge of Resistance

Around the same time that Witness for Peace was formed, the United States sent 7,000 troops to the island of Grenada with the purpose of overturning its leftist government. Some activists in the United States believed that this was a dress rehearsal for a full-scale invasion of Nicaragua. At a retreat in Pennsylvania, several progressive religious leaders discussed the situation and unanimously concluded that they needed an organization that could preemptively mobilize opposition to such an invasion. Toward that goal, Jim Wallis and Jim Rice of *Sojourners* magazine drafted a "Pledge of Resistance." By taking this pledge, activists vowed that if the United States intervened in Nicaragua, they would mobilize masses of US Christians to "go immediately to Nicaragua to stand unarmed as a loving barrier in the path of any attempted invasion."[62] On the US side, they called upon Christians to "encircle, enter, or occupy congressional offices in a nonviolent prayerful presence with the intention of remaining at those offices until the invasion ended."[63] The idea was to provide a US complement to the resistance work that Witness for Peace was doing in Nicaragua. *Sojourners* leaders sent copies of this pledge to President Reagan, every member of Congress, the CIA, and the Departments of State and Defense. Then they set out to gain pledge supporters throughout the country and to develop a mobilizing infrastructure.

This small initiative developed into a national organization when the American Friends Service Committee provided the funds to hire Ken Butigan, a theology student from Berkeley, California, to direct the Pledge of Resistance campaign. Butigan had been searching for a way to address the Nicaraguan situation ever since he had received a letter from a Nicaraguan who wrote, "We're telling you this: your government is killing our children. We're telling you now so that later you cannot say that you didn't know. We're asking you to take steps to stop this killing at a time when we have such hope for our country."[64]

Building upon the work of *Sojourners*, Butigan revised the statement to read, "If the United States . . . significantly escalates its intervention in Central America, I pledge to join with others . . . in acts of legal protest and civil disobedience as conscience leads me."[65] Then he launched a public event in October 1984 outside the San Francisco Federal Building, where 700 people signed the pledge. Encouraged by this success, Butigan attended a meeting of major solidarity and anti-intervention organizations in Washington, DC. At the meeting, he proposed that they coordinate Pledge of Resistance initiatives across the country. Those gathered in Washington agreed to form an "analyst group" that would monitor all US activities in Central America. These analysts would then consult with a "signal group," and together they would decide if the actions were bellicose enough to activate the network. Once they gave the green light, local Pledge of Resistance chapters would undertake a variety of actions to obstruct any major military escalation in Central America. By early 1985, more than 50,000 citizens were active in 200 local chapters. This budding organization had the capacity to rapidly generate political chaos nationwide.

Fairly quickly, solidarity leaders realized that an overt invasion of Nicaragua was unlikely. Instead, the Reagan administration continued its low-intensity warfare strategy, and thus Pledge of Resistance activists shifted their focus to challenging Contra aid bills. In June 1985, when Congress passed a Contra aid package of $27 million, the network responded by organizing demonstrations in 200 cities. The following year, activists challenged four separate Contra aid votes in Congress. By this point, nearly 70,000 US citizens had signed the pledge. Tens of thousands took action by occupying congressional offices, staging funeral processions, blocking arms shipments, running "Stop the Lies" advertisements in newspapers throughout the country, and renting planes to fly over sporting events, carrying banners that read, "U.S. Out of Nicaragua Now!" The campaigns continued throughout the 1980s, contesting US policies toward Nicaragua, El Salvador, Guatemala, and Honduras.[66]

School of the Americas Watch

A third solidarity movement targeted the United States' role in training military personnel from Central America. This occurred at Fort

Benning, Georgia, at the School of the Americas (SOA). The US government argued that the SOA was an important means of promoting democracy by helping Latin American militaries defeat Marxist insurgencies. Yet a growing number of critics, including former SOA instructors and students, condemned the school, asserting that it mainly taught psychological warfare, intelligence-gathering techniques (including torture), and commando operations that contributed to widespread violence and authoritarianism in the region.[67]

Under the leadership of Father Roy Bourgeois, a Maryknoll priest who had served as a missionary in Bolivia, US Catholics began protesting the SOA's work, which they argued contributed to the human rights abuses in Central America. Following the assassination of Archbishop Romero and the four churchwomen in El Salvador, Father Bourgeois was outraged to learn that the United States continued to finance, equip, and train the Salvadoran armed forces, even though they were implicated in these murders. To draw attention to this issue and to honor the martyrs' memory, Bourgeois decided to take action. Together with two others, he traveled to Fort Benning and purchased military uniforms at a local store. Impersonating officers, the three entered the base. With a map of the compound, they located the barracks where the Salvadoran soldiers were housed. After nightfall, Father Bourgeois climbed a tree outside these barracks, with a portable stereo strapped on his back. When the last lights went out, Bourgeois played a tape, at full volume, of Romero's final homily. The Salvadoran soldiers awoke to hear Romero's voice proclaiming, "No soldier is obliged to obey an order against God's law. No one has to carry out an immoral law. It is time to recover your conscience and obey it rather than orders given in sin. In the name of God, and in the name of this long-suffering people whose cries rise more thunderously to heave, I beg you, I order you: stop the repression!"[68] Father Bourgeois was quickly arrested and eventually served a year in prison for this action.

Prison did not deter Father Bourgeois. In fact, he was more committed than ever, particularly following the assassination of six Jesuits in El Salvador in 1989. In November of that year, the Farabundo Marti National Liberation Front launched a final offensive against the state, hoping to capture the city of San Salvador and declare victory for the revolutionary movement. During the battle, the FMLN fighters fled through the campus of the Jesuit University of Central America (UCA). Believing that the university was a launching point for the FMLN's operations and that the Jesuits were guerrilla sympathizers, the military regime targeted the campus. On the night of November 16, armed forces broke down the campus gates and entered the Jesuits' residence. All the Jesuits were there, except Jon Sobrino, who was in Thailand at the time. Sobrino recalled the events that transpired that night:

> Very late on the night of November 16th [1989] . . . an Irish priest woke me up. While half asleep, he had heard news on the BBC saying that something serious had happened to the UCA Jesuits in El Salvador. To reassure himself he had phoned London and then he woke me up. "Something terrible has happened," he told me. . . . On the way to the telephone, I thought, although I did not want to believe it, that they had murdered Ignacio Ellacuría. Ellacuría, a brave and stubborn man, was not a demagogue but a genuine prophet in his writings, and even more publicly on television. . . . On the other end of the telephone in London was a great friend of mine and all the Jesuits in El Salvador, a man who has shown great solidarity with our country and our church. He began with these words: "Something terrible has happened." "I know," I replied, "Ellacuría." But I didn't know. He asked me if I was sitting down and had something to write with. I said I had and then he told me what happened. "They have murdered Ignacio Ellacuría." I remained silent and did not write anything, because I had already been afraid of this. But my friend went on: "They have murdered Segundo Montes, Ignacio Martín-Baró, Amando López, Juan Ramón Moreno and Joaquín López y López." My friend read the names slowly and each of them reverberated like a hammer blow that I received in total helplessness. I was writing them down hoping that the list would end after each name. But after each name came another, on to the end. The whole community, my whole community, had been murdered. In addition, two women had been murdered with them. They were living in a little house at the entrance of the university and because they were afraid of the situation they asked the fathers if they could spend the night in our house because they felt safer there. They were also mercilessly killed.[69]

Details soon emerged. The soldiers had ordered Fathers Ellacuría, Moreno, Martín-Baró, Montes, and López to lie facedown in the garden, where they were assassinated. According to forensic reports, the priests were shot multiple times, including postmortem shots to the head, which symbolically represented the regime's intention to destroy their beliefs and ideas. Next, Father López y López came into the hallway. When he saw the bodies, he turned to go back inside but was shot immediately. The soldiers then proceeded into the Jesuit residence and killed the housekeeper and her daughter to ensure that there would be no witnesses. Before leaving the campus, the soldiers broke into the pastoral center, destroying books and documents, and then placed a sign on the university gates stating, "The FMLN executed enemy spies. Victory or Death, FMLN."[70]

The next morning, news of the murders was broadcast on the government radio. The reporters claimed that the FMLN was responsible, commenting, "The communists kill all those who don't serve them. . . . The government and armed forces condemn these assassinations committed by the FMLN in an attempt to destabilize democracy."[71] Archbishop Rivera y Damas, who succeeded Romero, immediately proclaimed that the armed forces were responsible for the Jesuit murders. Hours later, the archbishop received a death threat, warning that he would be next.

Outraged by these events, the international Jesuit community called for an investigation. The investigation found that the army had killed the Jesuits, the housekeeper, and her daughter. Furthermore, the United Nations Truth Commission found that nineteen out of the twenty-six officers responsible for these murders had been trained at the US School of the Americas.[72]

When Father Roy Bourgeois heard the results of the investigation, he became determined to end SOA training of Latin American military leaders. He moved to Columbus, Georgia, where he rented a small apartment directly adjacent to Fort Benning's entrance. He began working with a former soldier who had gone AWOL after she determined that US military involvement in Central America was unethical. Together, they painstakingly matched the names of SOA graduates, which they received under the Freedom of Information Act, with those cited by the United Nations for human rights violations. They discovered that—in addition to those who had killed Romero, the four churchwomen, and the six Jesuits—the School of the Americas had trained many officers who were responsible for civilian massacres throughout Latin America.[73]

With evidence connecting the SOA to the martyrs' assassins, Father Bourgeois went on a speaking tour—visiting churches, peace groups, and college campuses—to spotlight this issue. In the beginning, there was little strategic planning involved. Father Bourgeois reflected, "In the first year or two, we didn't have a long-range plan. What we had was this rage, this sense of immediacy. No one knew about the school in this country so we wanted to call attention to it in a dramatic way."[74]

Eventually, he did find a strategy that combined legislative work to shut down the SOA and acts of protest centering on the anniversary of the Jesuit murders. With time, his efforts paid off. In 1990, on the first anniversary of the Jesuit killings, Father Bourgeois called for a commemorative protest. Only 10 people attended. In November 1991, the commemorative protest drew 70 people. But momentum was accruing. In 1993, Representatives Joseph Kennedy and Joe Moakley introduced an amendment to Congress to close the SOA. Although the amendment was narrowly defeated, the media coverage brought greater attention to the cause. In 1996, 500 individuals, mostly laypeople, attended the commemorative protest at Fort Benning. In 1997, 2,000 protesters filled the street. More than 600 were arrested for trespassing onto the base in a mock funeral procession, carrying eight coffins to represent the six Jesuits, their housekeeper, and her daughter.[75] With each passing year, the numbers of protesters expanded, and numerous religious organizations, such as the Presbyterian Church (U.S.A.) and the Leadership Conference of Women Religious, endorsed the legislative resolutions. Eventually, the commemorative actions drew more than 20,0000 people from across the country. By 2000, there had been six legislative attempts to cut the SOA's funding.[76]

What was the effect of the SOA Watch movement? In 2000, the School of the Americas closed its doors. Yet in 2001, it reopened with a new name: the Western Hemisphere Institute for Security Cooperation. The institute had a new emphasis on human rights, democracy, and humanitarian relief. Yet SOA activists continued to monitor and protest the new institute, ensuring that it lived up to its stated commitment to human rights and democratic sustainability.[77]

Conclusion

As the Catholic Church opened itself to the modern world during the Vatican II Council, it became apparent that it needed to respond to growing global inequalities. The pope addressed poverty and underdevelopment in his encyclical *Popularum Progressio*. Latin America clergy were particularly attentive to these changes and began articulating their own views on how Catholics should respond, based on biblical teachings. In time, a new theology emerged that promoted liberation rather than modernization and economic neoliberalism. Liberation theology fostered the growth of social movements as peasants and urban workers organized unions and human rights groups and promoted land reform. In some places—like Nicaragua, El Salvador, and Guatemala—these organizations eventually became revolutionary movements.

The response to liberation theology and Central American revolutionary struggles varied widely. At the highest levels of the Vatican, there was clear opposition. Pope John Paul II and Cardinal Joseph Ratzinger tried to stop the movements. But among many lower-ranking clergy and laypeople, there was significant support. While Central American Catholics put their lives on the line to change the oppressive, neocolonial regimes that had ruled for so long, North American Catholics were trying to stop the US government from intervening or fueling the civil wars. Through their solidarity movements, US Catholics were able to challenge and obstruct US aid packages to the Contras. They successfully exposed the US role in training militaries that were responsible for human rights atrocities in Central America. They also questioned the legitimacy of the low-intensity US policies that were being practiced throughout the region. This is a clear instance of Catholic laypeople not obediently following the lead of the Vatican; they independently thought through the implications of Catholic Social Thought and came out on the side of the poor rather than on the side of the Vatican.

5

Compassion for Immigrants and the Sanctuary Movements

The United States is a country founded and built by immigrants. Yet public sentiment toward immigrants has not always been welcoming. Throughout US history, there have been various efforts to stem the tide of foreigners entering the country. By the start of the twenty-first century, immigration had become one of the most contested issues in the nation.

Various events and developments have kept this issue in the political spotlight. In 2010, Arizona passed a bill that required law enforcement officers to determine a person's immigration status during routine stops if there was a "reasonable suspicion" that the individual was undocumented. Critics of the Arizona policy were concerned that this would lead to racial profiling and open harassment of Hispanics. Supporters argued that it was a significant step toward identifying, prosecuting, and deporting those who had illegally entered the United States.

In 2014, 69,000 unaccompanied minors from Central America crossed into the United States. People were shocked that some of them were truly still children; according to the Pew Research Center review of US Customs and Border Patrol data, 27 percent were under the age of twelve.[1] While many of them came to the United States to be reunited with family members or to seek better economic opportunities, a shockingly high proportion (58 percent) stated that they were fleeing violence from organized crime groups in their communities. For some nations, the proportion was even higher: 72 percent of child immigrants from El Salvador feared that gangs would harm them.[2] While some Americans were eager to stop the flow of these undocumented young people, others mobilized to help them get legal assistance and to reunite them with their family members.

In 2016, the presidential election highlighted the different policy solutions of the two main political parties. Democratic nominee Hillary Rodham Clinton supported legislation that would create a pathway to citizenship for undocumented immigrants. She also supported the Deferred Action for Childhood Arrivals (DACA) program that protected from deportation those who came to the United States as children and who have no arrest records. Clinton planned to change detention policies for families who posed no flight risk or threat to the public. Rather than incarcerating or deporting undocumented immigrants, Clinton wanted to keep families together with supervised release policies. In contrast, Republican nominee Donald Trump called for tougher immigration laws and tougher enforcement. He promised that he would build a wall along the US-Mexico border and force Mexico to pay the estimated $5 to $10 billion that the construction would cost. He also promised to tighten criteria for asylum to reduce the overall number of refugees and the costs of social programs that assist them. Immigration was a priority to these presidential candidates and to the broader US population. A 2016 Pew Research Center poll indicated that 70 percent of Americans cited immigration as one of the most important issues that would influence how they would vote.[3]

In 2018, the issue gained new urgency as thousands of Central Americans and Mexicans came to US ports of entry to apply for asylum. Fleeing gang and cartel violence, adults came with their children in hopes of finding safety in the United States. Controversy exploded when the Trump administration took a "zero tolerance" approach to these refugees, separating families by placing parents and children in different detention facilities. Attorney General Jeff Sessions responded by stating, "If you are smuggling a child we will prosecute you, and that child will be separated as required by law. . . . If you don't like that, then don't smuggle children over our border. . . . We are dealing with a massive influx of illegal aliens across our Southwest border. We're not going to stand for this."[4] By its own estimates, the US government stated that between 2,000 and 3,000 children were in detention without their parents, including children who were under the age of five.[5] Critics denounced the practice as cruel and organized a national day of action. On June 30, 2018, approximately 750 protests took place. Tens of thousands of US citizens participated, under the motto "Families Belong Together."[6]

This chapter examines how progressive American Catholics responded to these and other immigration issues. Their responses were influenced by Catholic Social Teachings, which have long advocated that people of faith should welcome and assist immigrants. Yet US Catholic laypeople went beyond official social teachings, generating new and creative ways to help refugees and immigrants and to promote just policies.

Catholic Teachings on Immigration

The Catholic Church has an established history of welcoming immigrants. In fact, the experience of exile is a strong theme within the Judeo-Christian tradition, harkening back to the Hebrew experience recounted in the Old Testament. In Exodus 22:20, the scriptures mandate, "You shall not molest or oppress an alien, for you yourselves were once aliens in the land of Egypt." Jews were instructed to welcome refugees, since they themselves knew the experience of being exiled.

One of the earliest official Catholic statements on immigration was released in 1952, when Pope Pius XII published an Apostolic Constitution called *Exsul Familia Nazarethana*. In this document, the pope begins by stating that Jesus's own family members were immigrants:

> The émigré Holy Family of Nazareth, fleeing into Egypt, is the archetype of every refugee family. Jesus, Mary and Joseph, living in exile in Egypt to escape the fury of an evil king, are, for all times and all places, the models and protectors of every migrant, alien and refugee of whatever kind who, whether compelled by fear of persecution or by want, is forced to leave his native land, his beloved parents and relatives, his close friends, and to seek a foreign soil.[7]

Pius XII also recalled historical moments when Catholics left their homelands in search of new freedoms and opportunities. On this basis, he implored the faithful to welcome immigrants. The premise is that in welcoming the stranger or the refugee, Christians encounter Christ himself.

Pope John XXIII extended this theme in *Pacem in Terris* (1963). In a section entitled "The Right to Emigrate and Immigrate," John asserted that "every human being has the right to freedom of movement and of residence within the confines of his own country; and, when there are just reasons for it, the right to emigrate to other countries and take up residence there."[8] The pope stated that losing one's homeland through emigration is difficult; it is essential that the immigrants do not also lose their dignity and basic human rights.

When John Paul II became pope in 1978, he also advocated for immigrant rights. Even more than his predecessors, John Paul underscored the need to address the conditions that had generated a refugee crisis. In 1987, he released the encyclical *Sollicitudo Rei Socialis*, in which he described the expanding crisis as "the festering of a wound."[9] A few years later, the Pontifical Council released *Refugees: A Challenge for Solidarity*. In this document, Vatican leaders argued that world conditions, in which human rights were readily violated, would continue producing an ongoing stream of refugees. They also made a distinction between those who were emigrating to improve their socioeconomic positions and those who were fleeing life-threatening conditions. These religious leaders were concerned that these refugees were not receiving the protective measures they needed and that national policies were often hostile toward those who were escaping persecution and war-related violence. The council members called upon nations to treat refugees as people who had rights rather than people who needed assistance.[10] Furthermore, they asked the international community to not deport those seeking asylum due to cultural and political persecution, since this would place them once again in a life-threatening situation.

In 1995, John Paul II addressed the issue of immigration without proper documentation. In *The Church and Illegal Immigrants*, he stated that nations faced a social emergency as people flooded across borders without permission. Despite increasingly restrictive measures and policies, nothing was curbing the flow of such immigrants. Although the pope stated that illegal immigration should be prevented, he also noted that this was unlikely as long as businesses welcomed the opportunity to exploit cheap labor and as long as dire circumstances left people desperate. The only way to stop the influx is to address global underdevelopment and poverty and to promote human rights worldwide. Until that occurs, undocumented immigrants will be present in our communities, and the Catholic Church has a duty to minister to them. In fact, the pope stated that the church should help them in attaining residence permits, particularly when they have lived in a community for a long time.[11]

The US Conference of Catholic Bishops was another important source of teachings on immigration. Concerned about the expanding hostility toward immigrants, in 1995 the bishops released the statement *One Nation under God*, which underscored nations' rights to control their borders. The bishops also raised several other points of consideration. First, they stated that those fleeing persecution and violence should receive special attention. Second, they called for the elimination of temporary foreign labor programs that often exploited immigrants. Third, they argued that family unification should be the foundation of US immigration policy. Fourth, they underscored the importance of encouraging people who are highly skilled and educated to remain in their homelands or to return with the purpose of improving conditions in their own countries. Fifth, the bishops urged the US government to establish immigration laws that are completely transparent and fair. This means granting due process to those who seek asylum and treating those who are in the deportation process with dignity.[12]

In 2000, the US Bishops Conference released yet another statement, *Welcoming the Stranger among Us: Unity in Diversity*, which issues three mandates for US Catholics. The first is the "call to conversion." The bishops noted that many American Catholics have forgotten their own immigrant heritage and thus respond to new immigrants with fear or hostility. Conversion happens when they respond with openness, welcoming the newcomers. Next is the "call to communion," embracing multiculturalism within Catholicism. The US bishops rejected nativist attitudes that assert there is only one correct way to worship and that all immigrants must assimilate to these practices. Finally, there is the "call to solidarity," which emphasizes the church's role in promoting social justice and meeting the basic needs of immigrants by providing social services, legal assistance, medical care, and so forth. All people, even those who have breached immigration laws, should still be granted basic human rights.[13]

Catholic Lay Responses to Refugee and Immigrant Concerns

Catholic social teachings on immigration are notably progressive. Religious leaders have called for policy reform and respectful treatment of all immigrants, regardless of their legal status. While the religious leadership verbally welcomed immigrants and their causes, religious laypeople were putting these principles into action.

A novel form of political action emerged in the 1980s that was designed to physically protect refugees fleeing from Central America's civil wars (described in chapter 4). Known as the Sanctuary movement, it began in the spring of 1981, when a Quaker named Jim Dudley picked up a hitchhiker near the Arizona-Mexico border.[14] As the two men drove to Tucson together, they engaged in conversation; the hitchhiker revealed that his name was Nelson and that he was from El Salvador. After a while, Dudley was pulled over by the US Border Patrol. Nelson begged Dudley to not reveal that he was Salvadoran and to tell the officers that they were on a work-related trip. The officers arrested the hitchhiker and held Dudley for questioning, accusing him of violating immigration laws by aiding an undocumented immigrant.

The Border Patrol eventually released Dudley, who continued on to Tucson, where he stopped at the home of a fellow Quaker, Jim Corbett. Dudley recounted the incident, expressing concern over Nelson's fate. Both Quakers knew about the deadly repression in El Salvador: just a few months earlier, the four North American churchwomen had been raped, murdered, and tossed in graves alongside the road. They also knew that deported Salvadorans were frequently assassinated upon their return, since the Salvadoran regime assumed that they had fled because they had been engaged in subversive activities. Dudley and Corbett were troubled as they considered Nelson's fate.

Corbett could not sleep that night, consumed with worry about the young hitchhiker. The next morning, he contacted a local immigration rights organization, where he met a priest who had worked with refugees for many years. The priest informed Corbett that Nelson could not be deported if he signed a G-28 form, which would indicate that he had legal counsel. A signed G-28 would require that the Immigration and Naturalization Service (INS) contact the refugee's lawyer before taking any action. Immediately, Corbett called the Border Patrol to find out where Nelson was being held; he was discouraged to learn that they would not release this information. By coincidence, Jim Corbett had the same name as a well-known former mayor of Tucson. He used this to his advantage, using an authoritative voice to demand the location of the hitchhiker. Convinced that Corbett was the former mayor, the Border Patrol agent stated that Nelson was in a jail near the border. Corbett grabbed a G-28 form and headed to the jail to get the hitchhiker to sign it. When he finally located Nelson, he found him in a cell with two other Salvadorans who had also fled violence in their homeland. Corbett was convinced that all three men's lives would be in danger if they were deported. So he went back to get additional G-28 forms for the other men. When he returned to the jail, Corbett was told that he would have to wait to see the prisoners. He waited impatiently, growing worried that he would not be able to file the G-28 forms with the INS by the end of the day, as was required. After repeated requests to see the three men, the jail staff informed Corbett that the Border Patrol had already moved them.

Corbett was indignant. He believed that the prison staff had deceived him, intentionally stalling for time to move the Salvadoran refugees. Corbett became more determined than ever to find the hitchhiker. Eventually, his search led him to a regional INS detention center in Los Angeles, where he was informed that Nelson had been deported to El Salvador. This was illegal, since Corbett had filed the G-28 form on Nelson's behalf. The INS had disregarded the law and violated this refugee's rights, potentially sending him to his death.

As a result of this experience, Corbett devoted himself to aiding other Central Americans. He used his personal savings and assets to bail out Salvadorans while their asylum applications were under review. He even brought them to live on his ranch in Tucson. However, because the demand for assistance was overwhelming, Corbett quickly ran out of resources.

To continue the work, Corbett wrote to Quaker meetinghouses all over the country, explaining the refugees' needs and appealing for help. He detailed the INS's deceptive practices and the discrimination that Central Americans faced when applying for asylum. The Refugee Act of 1980 stated that anyone with a "well-founded fear of persecution based on race, religion, nationality, membership in a particular social group or political opinion" is eligible to apply for asylum. Yet data collected during the mid-1980s revealed that some groups faced bias within the court system. Between 1983 and 1986, US courts rarely granted asylum to Central Americans: only 0.9 percent of Guatemalans and 2.6 percent of Salvadorans were given amnesty. In stark contrast, more than 60 percent of Iranians, 32 to 51 percent of Eastern Europeans, and 38 percent of Afghani refugees were given asylum during this period.[15] The reason for these disparities is that the US courts stated that Central Americans were primarily economic refugees in search of a better financial situation rather than political refugees fleeing persecution. Critics offered a different explanation: the US government found it embarrassing to acknowledge that Guatemalans and Salvadorans were the victims of state-sponsored violence and human rights abuses when it was providing massive funding to these regimes. Whatever the explanation, Corbett was aware that there was limited utility in working within the system and that extralegal measures might one day be needed to keep these Central Americans safe.

That day came sooner than expected. Just a few weeks after soliciting the help of fellow Quakers, Corbett brought three Salvadorans to an INS office to apply for asylum. Although he had little hope that their applications would be approved, he thought doing this would buy them time to stay in the United States until the war in El Salvador ended. Having gone through this process many times, Corbett knew the routine: the refugees would submit their paperwork and then be released to the custody of a local minister to await their court appearance. But this day was different. Instead of being released, the applicants were arrested. Corbett concluded that it was no longer possible to work within the system. Playing by the rules was tantamount to turning refugees over to the authorities, who would deport them after an unfair hearing. Immediately, Corbett changed his strategy. He had extensive knowledge of the local terrain, based on years of goat farming. Using this knowledge, he began smuggling people across the US-Mexico border. He loaded them into his 1961 Chevy truck and brought them to homes of friends throughout the Tucson area. Border Patrol officials never bothered him since he looked like many other local ranchers driving their hired laborers to and from a job.

Corbett had a tough time finding housing for everyone, since the volume of refugees was enormous. According to some estimates, between 500,000 and 750,000 Central Americans crossed the US border each year in the early 1980s.[16] Consequently, Corbett approached the pastor of a local Presbyterian church, John Fife, and asked whether some of the refugees could be housed at his church. Although Fife was aware that providing shelter would make him vulnerable to prosecution for aiding and abetting undocumented individuals, he felt morally compelled to help. He brought the matter to the church elders, who voted to open their church to the refugees. Shortly thereafter, Fife's congregation began helping Corbett to transport people across the border.

It did not take long for the INS to figure out that the church was involved in Corbett's operation. Pastor Fife called his congregation together to decide how they should respond. They could stop helping Corbett and refuse to shelter the refugees. They could continue on until they were arrested. Or they could take the initiative and publicly announce why they were violating immigration laws. They chose the last option.

On March 24, 1982—the second anniversary of Archbishop Romero's assassination—leaders of the Southside Presbyterian Church of Tucson held a news conference to declare their church a Sanctuary and cited the biblical mandate: "If a stranger lives in your land, do not molest him. You must count him as one of your own countrymen. Love him as yourself, for you were once strangers, in the land of Egypt."[17] Furthermore, Fife declared that his church was following an ancient Hebrew tradition of designating safe havens for those fleeing violence. Since the US government was not providing protection, his church members felt that their faith required them to do so, even if this entailed breaking immigration laws, which they readily admitted they had done for several months. Fife stated directly:

> We are writing to inform you that Southside Presbyterian Church will publicly violate the Immigration and Nationality Act, Section 274(A)....
> We take this action because we because we believe that the current policy and practice of the United States Government with regard to Central American refugees is illegal and immoral.... We beg of you, in the name of God, to do justice and love mercy in the administration of your office. We ask that "extended voluntary departure" be granted to refugees from Central America and that current deportation proceedings against these victims be stopped. Until such time, we will not cease to extend the sanctuary of the church to undocumented people from Central America. Obedience to God requires this of all of us.[18]

News of the Tucson Sanctuary church spread rapidly, with favorable stories published in national newspapers, such as the *Washington Post*, and in the news program *60 Minutes*.[19] Within weeks, Southside Presbyterian Church had been contacted by dozens of other faith communities that wanted to join the effort. Because the Tucson Sanctuary group was overwhelmed with offers, it asked the Chicago Religious Task Force on Central America to coordinate the growing Sanctuary movement. Quickly, these efforts began to resemble a new underground railroad in which volunteers would transport refugees from the border regions to churches and synagogues throughout the country. Within a year of Southside Presbyterian's public declaration, thirty faith communities had also declared themselves Sanctuaries. By 1984, the network had expanded into thirty-four states.[20] The movement began as a Quaker initiative, but it rapidly became a truly ecumenical endeavor, including Protestants, Jews, and Catholic communities.

Although the Sanctuary movement began as a humanitarian response to Central Americans seeking safety, the Chicago Task Force quickly recognized the movement's potential for educating US citizens about the conditions in El Salvador and Guatemala. As Sanctuary activists transported refugees throughout the country, they would stop at faith communities along the way, and the refugees told their stories, recounting the violence in their homelands and the human rights abuses committed by these US-sponsored regimes. These encounters were powerful, connecting real humans to the atrocities occurring thousands of miles away. This prompted many North Americans to question US foreign policy toward Central America and US immigration practices. One Sanctuary activist explained:

> The Sanctuary movement was ingenious because, with the network of churches that developed through the underground railroad, you had refugees that were moving into communities around the United States and telling their stories. These were compelling stories, and that did two things. First, it gave people a human face to the reality in Central America, to this foreign policy debate that was going on in Washington. But it also taught people something about their own government, because in the face of these compelling stories, we were told that our government said they had no right to be here. So people began learning about asylum laws. You ended up with a lot of white, middle-class folks—some of them quite conservative and Republican—who saw the injustice of the situation. They saw that we actually have laws that should have allowed these

people to stay, but they weren't allowed to stay. That became the basis of a tremendous amount of activism.[21]

Over the next few years, the Sanctuary movement assisted an estimated 2,000 to 3,000 Central Americans.[22]

Within this ecumenical movement, Catholic laypeople were well represented. One reason they got involved was because of the connection to Catholic martyrs in Central America—particularly Archbishop Romero and the four North American churchwomen who were murdered in El Salvador. For some North American Catholics, those murders were politically transformative, shedding light on the devastating human costs of the region's civil wars. As Salvadorans and Guatemalans fled to the United States in search of protection, many of these Catholics were willing to provide support. At the peak of the movement in August 1988, there were 464 Sanctuary communities throughout the country. According to the files of the Chicago Religious Task Force on Central America, 78 of those Sanctuary groups were Catholic—a higher number than for any other denominational group.[23]

Not surprisingly, then, when the government finally cracked down on the Sanctuary movement, Catholic laypeople were among those who were arrested and prosecuted. In the early years, some activists felt that the religious nature of the movement provided them some protection. As one stated: "We did have some discussions about [infiltration] . . . but I felt that people [in the movement] were getting paranoid. . . . I thought, 'The government would never send agents into the churches.'"[24] They were wrong.

The first arrests occurred in February 1984 near Guerra, Texas, when Border Patrol agents pulled over a vehicle that was transporting three Salvadoran refugees. The officers promptly placed three Sanctuary activists under arrest: Sister Dianne Muhlenkamp, a Catholic nun with the Poor Hand Maids of Jesus of Indiana; Stacey Lynn Merkt of the Bijou House Religious Community of Colorado; and *Dallas Times Herald* reporter Jack Fischer. They were charged with transporting "aliens." Prosecutors decided to drop charges against Fischer. Muhlenkamp chose to plead guilty to a misdemeanor and was sentenced to a year's probation. Merkt, a refugee worker at Casa Romero (a refugee center run by the

Roman Catholic diocese of Brownsville, Texas), was convicted of three felonies. She initially received a ninety-day suspended sentence and two years' probation, but an appeals court later overturned her conviction.

From this point on, the crackdown expanded. In April 1984, Jack Elder was arrested for transporting Salvadorans. Elder, a Catholic layperson, was the director of Casa Romero in Texas. He faced three felony charges that could result in a maximum sentence of fifteen years in prison. Several months later, in December 1984, Stacey Merkt and Jack Elder were indicted again. They used their trials to draw attention to the brutality of the Central American wars and US involvement in the region. Merkt told news reporters, "I don't know whether to cry or yell about the injustices both here and there [in Central America]. I believe it is time to yell. I will persevere."[25] Elder stated:

> I'm not looking for a confrontation. . . . Not to be self-righteous about it, but there's a moral force behind what we're doing that has the potential to focus some light on foreign policy. . . . There is a war going on in El Salvador right now; there are bombing raids financed by the U.S. government. This is the issue that people are fleeing from.

When their trial concluded, Merkt was convicted of one count of conspiracy and was sentenced to eighteen months in prison. Elder was found guilty of conspiracy, helping undocumented immigrants enter the country, and transporting undocumented persons. He was sentenced to one year in prison.

The arrests continued. In January 1985, sixteen Arizona Sanctuary activists faced prosecution. Eventually, the number of activists charged was reduced to twelve, which included the movement founders, Jim Corbett and John Fife, and ten others (five of whom were Catholic). The Arizona activists were accused of various crimes, ranging from "harboring or shielding illegal aliens" to conspiracy, aiding, and abetting.[26] The charges were based on evidence that had been collected by government infiltrators who had posed as Sanctuary activists in a mission called "Operation Sojourn."

The Tucson activists presented an argument in the pretrial hearings that this was not strictly a case of immigrant smuggling, as the government charged. Defense attorneys argued that the immigrants were not "aliens"—to use the government term—since they had legitimate asylum claims. In addition, the defense argued that the Sanctuary activists were actually following US and international refugee law by protecting those who had a well-founded fear of persecution, given the overwhelming evidence of human rights abuses in Guatemala and El Salvador. Because the INS was not properly complying with the asylum process, the activists were fulfilling the law by providing protection that these Central Americans duly deserved. In addition, the activists posited that Sanctuary is a religious practice protected by the First Amendment. The defense attorneys called upon religious experts, who testified that the practice is grounded in Judeo-Christian traditions and scripture. Finally, the defense argued that government-paid informants in "Operation Sojourn" had violated the activists' constitutional right to practice their faith without government obstruction. Such surveillance, they claimed, was parallel to state interference and suppression in Soviet bloc nations and Nazi Germany.[27]

The prosecution countered each point. Responding to the claim that Sanctuary was a practice mandated by the defendants' faith, the prosecuting attorney asked if the pope had publicly taken a stand on Sanctuary practices. If it was required by one's Christian commitment, then why had millions of other Christians refused to participate in the movement? The judge also questioned whether Sanctuary practices reflected primarily a matter of individual conscience rather than a religious imperative. Regarding the infiltration and surveillance of church activities, the prosecution argued that religious affiliation did not give the defendants the right to break the law. In fact, the lead prosecutor claimed that "what was extraordinary about the Sanctuary case was not the government investigation, but rather that for the first time churches had been used to hatch criminal conspiracies."[28] They posited that the government had the right to prosecute all criminals, regardless of their faith affiliation.

The judge ruled in favor of the prosecution on every motion. Before the trial even started, the defendants felt that the legal cards were stacked against them. Nonetheless, they held to their position that they were humanitarians, not criminals, who were acting in true compliance both with federal and international refugee law and with God's law.

The trial lasted six months. The media covered it closely, largely because the accused included a nun, several priests, a minister, and religious laypeople, making it an unusual criminal case. Moreover, it had elements of high drama, including torture, faith, altruism, risk, spying, and betrayal. However, as the trial progressed, the defendants and their lawyers grew increasingly frustrated, since they were not allowed to discuss the human rights conditions in Central America or their own religious beliefs. In addition, the judge did not permit defendants to use terms such as "torture," "electroshock," or "death," deeming them to be inflammatory.[29] When the defendants argued that the judge was biased, they were threatened with contempt of court charges.

After the trial concluded, the jury deliberated for two weeks. When the verdicts came in, hundreds of supporters packed the courthouse, awaiting the news. The walls outside the building had been covered with banners. One banner conveyed the words engraved at the Statue of Liberty's base: "Give me your tired, your poor, your huddled masses yearning to breathe free." Finally, the verdict was announced: jurors convicted eight of the defendants, handing down convictions on eighteen of the thirty charges. The convicted defendants received a sentence of five years' probation.[30]

Although these arrests and trials were designed to end the movement, they had the opposite effect. Dozens of religious individuals and organizations had come forward to support the prosecuted Sanctuary activists, including Bishop Joseph Fiorenza of Galveston-Houston; Bishop John Fitzpatrick of Brownsville, Texas; and the National Federation of Priests' Councils.[31] The national media coverage brought widespread attention to the movement. As a result, the number of Sanctuary communities doubled during this time.[32] The movement eventually began to subside in the early 1990s as El Salvador and Guatemala negotiated an end to their civil wars. But the Sanctuary movement left a legacy and set of practices that would be revived years later.

The New Sanctuary Movement

At the beginning of the twenty-first century, the idea of Sanctuary resurfaced as US deportations of undocumented immigrants expanded. Those threatened with deportation faced the prospect of being separated from spouses and children who were US citizens. Such was the case for Elvira Arellano, an undocumented Mexican immigrant who had been living in Chicago for many years and was active in immigrant rights campaigns. Her son had been born in the United States and thus had citizenship. Arellano grew increasingly worried that she would be deported and separated from her son, and so she moved into her church and took sanctuary in the summer of 2006. Other groups began to organize in support of immigrants facing similar concerns.[33]

On May 9, 2007, the New Sanctuary Movement was officially launched when religious activists in Chicago, New York, Seattle, Los Angeles, and San Diego publicly announced the formation of a national interfaith network for immigrant rights. The date was intentional: this was the same day that the Comprehensive Immigration Reform Act of 2007 (S. 1348) was introduced in the US Senate, which proposed legal status and a pathway to citizenship for undocumented immigrants living within the United States. The movement released its mission statement, proclaiming: "As people of faith and people of conscience, we pledge to resist the . . . administration's policy proposals to target and deport millions of undocumented immigrants and discriminate against marginalized communities. We will open up our congregations and communities as sanctuary spaces for those targeted by hate, and work alongside our friends, families, and neighbors to ensure the dignity and human rights of all people."[34]

As they announced the New Sanctuary Movement, these religious activists explicitly stated that they were following the tradition of the 1980s Sanctuary movement. Yet there were some important differences. The 1980s movement provided aid to as many Central Americans as possible, with few limitations on who was eligible to receive Sanctuary assistance. The new movement, in contrast, has focused primarily on "mixed-status" families—that is, families in which some members are US citizens and some are undocumented—although it has stated that all immigrants deserve rights and compassionate treatment. In practice, this has meant that most of those who were given safe haven by religious communities were young, heterosexual married couples with US children rather than nontraditional families or single individuals. A second difference is that refugees in the 1980s actually took shelter in religious communities until they could be safely settled elsewhere. In the New Sanctuary Movement, Sanctuary refers to a broad array of practices. While some immigrants take up residence in churches and synagogues, others remain in their homes and continue in their jobs, working in partnership with a congregation that provides financial, legal, and moral support. Finally, the New Sanctuary Movement is distinct from its forerunner in that it explicitly aims to change immigration policy whereas its predecessor saw itself primarily as responding to a humanitarian crisis. Although the 1980s Sanctuary movement did eventually develop a policy focus, those activists were trying to change US foreign policies, not immigration policies.[35]

The New Sanctuary Movement encountered significant obstacles, since anti-immigrant sentiment had expanded since the 1980s. The greatest hostility was directed toward those who entered the United States illegally, since there is a misperception that the undocumented are taking away employment from US citizens while contributing to problems such as crime and drugs. In response to this growing sentiment, the US government implemented the Illegal Immigration Reform and Immigrant Responsibility Act in 1996, which instituted mandatory detention and deportation for the undocumented and for legal permanent residents who had criminal convictions, even for minor offenses. This constituted a major shift in policy; previously, detention and deportation were largely discretionary, and legal permanent residents could not be deported unless they had been convicted of an aggravated felony. Moreover, the new law could be applied retroactively.[36]

In addition to new legislation, the Federal Bureau of Investigation and the Immigration and Naturalization Service began conducting routine raids after the terrorist attacks of September 11, 2001. Shortly thereafter, the Department of Homeland Security and INS merged, indicating a new mentality in which all immigrants were seen as potential threats to national security. The previous responsibilities of the INS were delegated across three new government institutions: US Citizenship and Immigration Services, US Customs and Border Protection, and Immigration and Customs Enforcement (ICE). ICE implemented a plan in 2004 to remove all undocumented immigrants within a ten-year time frame. This plan, known as "Operation Endgame," required a significant increase in federal funding. By 2007, $12.5 billion was being spent annually on immigration enforcement and border protection.[37] According to sociologist Grace Yukich:

> In 2006 alone, raids and other enforcement operations led to the deportation of approximately 280,000 people: a 32% increase from 2003. After 2006, intensive raids, detentions, and deportations only increased,

with even more undocumented immigrants detained or deported without warning, leaving families and homes behind. . . . [There were over] 320,000 deportees in 2007 alone. Over the period stretching from 1997 to 2007, more than 100,000 of the millions deported were the parents of U.S. citizen children. A 2009 Human Rights Watch report estimated that over one million family members were separated by deportation from the United States between 1997 and 2007.[38]

As raids and deportations escalated, legislators passed new immigration laws. The Border Protection, Anti-Terrorism, and Illegal Immigration Control Act, introduced in 2005, stiffened penalties for those using false documents to gain employment, those who employed undocumented immigrants, and anyone who provided assistance to the undocumented. Outraged by the new legislation, immigrant rights groups took to the streets. They organized a walkout in Philadelphia, which they called "A Day without Immigrants," to show how much local economies depended on their work. In addition, tens of thousands marched in Washington, DC, and Chicago. In March 2006, as new legislation was being debated in Congress, an estimated 1 million demonstrators marched in cities throughout the country.[39]

These acts of protest had an effect. By May 2007, the Senate introduced the Comprehensive Immigration Reform Act, which provided a route to citizenship for some undocumented workers and repealed the more severe punishments of earlier bills. This inspired activists to keep the pressure on policy makers. When the legislation eventually stalled in Congress, undocumented immigrants knew that they were still in danger of being deported and separated from their families.

This was the context that revived the practice of Sanctuary. The New Sanctuary Movement expanded rapidly, mobilizing hundreds of faith communities throughout the United States.[40] Some congregations offered the undocumented assistance in navigating the legal system. Others pressured politicians to develop new immigration policies. And some provided shelter to "mixed-status" families to deter deportation. Although ICE agents can legally enter a place of worship to make arrests, they rarely do; the agency recognizes that breaking down the doors of Sanctuary churches and synagogues would be perceived as disrespecting the sanctity of religious institutions.

New Sanctuary Movement activists became hopeful in 2012 when President Barack Obama announced the Deferred Action for Childhood Arrivals (DACA) program, which enabled undocumented immigrants who were brought into the country as children to obtain work permits, attend public schools and universities, and apply for deportation exemptions. Approximately 800,000 undocumented youth applied for DACA status. In 2014, President Obama introduced the Deferred Action for Parents of Americans and Lawful Permanent Residents (DAPA) program, which would allow undocumented immigrants who have children who are US citizens or residents to apply for a three-year renewable work permit and exemption from deportation. Sanctuary activists were optimistic that their pressure was making a difference as political leaders sought solutions to immigration concerns.

Yet the optimism diminished rapidly when Donald Trump was elected president of the United States in November 2016. When Trump assumed office in January 2017, he rescinded the immigration programs that Obama had enacted. He revoked DAPA in June 2017, although the program faced legal obstacles and had never actually been implemented. He repealed DACA in September 2017. Suddenly, youth and their parents once again faced the serious prospect of permanent family separation.

The New Sanctuary Movement refused to capitulate in the face of Trump's policies. In fact, Sanctuary religious communities were more committed than ever, and their example caught on: soon, numerous cities were declaring themselves Sanctuary cities, meaning that police would refuse to inquire about a person's immigration status or to detain people solely on the basis of their immigration status. Sanctuary cities stated that they would limit their cooperation with federal immigration enforcement. Dozens of college campuses also followed suit, declaring that they would not turn over any information to federal officials about their students' immigration status. The idea of welcoming the immigrant—taught so strongly within the American Catholic tradition—had spread beyond faith communities, inspiring city and university officials to embrace their undocumented residents and students. Because this issue continues to be debated and legislative initiatives are still under way, the story of the New Sanctuary Movement is still unfolding.

Conclusion

Catholic leaders in the United States have long endorsed immigrant rights and policy reform. They have called upon their parishioners to welcome immigrants, regardless of their legal status, and to treat them with dignity. Some have gone even further. Starting in the 1980s, when some US Catholics realized that Central American refugees' lives were at stake, they followed their moral convictions and assisted them. Recognizing that they could not work within the legal system without jeopardizing the refugees' safety, they began to work outside of it, assisting Central Americans across the border and providing them with safe haven until the civil wars ceased or until the US government changed its policies. These Catholics, along with other people of faith, helped thousands of refugees. This tradition was revived decades later, in the early twenty-first century, as anti-immigrant sentiments expanded and new policies led to increasing numbers of arrests and deportations. As families of mixed immigration status feared that they would be separated, faith communities throughout the United States once again declared themselves sanctuaries, providing assistance and challenging the government to adopt more compassionate policies. As the struggle over immigration continues, US Catholics will continue to be a force for progressive change.

Earth Ethics and American Catholic Environmentalism

In 1962, Rachel Carson's book *Silent Spring* spelled out the environmental dangers of rampant industrial growth. Carson focused particularly on the synthetic pesticide DDT, which was widely used at the time and was endangering fish and numerous bird species, from hummingbirds to bald eagles. She warned that it was only a matter of time until it harmed people, arguing that "if humankind poisoned nature, nature would in turn poison humankind."[1] By 1969, Carson's warnings appeared prophetic. In January of that year, an oil rig ruptured off the coast of Santa Barbara, California. More than 3 million gallons of crude oil were spilled into the ocean, creating a thirty-five-mile-long oil slick that killed thousands of fish, sea mammals, and birds.[2] Several months later, Cleveland's Cuyahoga River—filled with chemicals, sewage, and industrial waste—caught fire when sparks from a passing train ignited debris floating on the water. Seeing dramatic photos of the river in flames, US citizens were shocked, even though the highly polluted body of water had caught fire numerous times before.

These events and others compelled American citizens to demand changes, leading to the birth of the contemporary environmental movement in the 1960s. Activists mobilized for protective policies, and their efforts paid off. President Lyndon Johnson signed nearly 300 conservation measures into law. Some of these acts preserved federal lands from commercial economic development. Congress also passed laws to limit pollution; these included the Clean Air Acts, the Clean Water Acts, the Pesticide Control Act, the Ocean Dumping Act, the Federal Water Pollution Control Act Amendments, the Toxic Substance Control Act, the Endangered Species Act, and the Federal Land Policy and Management Act. To enforce these new federal environmental regulations, the Environmental Protection Agency (EPA) was created in 1970.[3] That same year, environmental groups promoted public awareness by implementing the first Earth Day celebration. Roughly 20 million Americans participated in teach-ins, celebrations, and protests on college campuses and at city halls throughout the United States.[4]

Although environmentalists were a growing force in American politics, there were also a growing number of problems. In the 1970s, there was the Love Canal crisis (1978) in upstate New York, where a local chemical company had buried more than 21,000 tons of toxic waste, which seeped into people's homes, forcing them to relocate and causing nervous disorders and cancer. This was followed in 1979 by an accident at the Three Mile Island power plant near Harrisburg, Pennsylvania, where a partial meltdown of a nuclear reactor released radioactive gases into the atmosphere. In the 1980s, the world witnessed another major nuclear accident in Chernobyl, Ukraine (1986), as well as the worst oil spill in history when the *Exxon Valdez* oil tanker hit a reef off the Alaskan coast in 1989, dumping 11 million gallons of oil into the ocean.

Where did US Catholics stand during the emergence and expansion of the environmental movement? Although there were small environmentally oriented trends within Catholicism in the first part of the twentieth century, the Catholic hierarchy and many laypeople were reluctant to address the growing ecological crisis until much later. One layperson reflected on this lack of attention to environmentalism within American Catholicism:

Elizabeth Johnson, C.S.J., a theologian and professor at Fordham University in New York, was talking to Catholic school teachers about ways to integrate environmental concerns into classroom lessons. Personally, I considered environmental concern a white privilege. I did not have time to teach it to my inner-city students. Sister Johnson argued that social justice and environmental activism are necessarily linked and gave examples of ways to integrate ecology into an inner-city school's daily life. It was intriguing, but I didn't quite buy it. I do not think I was alone in downplaying the environment. While a recent Gallup poll indicates that over half of all Americans believe environmental quality in this country is getting worse and that our leaders are not doing enough about it, I did not see the same level of concern reflected in my experience as an American Catholic. I have never heard a homily about ecology, although in various parishes I have heard dozens about abortion or war. I receive countless direct mailings from Catholic organizations, but I do not recall ever receiving one about the environment. There are many books that discuss religion and environmental awareness. But where is the action?[5]

This individual's observations reflect this notion that environmentalism was not initially a central part of American Catholic ethics and activism. Why? After decades of political engagement with labor, poverty, peace, gender equality, and immigration, why did US Catholics largely overlook these growing environmental problems in the twentieth century? And what caused this to change in the early twenty-first century, culminating in Pope Francis's encyclical *Laudato Si* ("On Care for Our Common Home")?

This chapter addresses these questions. It summarizes early Catholic efforts to promote environmentalism and describes the initial responses of the Catholic Church, which often prioritized human needs over environmental matters. It also shows how the Catholic Church and Catholic laypeople started placing greater emphasis on the environment toward the end of the twentieth century. The chapter then surveys the main themes of various Catholic teachings and publications—from the US Catholic Bishops Conference's *Renewing the Earth* (1991) to Pope Francis's *Laudato Si* (2015)—that have given impetus to more Catholic environmental action. Finally, it describes the work of two activist groups: the National Religious Partnership for the Environment, an ecumenical organization, and Catholic Climate Change.

Precursors to Catholic Environmental Movements

A "green revolution" philosophy existed among Catholic laypeople and clergy, dating back to the 1920s. It was evident in two separate movements: (1) the farming communes proposed by Peter Maurin of the Catholic Worker movement, which was promoted by laypeople; and (2) the National Catholic Rural Life Conference (NCRLC), which was largely promoted by Catholic clergy.

Peter Maurin and the Catholic Worker Farms

Peter Maurin cofounded the Catholic Worker movement with Dorothy Day in 1933, as discussed in chapter 1. While both Maurin and Day were concerned about workers' rights, Maurin felt the solution was to return to Christian communalism. In this context, the Christian community would take responsibility for caring for the poor—not the government, with its dehumanizing welfare programs. This belief was the basis for the houses of hospitality that Catholic Workers formed in urban centers throughout the United States and, eventually, the broader world. Yet Maurin believed that the situation was about much more than unemployment and poverty. He believed that work was a necessary component of human dignity and that dignity was best found on small agricultural communes. Moreover, he felt that a so-called green revolution would mean that humans would live in closer community with one another and in closer harmony with the natural environment.[6]

Although Day was truly an urban-focused Catholic Worker, she recognized the value of Maurin's vision, and together they sought out opportunities to create this type of Catholic agricultural commune. Maurin called these communes "agronomic universities," envisioning them as places where workers and others, including scholars, could create an ethical economic and social system rooted in a profound respect for the land.[7] The communes would be based on subsistence farming practices that were not profit-oriented. Maurin declared that the commune members "would only eat what they could raise, and raise what they could eat. In order to conserve the energy of the land, the Catholic Workers planned to rotate crops and fertilize them only with organic compost."[8] Although the Catholic Worker farms failed, Maurin's vision of a green revolution was influential, especially for those seeking an alternative to an unsustainable capitalist system based on the production and acquisition of more and more material objects and the exploitation of the earth.

John Rawe and the National Catholic Rural Life Conference

Around the same time that Maurin was calling Catholic Workers to form agricultural communes, Jesuit priest John Rawe was also preaching the virtues of a green revolution. For Rawe, this meant the following:

> It is a green revolution because it is far removed from any battleground reddened by the selfish blood of class hatred, far removed from the red rags of Communistic tyranny and the wriggling swastikas of frenzied dic-

tatorships. It is a green revolution because it takes place out in the green fields where the land, owned by the patient, productive, profitable, democratic, free, personal laborer is blessed and gladdened with the divine benedictions of life-giving moisture and smiling sunshine. It is a green revolution because it deals with deep planting and sturdy growth and not with wanton destruction and economic ruin; because it buries its roots in the soil, broken for cultivation and divided for ownership in such a way that human nature, individual and social, can grow to a bountiful maturity in sufficient prosperity, wider freedom, wholesale family life, and a closer union with the eternal God and fellow man in religion, in the arts, in the whole of life.[9]

Rawe believed that family farming promoted important values such as hard work, perseverance, and thrift. It countered the growing trends toward consumerism and materialism while promoting a family- and community-minded culture. Moreover, family farming offered freedom from the exploitation and alienation of industrial factory jobs. Rawe saw family farming as an alternative to both capitalism and communism.

Father Rawe's preaching inspired Edwin O'Hara, a priest in Oregon who had been studying the demographics of American Catholics and had discovered that most lived in urban centers. These urban Catholics were more likely to have smaller families and to move away from their faith tradition. O'Hara wanted to address the decline of urban Catholicism while simultaneously ensuring that the church was responsive to rural populations. Toward this end, in 1923, he created the National Catholic Rural Life Conference, which developed a Catholic rural philosophy. This philosophy held that farming could forge a unique relationship between individuals and nature, which in turn generated security and stability. The organization preached an environmental ethic that was, first and foremost, concerned about the detrimental effects of commercialized agriculture and "finance capitalism" that did not value families and sustainable farming.

The NCRLC promoted its vision through various publications and by teaching these ideas to priests, primarily located in the Midwest, who disseminated them to their rural parishes. Eventually, the conference organized schools for priests, religious Sisters, and laypeople. The courses covered the religious premises of this rural philosophy as well as practical matters such as the management of farming cooperatives, soil conservation and enrichment, climatic considerations, and sustainable agricultural practices rather than industrial approaches. By 1944, sixty courses had been offered that enrolled 1,700 priests, 9,000 Sisters, and 12,000 lay Catholics.[10]

Yet the movement began to wane in the late 1940s, largely due to the growth of American industry in the post–World War II era, which drew more Catholics to urban centers and promoted large agribusinesses in rural areas. Yet even as the NCRLC was declining, its members issued warnings about the growing environmental threats associated with such industrialization. In 1941, the conference printed an article proclaiming that swallows would no longer return to the region because of toxic pesticides used in the "commercialized factories-in-the-fields." In 1948, it printed an article warning of DDT's adverse effects—fourteen years before Rachel Carson articulated the same concern in *Silent Spring*. By the early 1950s, the conference was opposing strip mining.[11] Yet the movement never took hold within mainstream American Catholicism—either within the official hierarchy or among urban and suburban laypeople—and its philosophy was at odds with the industrial approach that dominated the American economy.

Absence of Catholic Environmentalism, 1950s–1980s

Ironically, the influence of these early Catholic environmental movements diminished precisely at a time when environmental threats were expanding. Widespread use of agricultural pesticides, expanding industrial pollution, and toxic waste contamination created numerous disasters. While these problems prompted the emergence of secular environmentalism in the United States, many Catholic leaders and laypeople were largely silent on environmental concerns from the 1950s through the 1980s.

What accounts for the absence of Catholic environmentalism when American Catholics had been at the forefront of other progressive causes, such as labor issues, immigration, and peace? There are several possible explanations.

One explanation is that Roman Catholics placed primary emphasis on human needs, such as development and employment, over environmental concerns. For some, human and economic development required scientifically engineered high-yield seeds to meet the needs of the hungry. Others believed that tightening environmental regulations might hurt businesses and thus contribute to unemployment. This sentiment was clearly articulated by one writer for the *National Catholic Reporter*, who stated:

> Faced with the choice of saving the redwood forests or one child's brain potential, which will be damaged by lack of protein, then I say good-bye redwoods, and good-bye trumpeter swans, and good-bye wild rivers, which only a family making [a substantial amount of income] can afford to enjoy. . . . Sorry, but people do come first, last, and always.[12]

Similarly, some Catholics argued that human development required the use of natural resources and other forms of energy to promote modernization, which in turn created employment. Some embraced nuclear energy as an inexpensive energy source that would provide a stable basis for economic advancement. The American Catholic magazine *Commonweal* published an article that depicted environmentalists' concerns about nuclear accidents as "hysterical" and their rejection of nuclear energy as "knee-jerk opposition." The *Commonweal* author wrote that the call for alternative energy sources "through windmills, firewood, solar energy converters and the like were all very quaint but, with the possible exception of solar energy, all geared to life in another century."[13] Even after the Three Mile Island and Chernobyl nuclear accidents, there was little concern about nuclear energy in American Catholic circles. Those Catholic writers who did respond often underscored the familiar themes of Catholic teachings, such as the "condemnation of a heartless capitalist economy and the military industrial complex, denunciation of America's profligate consumer society, and sympathy for the world's hungry and poor."[14] Environmentalism was not a high priority.

A second explanation for the lack of Catholic engagement in the environmental movement is that US Catholics were heavily involved in other causes during this period. Many focused their efforts on the US civil rights movement, the anti–Vietnam War movement, and liberation struggles in Latin America and other world regions. Others supported Cardinal Joseph Bernardin's "seamless garment" principle of protecting all forms of human life. With the Supreme Court's decision to legalize abortion in *Roe v. Wade* (1973), some Catholics dedicated their time to the pro-life movement. Others organized against the death penalty or the proliferation of nuclear weapons. This commitment to protecting human life may have felt at odds with environmentalists, who opposed the prioritization of human life at the expense of other species.[15]

A third possible reason for the absence of a Catholic environmental movement is that some viewed environmentalism as incompatible with two Catholic teachings: (1) the belief that God gave humans dominion over the earth and (2) the Catholic prohibition on birth control. Regarding the dominion teaching, this concern was heightened when historian Lynn White published an article in *Science* magazine in 1967 entitled "The Historical Roots of Our Ecological Crisis."[16] In this article, White argued that the Christian Genesis story—where God instructs Adam to subdue and have dominion over the earth—led to an anthropocentric worldview in which humans believe it is their right to wantonly use the earth and its resources.[17] The second Catholic concern arose with the 1968 release of Paul Ehrlich's best-selling book, *The Population Bomb*. Ehrlich, a biology professor at Stanford University, argued that population growth had created a crisis in which hundreds of millions of people would starve to death and the earth's capacity to support the human race would collapse. He called for drastic measures to reduce the world's population, which included birth control and family planning.[18] Ehrlich did not mince words in condemning the Catholic prohibition on contraception, writing that it "contributes to misery and starvation for billions, and perhaps the end of civilization as we know it."[19] As discussed in chapter 3, many Catholics agreed with Ehrlich and spoke out against the encyclical *Humanae Vitae* (also released in 1968), which upheld the contraception ban. Charles Curran, a priest and theology professor at Catholic University, wrote that the encyclical demonstrated "an almost total disregard for the dignity of millions of human beings brought into the world without the slightest possibility of being fed and educated decently."[20] Still, numerous Catholics were fearful that Ehrlich's view would promote abortion, making them reluctant to embrace environmentalism.

A final reason why environmentalism did not initially take root in American Catholicism is that some Catholic environmentalists drew on the insights of Native American traditions, Eastern religions, and New Age ideas, which were foreign and sometimes repellent to traditional Catholics. No one exemplified this trend more than Matthew Fox, a former Dominican priest, who preached a "creation spirituality" that rejected the Catholic doctrine of "original sin" and advocated a belief in the "original blessing" of the earth. Fox's creation spirituality drew from the Bible, medieval mystics Meister Eckhart and Hildegard of Bingen, Jungian psychology, feminism, meditation practices, yoga, and the witchcraft teachings of Starhawk. Furthermore, in his journal *Creation,* he promoted New Age ideas, such as the belief that animals can be our spiritual guides. He even claimed that he took spiritual advice from his dog. After being silenced by the Vatican for a period, he was ordered to leave his position at Holy Names College in Oakland, California, and move to a Chicago monastery. When Fox refused, he was dismissed from the order and became an Episcopalian priest in 1994.[21] Fox's Catholic form of environmental spirituality seemed far-fetched and strange to many US Catholics.

Beginnings of Catholic Environmental Ethics

Eventually, American Catholics did begin paying attention to environmental concerns. This shift was due to a variety of developments, one of which was the election of John Paul II to the papacy in 1978. The new pope addressed environmental issues in his first encyclical, *Redemptor Hominis* (1979), also known as "Redeemer of Man." In this document, he departed from the optimism of his predecessors who believed in the progress that technology could bring. Instead, John Paul II expressed concern that humanity was not progressing but rather regressing. He specifically noted that the dominant economic order was "depleting the earth's resources of raw materials and energy at an ever increasing rate and putting intolerable pressures on the geophysical environment."[22] He also challenged the dominant view that God gave humans dominion over the earth to use its resources for their own purposes. The pope stated that the earth does provide for human needs but that humanity had an obligation to guard the earth and to avoid needless exploitation and destruction.

Although the pope did not address the issue again for nearly a decade, other Catholic thinkers began writing in earnest about environmentalism in the 1980s. Most notable were Bernard Häring's *Free and Faithful in Christ* (1981), John Carmody's *Ecology and Religion* (1983), Sean McDonagh's *To Care for the Earth* (1986), and Thomas Berry's *The Dream of the Earth* (1988). Eventually, in 1987, John Paul II revisited the topic in the encyclical *Sollicitude Rei Socialis* ("On Social Concern"), in which he argued that development practices had consistently prioritized economic concerns over moral considerations. The pope argued that respect for the natural world must be an essential part of any morally responsible development practice.[23]

Changes in US political dynamics also promoted openness to environmentalism among American Catholics. When Ronald Reagan was elected president in 1980, he was hostile to the environmental movement. He gained notoriety when a proposal was made to create the Redwood National Park in Northern California and he replied, "A tree is a tree. How many more do you have to look at?"[24] Eventually, however, Reagan was pressured into firing his antienvironmental appointees, including Secretary of the Interior James Watt and the EPA's leader, Anne Gorsuch, and replacing them with environmentally friendly leaders.

When Reagan left office and Republican George H. W. Bush took over the presidency in 1989, he took environmental matters seriously. Bush appointed William K. Reilly, a Catholic, to head the EPA. Reilly in turn wrote an article in *Commonweal*, imploring Catholics to take up the cause. Environmental concerns were becoming more mainstream and less alienating to U.S. Catholics during this period.[25]

By the beginning of the 1990s, Catholics had begun to advocate for environmental measures. On January 1, 1990, Pope John Paul II addressed the issue in "The Ecological Crisis: A Common Responsibility," his message for the World Day of Peace, which emphasized that Catholics had a moral obligation to act. The pope linked environmental degradation to the blind embrace of technology, rampant consumerism, and instant self-gratification. He stated: "Technologically enhanced exploitation of the earth for military and industrial purposes alienates humankind from nature, and turns us from 'guardian' to heedless exploiter and destroyer."[26] He further stated:

Modern society will find no solution to ecological problems unless it takes a serious look at its lifestyle. In many parts of the world, society is given to instant gratification and consumerism while remaining indifferent to the damage which they cause. . . . Simplicity, moderation, and discipline, as well as a spirit of sacrifice, must become part of everyday life, lest all suffer the negative consequences of the careless habits of the few.[27]

This message generated hope among environmentalists that the Roman Catholic Church was finally prioritizing this issue. Yet many were disheartened when subsequent encyclicals, such as *Evangelium Vitae*, focused on abortion and euthanasia and barely mentioned environmental concerns. Those outside the church, however, championed the cause. For example, a group of eminent scientists, including thirty-two Nobel laureates, released "An Open Letter to the American Religious Community" in 1991. The scientists called upon faith communities to fight the expanding global warming crisis.[28] That same year, the National Conference of Catholic Bishops released a pastoral declaration called *Renewing the Earth: An Invitation to Reflection and Action on the Environment in Light of Catholic Social Teaching.*"[29]

In *Renewing the Earth*, the bishops highlighted seven Catholic themes that support environmentalism. The first is a "*sacramental view of the universe.*" The bishops argued that humans can encounter the divine in the natural world and that this sacred experience should be the basis for environmental responsibility. Second is a "*consistent respect for human life*, which includes respect for all creation." Third is a "worldview affirming the ethical significance of *global interdependence and the common good*." Pope John XXIII had emphasized the world's increasing interdependence in his 1963 letter *Pacem in Terris*. The bishops built upon this premise by emphasizing that the most serious environmental problems are global in nature, and thus everyone is responsible for addressing them. This leads to the fourth theme: an "*ethic of solidarity*, promoting cooperation and a just structure of sharing in the world community." Solidarity requires us to sacrifice self-interest in favor of the well-being of the earth and all its inhabitants. Fifth is "an understanding of the *universal purpose of created things*, which requires equitable use of the earth's resources." In other words, Catholics should work toward an economy that is environmentally sustainable and that shares the earth's abundance with all humanity. The sixth theme is the "*option for the poor*," which indicates that the poor are disproportionately affected by environmental degradation and "most directly bear the burden of current environmental careless-ness." The final theme is about "*authentic development*, which offers a direction for progress that respects human dignity and the limits of material growth." Such development must demonstrate a respect for nature and insist that affluent countries reduce their consumption of natural resources.[30]

While this was a significant advance, the US bishops' views were still rooted in traditional Catholic beliefs. For example, the document re-tained an anthropocentric focus that emphasized humanity as God's highest creation. It also opposed any type of population control policies and insisted that "environmental progress cannot come at the expense of workers and their rights. . . . [S]olutions must be found that do not force us to choose between a decent environment and a decent life for workers."[31] Yet precisely because it resonated with traditional Catholics, *Renewing the Earth* became a landmark piece that linked Catholic values with preservation of the earth. By 1996, forty-eight environmental state-ments had been issued by bishops and regional conferences throughout the world.[32] The new commitment of Catholic leaders was matched by laypeople's strong commitment: according to one survey in the early 1990s, Catholics held the most pro-environment attitudes of all major Christian groups in the United States.[33]

Catholic Environmental Organizations

National Religious Partnership for the Environment

With this turn toward environmental ethics, many US Catholics were ready to put their beliefs into action. They found an important opportu-nity in 1992, when religious leaders organized an ecumenical conference in Washington, DC, to discuss the scientists' "Open Letter to the Reli-gious Community." Members of Catholic, Protestant, Evangelical, and Jewish groups gathered to discuss the need for a theologically based and scientifically informed religious initiative. During the conference, scien-tist Carl Sagan and Senator Al Gore presented the film *Blue Planet*. The film galvanized a sense of urgency, as one organizer recounted:

The presiding bishop of the Episcopal Church . . . gets up and says, "Until I saw that film last night and prayed about it afterwards, I didn't realize the depth of my love of creation, and my distress at its current condition." Then he sat down. And that was another one of those open-the-door moments. . . . I remember thinking, "this is irresistible." There was a whole day meeting, and we basically identified some of the priorities or values that would be important for the religious community to explore, albeit in different groups. This is the advantage of everybody largely starting out from scratch together, which is not usually the case in our religious lives. . . . This is new, but you know that it is inescapably religious. It affects the religious imagination.[34]

At the conference's conclusion, the group decided to establish an organization to continue its mission. In 1993, the National Religious Partnership for the Environment (NRPE) was officially launched as an alliance of the US Conference of Catholic Bishops, the National Council of Churches, the Coalition on the Environment and Jewish Life, and the Evangelical Environmental Network. Over the course of subsequent years, the organization mobilized faith communities to pressure Congress to pass climate change legislation. NRPE leaders also published "An Open Letter to Automobile Executives" and held conversations with representatives from Ford, General Motors, and the United Auto Workers to encourage the production of more fuel-efficient vehicles. They wrote editorials and obtained media coverage of their initiatives, such as the "What Would Jesus Drive?" campaign, in outlets such as the *New York Times*, *Washington Post*, and *ABC World News Tonight*. They also put together resource kits for more than 100,000 congregations in the United States, which included every Catholic parish. These kits encouraged laypeople to advocate for species protection, preservation of national parks and public lands, and clean power plans.[35]

Catholic Climate Covenant

A second Catholic environmental organization is the Catholic Climate Covenant (CCC), a coalition of sixteen Catholic groups, formed in 2006 under the direction of the US Conference of Catholic Bishops. The

CCC, which is deeply rooted in traditional Catholic Social Teachings, emphasizes the values of "prudence, poverty, the common good, and solidarity." Dan Misleh, CCC's executive director, explained how these values promote a commitment to environmentalism:

> We especially want to focus on the needs of the poor, the weak, and the vulnerable in the debate often dominated by more powerful interests. Inaction and inadequate or misguided responses to climate change will likely place even greater burdens on already desperately poor peoples. Action to mitigate global climate change must be built upon a foundation of social and economic justice that does not put the poor at greater risk. . . . Working for the common good requires us to promote the flourishing of all. . . . It's not just the environment for the environment's sake. We're not just about saving the spotted owl; we're also about saving people, and people are the ones that are primarily impacted by the environment. I mean other forms of life are as well, but if we believe that we are created in God's image and likeness and the pinnacle of creation, then our primary concern ought to be how people are impacted. . . . We have lots of debates on climate change, about what it's doing to the polar bears or what it's going to do to amphibians in the rain forest, that's a very important discussion. But our added value, as a faith community, is what's it going to do for poor people or to poor people?[36]

Precisely what does the CCC do to address climate change? Its members have been active in educational and policy work. They teach lay Catholics how to visit their legislators and lobby for climate change policies. They have given testimony to the EPA on the effects of repealing the Clean Power Plan in West Virginia. They have collected the signatures of hundreds of Catholic leaders on a petition asking the US government to rejoin the Paris climate agreement. They have provided educational materials to laypeople interested in organizing Earth Day or Feast of Saint Francis events.

On a grassroots level, they work with parishes to form "creation care teams," which implement programs in their local communities to reduce their carbon footprint. Teams have successfully established a variety of projects, from setting up church recycling and composting programs and reducing use of bottled water at churches to organizing ballot initiatives against fracking, starting community gardens, and installing solar panels on parish buildings.[37]

Pope Francis and *Laudato Si*

After nearly twenty-five years of Catholic environmental action, Pope Francis released the encyclical *Laudato Si* ("On Care for Our Common Home") in 2015. This is the most direct Catholic Social Teaching on the environment to date, and it has now firmly established environmentalism as a central part of Catholic beliefs and values. In the encyclical, Francis began by documenting the extent of environmental damage and appealing for urgent action. Francis's appeals were firmly grounded within the Catholic tradition, emphasizing the needs of the poor as well as the needs of the earth. He also dispelled arguments that overpopulation is the cause of environmental problems, claiming that such positions diminish the responsibilities of the wealthy to reduce their consumption.

Yet Francis did not merely stick to traditional Catholic values. In the encyclical, he challenged the previous Catholic view of humanity as the pinnacle of God's creation. He stated that there is no biblical basis for "a tyrannical anthropocentrism unconcerned for other creatures," which has lead humankind to exploit the earth for its own purposes.[38] He also challenged the technocratic paradigm, which holds that technology and modernization can solve world poverty and environmental problems. Instead, Pope Francis proposed other solutions. At the societal level, he called for the development and implementation of renewable energy sources, legislation to protect biodiversity, and policy initiatives to address climate change. At the individual level, Francis called upon people to change their consumption patterns to reduce wastefulness and to minimize their impact on the earth.

Conclusion

American Catholics' commitment to environmentalism has grown over time. Although there were some early efforts to promote sustainable farming and a sacred connection to the earth, most Catholics—including progressive Catholics—were reluctant to embrace the cause until the

1990s. At that point, however, they took up the issue with great commitment and energy. Clergy and religious leaders wrote dozens of documents that linked Catholic values to environmental activism. Laypeople established organizations that encourage local communities to implement environmentally sound practices and to pressure the US government to pass legislation that protects the earth and its resources. And Pope Francis made earth ethics the focus of his first papal encyclical. In this sense, the story of Catholic environmental activism is just beginning.

Conclusion

Contributions of Progressive US Catholic Movements

This book has highlighted a variety of progressive social movements that US Catholics have organized and mobilized. These movements have formed houses of hospitality and agricultural communes to welcome the destitute as guests rather than charity cases. They have organized unions, employing nonviolent tactics to improve the wages and living conditions of farmworkers. They destroyed draft cards to obstruct the conscription process and to save the lives of young men who would have been sent to fight in Vietnam. They have broken into military bases and industries to damage weapons of mass destruction. They have challenged traditional church teachings on gender roles and contraception. They have risked their own safety to shelter refugees fleeing the violence of Central America's civil wars. They have lived and worked in Nicaraguan war zones to deter combat attacks during the US-backed Contra War. They have sponsored legislation to cut funding from a US military facility that trained Latin American security forces in counterinsurgency tactics that included torture and psychological operations. They have organized local campaigns to help their fellow parishioners lower their carbon footprint, and they have organized national campaigns to fight global climate change.

These are all illustrations of "lived religion." In other words, these movements reveal how progressive American Catholics put their religious beliefs into action when they encountered social injustices and suffering. These movements reflect laypeople's moral responses to "hot cultural moments" of labor exploitation, war, human rights abuses, gender inequality, climate change, and expanding hostility toward immigrants. These movements reveal the core principles of these activists' faith.

In this conclusion, I reflect on these movements' contributions and enduring legacies. The book began with an overview of the values that undergird Catholic Social Thought; it concludes with the lessons derived from activists' experiments in living these values. Additionally, here I analyze how these movements have influenced official church teachings. I show how Catholic Social Thought has often been produced because laypeople have pushed the religious hierarchy to respond to the pressing issues of their era. Consequently, I challenge the idea that such teachings are strictly a top-down phenomenon, with church leaders declaring what members should believe and what actions they should take.

Key Themes in Progressive Catholic Movements

Reflecting on the experiences of these progressive movements, several themes emerge. The first theme is that *charity is not enough; socially engaged Catholics must also transform social structures.* Unquestionably, charity and "works of mercy" are needed to address people's immediate need for food, shelter, and safety. Yet even though such actions are important and laudable, they only address the symptoms of deeper problems. Charity does nothing to address the root cause of injustices.

Many of the movements described in this book have emphasized that authentic justice requires the transformation of oppressive social structures. One of the first to underscore this point was the Catholic Worker movement. Movement cofounder Dorothy Day is best known for starting houses of hospitality that feed and shelter the indigent, yet she was always challenging the economic, political, and military systems that created conditions of poverty. She once wrote: "We need to change the system. We need to overthrow, not the government, as the authorities are always accusing the Communists of conspiring to teach to do, but this rotten, decadent, putrid industrial capitalist system which breeds such suffering."[1] Similarly, liberation theology and its supporters highlighted the need for comprehensive social change by noting that exploitive systems actually constitute "structural sin." The only way to end such sin is to build just political, economic, and cultural systems.

A second theme is that *protest is not enough; sometimes resistance is necessary.* This theme is particularly evident in the American Catholic peace movement. Beginning with the Vietnam War, numerous activists realized that protest was nothing more than stating one's opinion or opposition. Holding an antiwar demonstration did little to stop the war. Vigiling outside a nuclear weapons fabrication site did little to impede the escalating arms race. Consequently, some called for a shift from protest to resistance, which meant obstructing war efforts. This was also evident in the 1980s Sanctuary movement; in this case, progressive Catholics and other religious activists decided that protesting US immigration policies was ineffective, since Central American refugees were being deported to their homelands, where they faced the likelihood of imprisonment and even assassination. The Sanctuary activists needed to do more than protest; they needed to interfere with the immigration system by assisting refugees across the border and helping them evade deportation.

The third theme in these movements is that *following your religious convictions may require you to break the law*. On this point, we have multiple examples: Catholic Workers refusing to participate in legally mandated New York City atomic drills, Plowshares activists damaging government-owned weaponry, and anti–Vietnam War activists burning their draft cards in violation of federal law—to name just a few. Of course, much of the activism described in this book was legal—such as climate change initiatives and lobbying efforts to cut aid to the Contras. Yet, when lives hang in the balance and atrocities are imminent, these activists chose to follow moral law over state and federal laws.

A fourth theme is closely related to this point: *working for peace and justice may demand significant personal sacrifices*. Some of the individuals in these movements paid a high price for their activism. Womenpriests and their supporters have been excommunicated. Those who committed civil disobedience at the School of the Americas routinely faced prison sentences of six months, and some Plowshares activists have been given prison sentences as long as eighteen years.[2] Others have literally risked their lives, such as the Witness for Peace activists who lived in Nicaragua's war zones. And, as part of the Central America solidarity organization Pledge of Resistance, one man—S. Brian Willson—sat in front of a government munitions train carrying weapons to El Salvador.[3] As the train barreled toward him, he decided that he would not leave the tracks, since he knew that lives would be lost if the weapons were delivered. Those lives were not worth any less, he stated, than his own. Willson held his ground and was hit by the train, which severed his legs. Miraculously, he survived to build a stronger bond of solidarity with Central Americans who had lost limbs from land mines planted during the wars.[4] All these activists were prepared to sacrifice their freedom, their security, and sometimes even their lives for the cause of peace and justice.

The fifth and final theme is that *church positions on social issues are not timelessly true or unchangeable.* As laypeople have organized and resisted injustices, their actions have sometimes pushed the religious hierarchy to rethink its traditional views. For example, the Roman Catholic Church, once so closely aligned with the wealthy and privileged classes, reconsidered its alliances when the poor began turning to labor organizations, to unions, and, in some regions, to armed revolutionary groups. Realizing that the Roman Catholic Church had lost its connection to the impoverished, and recognizing that Christ himself sided with the oppressed, church leaders shifted allegiance from the elites to the marginalized. Similarly, the Catholic Church has traditionally held a theology that positions humans at the pinnacle of creation, possessing dominion over the earth and its resources. As a result of environmental activism, which challenged this anthropocentric view, the Catholic hierarchy has been shifting toward a new environmental ethic that emphasizes stewardship of the earth rather than dominance.

Movement Influences on Catholic Social Teachings

The last theme indicates that movements have helped to shape Catholic social teachings. To what extent have progressive activists pushed religious leaders toward more progressive stances? While it is impossible to fully gauge their impact, there is evidence that religious leaders have been listening to and reflecting upon activist views.

Consider the influence of Catholic peace activists, who have worked to end war and the nuclear arms race and have called upon the Roman Catholic Church to reject the just war doctrine. One could argue that these activists have largely failed. After all, in 2018 the United States still had more than 4,000 active warheads in its nuclear stockpile and wars and terrorist attacks continue in countries such as Syria, Afghanistan, and Nigeria.[5] It seems that there is little peace in the world.

While wars and nuclear weapons are still real concerns, the Catholic peace movement has seen progress toward its goal of getting the church hierarchy to reconsider the just war tradition. Pope Francis, together with the Catholic peace organization Pax Christi International, sponsored a conference in Rome in April 2016 to discuss this issue. Called the "Nonviolence and Just Peace" conference, this event brought together approximately eighty-five individuals, including bishops, clergy, theologians, academics, and peace activists. Conference participants came from all regions of the world: the Philippines, Sri Lanka, Pakistan, Afghanistan, Iraq, Thailand, Democratic Republic of Congo, El Salvador, South Sudan, Colombia, Burundi, Guatemala, Mexico, Palestine, the United States, and other countries.[6]

Participants were asked to discuss four main issues. First, each individual shared his or her personal experiences with nonviolence—both as a spiritual commitment and as a practical strategy in violent conflicts. Second, they discussed Jesus's approaches to nonviolent action, noting how such insights might inform theology. Third, they reflected on how Catholics have promoted "just peace"—a concept introduced in the mid-1980s that includes nonviolent direct action, conflict transformation work, human rights, civil liberties, and sustainable and fair economic development.[7] Fourth, they articulated reasons for rejecting the just war principles and discussed ways to move beyond war.[8]

By the end of the conference, participants concluded that it was time for the Roman Catholic Church to replace its just war doctrine with just peace policies and practices. No one was more adamant about this than those who lived in conflicts areas where violence was pervasive. One participant, peace researcher Maria J. Stephan, described the group's deliberations:

> Given the power of modern warfare, and the second- and third-order effects of unleashing conflicts (even for presumably "just" causes), many participants at the Rome conference came seeking a bold new direction for the church. The fact that most came from contexts of extreme violence and injustice in Africa, the Americas, Asia, Europe, and the Middle East made the conversations all the more visceral and meaningful.
>
> For some at the Rome conference, the pope's endorsement of the gathering was long overdue for the church. Many of those in attendance, like Sister Nazek Matty from Erbil, Iraq, had known war for years and were sick of it. She and other participants pressed the church to place greater focus on nonmilitary responses to the Islamic State and expand the creative imagination to fight injustices with active nonviolent means. During

one of the plenary sessions, Rev. Francisco José de Roux, a Jesuit priest from Colombia, decried how, since the mid-1960s, supporters of both the government and FARC insurgents, including local priests, have justified violence in the name of a "just war." The outcome? Nearly 50 years of civil war. Other Catholic leaders in Colombia have supported nonviolent civic action and "zones of peace" to keep armed groups out of local communities and have helped advance peace talks expected to culminate in a final settlement later this year. By putting a just-peace approach at the center of its work, the Catholic Church in Colombia opened multiple avenues to effective nonviolent action.

One key exchange at the conference illustrated how just peace could make a big difference. Ugandan Archbishop John Baptist Odama of Gulu described how, after a round of bloody tit-for-tat killings in the government's long-running war against Joseph Kony's Lord's Resistance Army, an inter-religious group won the trust of the two sides and employed effective shuttle diplomacy to stop the violence. The group helped mediate a cease-fire between the two sides, showing that nonviolent tools can open channels of communication and produce results even in the fight against extremism. . . .

While one could argue that the just-war doctrine helps policymakers and ordinary citizens navigate the most difficult situations, many at the Vatican conference disagreed, arguing instead that the emphasis on just war limited the potential for creative alternatives to violence. Cardinal Peter Turkson, the president of the Pontifical Council for Justice and Peace, one of the two co-conveners of the conference along with Pax Christi International, expressed concern that just war has too often been used to rationalize wars that produce more harm than good. Marie Dennis, co-president of Pax Christi, similarly noted that just war has been "used and abused by political leaders."[9]

These convictions led the conference participants to write "An Appeal to the Catholic Church to Re-commit to the Centrality of Gospel Nonviolence." In this document, they stated that the just war doctrine should be rejected, since it has too often been used to legitimate war rather than to avoid or limit it. Adherence to a just war position also weakens the imperative to find alternative ways to address conflict. Thus they called upon Pope Francis to release an encyclical that rejects war and firmly promotes nonviolence and peace-building. They also recommended that the church integrate nonviolent practices and teachings into its daily activities, from the parish level to Catholic universities and national Catholic organizations. Finally, the participants implored the church to "no longer use or teach 'just war theory' . . . [and to] continue advocating for the abolition of war and nuclear weapons."[10]

The pope, who had initiated the conference, carefully contemplated these recommendations. Certainly, this document shaped his decision to focus his 2017 New Year's Day message on the theme of nonviolence. In this speech, Francis declared that Jesus taught nonviolence and thus his followers must choose this over violent alternatives. He stated:

> To be true followers of Jesus today . . . includes embracing his teaching about nonviolence. Jesus himself lived in violent times. . . . But Christ's message in this regard offers a radically positive approach. He unfailingly preached God's unconditional love, which welcomes and forgives. He taught his disciples to love their enemies and to turn the other cheek. When he stopped her accusers from stoning the woman caught in adultery and when, on the night before he died, he told Peter to put away his sword, Jesus marked out the path of nonviolence. He walked that path to the very end, to the cross.[11]

Did Pope Francis's public endorsement of nonviolence signal an official shift away from just war principles? He has not formally announced such a change. Moreover, a significant number of Catholic leaders still support just war principles, and the pope himself has recently stated that every nation has the right to defend and protect its citizens. Nonetheless, Catholic peace activists have made this a matter of serious discussion and debate, pushing the pontiff and the Catholic Church to endorse and promote nonviolence. Indeed, Catholic leaders are speaking more earnestly about nonviolence than they have at any other point in contemporary history.

Activist Experience and the Hermeneutical Circle

The 2016 "Nonviolence and Just Peace" conference also illuminates the dynamics and processes that produce Catholic Social Thought. As discussed in the introduction, Catholic Social Teachings are produced through the "hermeneutical circle" or the "circle of praxis." This is a multi-step process often summarized as "see-judge-act." In the first step ("see"), one observes a social injustice. Catholics should meet those who are suffering, collect as much information and data as they can, and gain direct experience. The second step ("judge") entails social analysis or understanding the roots of the problem. The third step (also part of "judge") entails theological analysis. It requires one to ask: What is a biblically appropriate response to this injustice? The fourth and final step is to take action ("act"), based on one's own social and biblical analysis. As Thomas Massaro stated, "As popes, bishops, and other church leaders surveyed the world and felt moved to write and promulgate major documents of church teaching about social issues, they were engaged in nothing other than a high-level experience of the see-judge-act process."[12]

Progressive Catholic activists have contributed to this process at numerous points. They have direct experience with social injustices or have observed them firsthand (the "see" stage). That is, activists are the ones working with laborers who suffer in the factories and the agricultural fields. They are the ones who encountered Central Americans crossing the border, desperate to escape the political repression and violence of their homelands. They are the ones who faced conscription and the prospect of fighting an unjust war in Vietnam. Few high-ranking Catholic leaders have had such experiences. Consequently, it is these activists who were largely responsible for creating a sense of urgency and pushing the religious hierarchy to articulate a biblically based response to these social problems. And very often, these Catholic activists were the first to take action (the "act" stage)—by sheltering refugees, by interfering with the testing and production of nuclear weapons, and by forming Catholic farming communes to withdraw from the capitalist economy.

Far from the view that church leaders discuss social issues and then announce what their faithful members should believe and do, we can see that the process of determining official Catholic teachings is a bidirectional and iterative process. Often, the impulse comes from below. For example, Catholic laypeople openly discussed the burdens and problems that the contraceptive ban created for their marriages and families, (unsuccessfully) pushing the religious hierarchy to reconsider its stance on birth control. The National Conference of Catholic Bishops wrote *The*

Challenge of Peace, and Pope Francis instigated the "Nonviolence and Just Peace" conference only after decades of Catholic peace activism. Similarly, the Vatican II Council endorsed the Catholic right to conscientious objection to war after Dorothy Day and PAX activists petitioned it to do so, based on their experiences with young Catholic men opposed to conscription in World War II and especially in the Vietnam War.

At other times, the impulse and direction for Catholic Social Thought and activism come from above: the church takes a stand and releases a document that guides laypeople's activism. This is evident in the work of the Catholic Climate Covenant. The executive director of the CCC, Dan Misel, is a layperson who has stated that his movement organization takes action based on the bishops' directives. He observed:

> The basic division of labor has been, and will continue to be, that the Bishops' Conference sets the public policy agenda, and the Catholic Coalition on Climate Change help[s] promulgate that public policy. . . . I implement what they say. I help when the Bishops put out a particular piece, or at least get some direction to how they want the public policy to unfold. Then with my connections to diocese and other organizations across the country, I can help them generate the ground troops, I guess you'd say.[13]

This iterative, bidirectional process of determining Catholic Social Thought reveals that the Roman Catholic Church is a living, changing institution of the people. While bishops and pontiffs may state that their encyclicals and official documents were developed by a group of religious leaders and theologians, who drew upon scripture and natural law, there is little doubt that activists have left their imprint and will continue to do so. Progressive Catholic activists in the United States will persist in the struggle for justice—not only in the areas described in this book but also with issues of racism and discrimination, the death penalty, police brutality, and sexual abuse and harassment. They will live out their religious beliefs in these "hot cultural moments" and in the places where people are suffering most.

ACKNOWLEDGMENTS

At NYU Press, I give my heartfelt thanks to Jennifer Hammer for her initial vision of this book and her faith in my scholarly abilities. I also thank her profusely for her patience, which I tested repeatedly as this manuscript developed more slowly than anticipated. I also wish to express my gratitude to Susan Ecklund for her excellent copyediting and to Alexia Traganas for her assistance in moving the manuscript through the production process.

I am indebted to two anonymous reviewers, who offered valuable feedback on an earlier version of the book. One reviewer offered generous words of encouragement to keep my writing accessible so that readers could see the passion and vitality of these Catholic activists and avoid getting entangled in weighty church documents and theological arguments. The other reviewer urged me to pay attention to women and underrepresented racial and ethnic groups who were involved in these struggles. I am grateful for this reminder and hope that I have captured at least some of the diversity that characterizes these movements.

Closer to home, I am grateful to many people in the Department of Sociology at the University of New Mexico. Shortly after I agreed to write this book, I found myself serving as department chair once again. As anyone who has served in this role knows, it has the potential to derail one's best scholarly intentions. Fortunately, many people helped to keep my administrative duties from becoming too burdensome. I thank our highly skilled staff members, who keep the department functioning smoothly on a daily basis: Dorothy Esquivel, Shoshana Handel, and Kaleigh Hubbard. I especially thank my faculty colleagues Christopher Lyons, Lisa Broidy, Kristin Barker, and Richard Wood, who shared my workload and provided support, friendship, and incredibly good judgment on various departmental matters.

Finally, I thank my family. Our children—Linnea, Malaya, Dante, and Aldo—fill our home with energy, activity, and laughter. It is my hope that they embrace the values of justice and compassionate action that this book conveys. I'm eternally grateful to have Kathryn-Sonja Erickson Inoferio as my sister as well as my dearest friend. I thank my parents, Millard and Virginia Erickson, for giving me an interest in religion while emphasizing the importance of thinking critically about it. Finally, I thank my husband, Claude Morelli, to whom this book is dedicated. He is the most committed, responsible, and loyal partner that I could ever hope for. Throughout the period when I was writing this book, he did more than his share of household duties and parenting tasks. I'm grateful for his acts of kindness, his dedication, his humor, companionship, intellectual prodding, support, and love.

NOTES

INTRODUCTION

1 Ana is not her real name; I use a pseudonym here to protect her identity.
2 Olson, "How to Address Child Migration from Central America," 2.
3 I choose to use the term "Catholic Social Thought," since it includes not only the official teachings of the Vatican but also many of the unofficial teachings from other Catholic actors. "Catholic Social Teachings" refers to official church teachings.
4 Bock, *Wilhem von Ketteler, Bishop of Mainz*.
5 Schäfer, "*Rerum Novarum*," 3–17.
6 Massaro, *Living Justice*.
7 Schäfer, "*Rerum Novarum*," 12.
8 Sharkey, *Sociology and Catholic Social Teaching*.
9 This legislation was overturned by the Supreme Court a decade later.
10 Curran, *American Catholic Social Ethics*.
11 These themes are from the US Conference of Catholic Bishops, *Sharing Catholic Social Teaching*.
12 King, *Why We Can't Wait*, 65.
13 Donahue, "The Bible and Catholic Social Teaching."
14 Pope, "Natural Law in Catholic Social Teachings."
15 Massaro, *Living Justice*, 91–92.
16 Gaillardetz, "The Ecclesiological Foundations of Modern Catholic Social Teaching."
17 Phan, *Social Thought*.
18 McGuire, *Lived Religion*, 12.
19 Hall, *Lived Religion in America*. Also see Nepstad, "Popular Religion, Protest, and Revolt," 105–124.
20 Hall, *Lived Religion in America*; Orsi, *The Madonna of 115th Street*.
21 Orsi, "Is the Study of Lived Religion Irrelevant to the World We Live In?," 172–173.
22 McKenna, *A Concise Guide to Catholic Social Teaching*.
23 Hinze, "Commentary on Quadragesimo Anno," 151–174.
24 O'Brien, *American Catholics and Social Reform*.
25 Ellis, "Peter Maurin."
26 For an evaluation of the Catholic Worker farming communes, see Stock, "The Perennial Nature of the Catholic Worker Farms," 143–173.

27 Keller quoted on Prentiss, *Debating God's Economy*, 165.
28 Keller, *Christianity and American Capitalism*.
29 For further information, see Sirico and LeMothe, *The Entrepreneurial Vocation*.

CHAPTER 1. DIGNITY AND JUST TREATMENT OF WORKERS
1 Stearns, *The Industrial Revolution in World History*.
2 Evans, *The Forging of the Modern State*.
3 Rodgers, *The Work Ethic in Industrial America*.
4 Marx, *Critique of Hegel's "Philosophy of Right,"* 131–132.
5 Cahill, "The Catholic Social Movement," 5.
6 Paulhus, "Social Catholicism and the Fribourg Union."
7 Mich, *Catholic Social Teachings and Movements*, 32.
8 Kaufman, "Rise and Fall of a Nation of Joiners," 553–579.
9 Weir, *Beyond Labor's Veil*.
10 Mich, *Catholic Social Teachings and Movements*, 40–41.
11 Browne, *The Catholic Church and the Knights of Labor*.
12 Mich, *Catholic Social Teachings and Movements*, 21.
13 Mich, 21.
14 *Rerum Novarum*, no. 22.
15 *Rerum Novarum*, no. 19.
16 *Rerum Novarum*, no. 32.
17 *Rerum Novarum*, no. 43, no. 44.
18 Mich, *Catholic Social Teachings and Movements*, 80.
19 Hinze, "Commentary on Quadragesimo Anno."
20 *Quadragesimo Anno*, paragraph 83.
21 Greeley, "*Quadragesimo Anno* after Fifty Years," 47.
22 Novak, *The Catholic Ethic and the Spirit of Capitalism*.
23 Forest, *Love Is the Measure*.
24 Roberts, "Dorothy Day," 115–133.
25 Curran, *American Catholic Social Ethics*, 130.
26 Ellis, "Peter Maurin," 16.
27 Forest, *Love Is the Measure*, 21.
28 For more on Dorothy Day's conversion experience, see Connor, "Dorothy Day's Christian Conversion," 159–180.
29 Forest, *Love Is the Measure*, 43.
30 Day, *The Long Loneliness*, 136.
31 Day, 139.
32 Miller, *Dorothy Day*.
33 Day, "To Our Readers," 1.
34 Webb, "Dorothy Day and the Early Years of the 'Catholic Worker,'" 71–88.
35 Matthew 25:35–40.
36 Sicius, "Peter Maurin's Green Revolution," 1–14.
37 Segers, "Equality and Christian Anarchism," 196–230.

38 Day, "The Church and Work," 1, 3, 7–8.
39 Forest, *Love Is the Measure*, 95.
40 Miller, *Dorothy Day*, 259.
41 Forest, *Love Is the Measure*, 66.
42 Mich, *Catholic Social Teachings*, 66.
43 Miller, *Dorothy Day*, 283.
44 John Heid, quoted in Nepstad, *Religion and War Resistance in the Plowshares Movement*, 56.
45 Novitsky, "Peter Maurin's Green Revolution," 83–103.
46 Sicius, "Peter Maurin's Green Revolution," 11.
47 Forest, *Love Is the Measure*, 70.
48 Taylor, *Chavez and the Farm Workers*, 81.
49 For more on this method, see Alinksy, *Rules for Radicals*.
50 Pawel, *The Crusades of Cesar Chavez*.
51 Rose, "Traditional and Nontraditional Patterns of Female Activism," 26–32.
52 Chávez, "Huelga!," 3.
53 Ganz, "Resources and Resourcefulness," 1003–1062.
54 Mich, *Catholic Social Teachings*, 168.
55 Chávez, "Nonviolent Trade Unionism," 366–367.
56 Mich, *Catholic Social Teachings*.
57 Quoted in Smith. *Grapes of Conflict*, 98.
58 Rose, "Traditional and Nontraditional Patterns of Female Activism."
59 Garcia, "Cesar Chavez and the United Farm Workers Movement."
60 Forest, *Love Is the Measure*, 122.
61 Garcia, "Cesar Chavez and the United Farm Workers Movement."
62 Ganz, *Why David Sometimes Wins*.
63 Garcia, "Cesar Chavez and the United Farm Workers Movement."
64 For more on the UFW's mistakes and challenges, see Garcia, *From the Jaws of Victory*.
65 Mich, *Catholic Social Teachings*, 67.
66 Campbell, "The Catholic Earth Mother," 274–275.
67 For more on this, see O'Gorman and Coy, "Houses of Hospitality," 239–272.
68 Mich, *Catholic Social Teachings*, 68.
69 Mich, 69.
70 McNeal, *Harder Than War*.
71 Klejment, "The Spirituality of Dorothy Day's Pacifism," 1–24.
72 Nepstad, *Nonviolent Struggle*, 1.

CHAPTER 2. PEACE, NONVIOLENCE, AND DISARMAMENT

1 Pant, "Hiroshima," 59–86.
2 For more information, see Brock, *Varieties of Pacifism*; Hershberger, *War, Peace, and Nonresistance*; Hornus, *It Is Not Lawful for Me to Fight*; Nuttall, *Christian Pacifism in History*.

3 Akers, *The Lost Religion of Jesus*.
4 Quoted in Nepstad, *Nonviolent Struggle*, 36.
5 Nepstad, 36–37.
6 Cadoux, *The Early Christian Attitude toward War*.
7 Bainton, *Christian Attitudes toward War and Peace*; Merton, *Seeds of Destruction*.
8 For further elaboration of the just war criteria, historical development, and key debates, see the following: O'Donovan, *The Just War Revisited*; Steinhoff, *On the Ethics of War and Terrorism*; Walzer, *Just and Unjust Wars*.
9 These principles are derived from the just war tradition within Christianity.
10 Wink, "Beyond Just War and Pacifism," 113.
11 *Pacem in Terris*, no. 130.
12 *Pacem in Terris*, no. 167.
13 Hollenbach, *Justice, Peace, and Human Rights*.
14 *Pacem in Terris*, no. 110.
15 McNeal, *Harder Than War*.
16 Ryan, quoted in *Social Doctrine in Action*, 216–217.
17 Quoted in McNeal, *Harder Than War*, 23.
18 Day, *Loaves and Fishes*, 69.
19 McNeal, *Harder Than War*, 47.
20 Wittner, *Rebels against War*, 265.
21 McNeal, *Harder Than War*.
22 Forest, *Love Is the Measure*; McNeal, *Harder Than War*.
23 McNeal, *Harder Than War*, 102.
24 McNeal.
25 Forest, *Love Is the Measure*, 112.
26 Kaiser, *American Tragedy*.
27 Topmiller, "The Buddhist Anti-war Movement," 143–167.
28 Guzder, *Divine Rebels*, 39.
29 Hess, "South Vietnam under Siege," 143–167.
30 Ngo et al., "Association between Agent Orange and Birth Defects," 1220–1230; Young et al., "Environmental Fate and Bio-availability of Agent Orange," 359–370.
31 Meconis, *With Clumsy Grace*.
32 Moon, "'Peace on Earth,'" 1033–1057.
33 Ciernick, "A Matter of Conscience," 33–50.
34 McNeal, *Harder Than War*, 148.
35 Moon, "'Peace on Earth,'" 1043.
36 Guzder, *Divine Rebels*, 41.
37 Moon, "'Peace on Earth,'" 1044.
38 Ryan, "The One Who Burns Herself for Peace," 21.
39 Guzder, *Divine Rebels*, 41.
40 Guzder, 42–43.
41 Ryan, "The One Who Burns Herself for Peace."
42 Day, "Suicide or Sacrifice?," 1, 7.

43 Meconis, *With Clumsy Grace*, 19–20.
44 Berrigan, *Fighting the Lamb's War*, 89.
45 Lewis, "Philip Berrigan, Former Priest and Peace Advocate," A36.
46 Nepstad, *Religion and War Resistance in the Plowshares Movement*, 48.
47 McNeal, *Harder Than War*, 97.
48 Berrigan, *Prison Journals of a Priest Revolutionary*, 15–16.
49 Cornell, "Nonviolent Napalm in Catonsville," 203–208.
50 Merton quoted in Meconis, *With Clumsy Grace*, 36–37.
51 For a more detailed account of Dorothy Day's changing views about draft board raids, see Klejment, "War Resistance and Property Destruction," 272–309.
52 Quoted in Klejment and Roberts, "The Catholic Worker and the Vietnam War," 153–169.
53 Isaiah 2:4.
54 Dunn, *The Politics of Threat*.
55 Nepstad, *Religion and War Resistance*.
56 Berrigan, "Swords into Plowshares," 55, 65.
57 Nepstad, "Disruptive Action and the Prophetic Tradition," 97–113.
58 Quoted in Nepstad, *Religion and War Resistance*, 62.
59 Quoted in Nepstad, 63–64.
60 Castelli, *The Bishops and the Bomb*, 13–18.
61 McBrady, "The Challenge of Peace," 129–152.
62 Castelli, *The Bishops and the Bomb*.
63 Lonsdale, "Nuclear Strategy and Catholicism," 186–207.
64 US Conference of Catholic Bishops, "The U.S. Bishops on Peace and War."
65 McBrady, "The Challenge of Peace."
66 Lonsdale, "Nuclear Strategy and Catholicism."
67 National Conference of Catholic Bishops, *The Challenge of Peace*, no. 73.
68 National Conference of Catholic Bishops, no. 223.
69 "The Pastoral and the New Moment," 291.

CHAPTER 3. EQUALITY FOR WOMEN AND CATHOLIC FEMINISM

1 Pope Pius XII, *Papal Teaching*, 109.
2 Friedan, *The Feminine Mystique*, 57, 472.
3 Braude, "A Religious Feminist," 555–572.
4 Henold, *Catholic and Feminist*, 18.
5 Katzenstein, *Faithful and Fearless*; Kucinskas, "The Unobtrusive Tactics of Religious Movements," 537–550.
6 Quoted in Mich, *Catholic Social Teachings*, 349.
7 Dolan, *The American Catholic Experience*, 414–415.
8 O'Gorman and Crowley, "Interview with Patty Crowley," 457–467.
9 McClory, "Patty Crowley, Giant of Catholic Laity, Dies at 92."
10 Steinfels, "The Life and Death of a Leading Lay Catholic."

11 Henold, *Catholic and Feminist*, 20.
12 Ruether, "The Place of Women in the Church."
13 Henold, *Catholic and Feminist*, 46.
14 Henold, 197.
15 Weaver, "American Catholic Women since the Vatican II Council," 200–208.
16 Katzenstein, *Faithful and Fearless*, 107.
17 Katzenstein, "Discursive Politics," 36 (emphasis added).
18 Lauer, "Women and the Church," 367.
19 Daly, "Letter to the Editor," 603.
20 Henold, *Catholic and Feminist*, 37.
21 Henold, 36.
22 Maron, "Interview with Mary Daly," 21–24.
23 Maron.
24 Maron.
25 Mich, *Catholic Social Teachings*, 373.
26 Mich, 374.
27 Quoted in Mich, 373.
28 Weaver, *New Catholic Women*, 167–168.
29 Callahan, *The Illusion of Eve*, 36–37.
30 Lauer, "Women and the Church," 367.
31 Ruether, "A Catholic Mother Tells."
32 Weaver, *New Catholic Women*, 112.
33 Ruether, "Should Women Want Women Priests or Women-Church?," 63–72.
34 Henold, *Catholic and Feminist*, 189.
35 Swidler and Swidler, *Women Priests*.
36 Katzenberg, "Discursive Politics," 38.
37 Quoted in Moon, "Womenpriests," 115–116.
38 "Introduction: Women Priests Project," accessed December 27, 2018, www.womenpriestsproject.org.
39 Ruether, "Should Women Want Women Priests or Women-Church?"
40 Rue, "Crossroads," 2.
41 Moon, "Womenpriests," 120.
42 Fiorenza, *Discipleship of Equals*.
43 Katzenberg, "Discursive Politics," 39.
44 Ruether, *Women-Church*, 5 (emphasis added).
45 Hunt, "Women-Church," 85–98.
46 Katzenstein, *Faithful and Fearless*, 108.
47 Gaventa, *Power and Powerlessness*.
48 Katzenstein, "Discursive Politics," 47–48.
49 Ruether, "Should Women Want Women Priests or Women-Church?," 72.
50 Tentler, *Catholics and Contraception*.
51 Quoted in Tentler, "Souls and Bodies," 298.
52 Tentler, 306.

53 Ryder and Westoff, *Reproduction in the United States.*
54 Tentler, "Souls and Bodies," 304.
55 Westoff and Bumpass, "The Revolution in Birth Control Practices of U.S. Catholics," 41–42.
56 Dillon, *Catholic Identity.*
57 Davis, *Sacred Work.*
58 Henold, *Catholic and Feminist.*
59 Ruether, "Catholics and Abortion."

CHAPTER 4. LIBERATION THEOLOGY AND THE CENTRAL AMERICA
SOLIDARITY MOVEMENT

1 Quoted in Harbury, *Bridge of Courage,* 47–51.
2 Smith, *The Emergence of Liberation Theology,* 12.
3 Carroll, *What Is Liberation Theology?*
4 Cabal, *The Revolution of the Latin American Church,* 7.
5 Rostow, *The Stages of Economic Growth.*
6 Frank, *Latin America.*
7 Nepstad, *Convictions of the Soul,* 45.
8 Schlesinger and Kinzer, *Bitter Fruit.*
9 Cullather, *Secret History.*
10 Berryman, *The Religious Roots of Rebellion.*
11 Handy, *Gift of the Devil.*
12 Brett, "The Impact of Religion in Central America," 297–341.
13 Nuñez, *Liberation Theology.*
14 Smith, *The Emergence of Liberation Theology,* 16.
15 Gerassi, *Revolutionary Priest,* xiii.
16 Quoted in Smith, *The Emergence of Liberation Theology,* 125.
17 Quoted in Mich, *Catholic Social Teachings and Movements,* 160.
18 Quoted in Mich, 158.
19 Quoted in Smith, *The Emergence of Liberation Theology,* 126.
20 Quoted in Smith, 18.
21 Quoted in Smith, 18.
22 Mich, *Catholic Social Teachings,* 242.
23 Berryman, "Basic Christian Communities and the Future of Latin America," 27–40.
24 Cox, *Religion in the Secular City,* 108; Cook, *The Expectation of the Poor,* 7.
25 Lernoux, "The Long Path to Puebla."
26 Gutierrez, *A Theology of Liberation,* 11.
27 Segundo, *A Theology for Artisans of a New Humanity,* 73.
28 Gutierrez, *A Theology of Liberation,* 175.
29 Luke 23:2.
30 Gutierrez, *A Theology of Liberation,* 229.
31 Gutierrez, 133.

32 Muñoz, "Ecclesiology in Latin America," 153–154.
33 Smith, *The Emergence of Liberation Theology.*
34 Boff and Boff, *Salvation and Liberation*, 18, 32, 57.
35 Gutierrez, *A Theology of Liberation*, 168.
36 Boff and Boff, *Salvation and Liberation*, 10.
37 Bonino, *Doing Theology in a Revolutionary Situation*, 35, 40.
38 Gutierrez, *The Power of the Poor in History*, x, 113.
39 Boff and Boff, *Salvation and Liberation*, 22.
40 Bonino, *Doing Theology in a Revolutionary Situation*, 35.
41 Nepstad, *Convictions of the Soul.*
42 Booth and Walker, *Understanding Central America*, 154.
43 Booth and Walker, 154.
44 Lernoux, *Cry of the People.*
45 Peterson, *Martyrdom and the Politics of Religion*, 61.
46 Erdozaín, *Archbishop Romero*, 74.
47 Sobrino, *Archbishop Romero*, 99–100.
48 Brett and Brett, *Murdered in Central America.*
49 Berryman, *Liberation Theology.*
50 Gibellini, *The Liberation Theology Debate*, 46.
51 Ratzinger and Messori, *The Ratzinger Report.*
52 Cox, *The Silencing of Leonardo Boff.*
53 Randall, *Christians in the Nicaraguan Revolution*, 33–34.
54 Quoted in Nepstad, *Convictions of the Soul*, 61.
55 Quoted in Nepstad, 66.
56 Smith, *Resisting Reagan*, 70.
57 Griffin-Nolan, *Witness for Peace.*
58 Smith, *Resisting Reagan*, 76–77.
59 Smith, 77.
60 Nepstad, *Convictions of the Soul*, 73, 127–128.
61 Smith, *Resisting Reagan*, 78.
62 Smith, 79.
63 Smith, 79.
64 Smith, 79.
65 Smith, 80.
66 Smith, 84.
67 Gill, *The School of the Americas.*
68 Quoted in Nepstad, *Conviction of the Soul*, 138.
69 Sobrino, *Companions of Jesus*, 4–5.
70 Doggett, *Death Foretold*, 70.
71 Nepstad, *Convictions of the Soul*, 142.
72 Nepstad, "School of the Americas Watch."
73 Nepstad, *Convictions of the Soul*, 145.
74 Nepstad, 145.

75 Nepstad, 146.

76 Gallo-Cruz, "Negotiating the Lines of Contention," 21–45.

77 Gallo-Cruz.

CHAPTER 5. COMPASSION FOR IMMIGRANTS AND THE
SANCTUARY MOVEMENTS

 1 Gonzalez-Barrera, Krogstad, and Hugo Lopez, "Children 12 and under Are Fastest Growing Group of Unaccompanied Minors at U.S. Border."

 2 Shah, "The Crisis in Our Own Backyard."

 3 "Top Voting Issues in 2016 Election."

 4 Williams, "Sessions."

 5 Domonoske and Gonzales, "What We Know."

 6 Lang, Zauzmer, and Natanson, "Thousands March in Washington."

 7 *Exsul Familia Nazarethana*, 1.

 8 Quoted in Cooney, "There Are No Strangers among Us," 121.

 9 Cooney, 129.

10 Pontifical Council Cor Unum, *Refugees: A Challenge for Solidarity*.

11 Cooney, "There Are No Strangers among Us," 134–145.

12 Cooney, 147–150.

13 Mooney, "The Catholic Bishops Conferences of the United States and France," 1455–1470.

14 This account of the Sanctuary movement is drawn from the following sources: Coutin, *The Culture of Protest*; Crittenden, *Sanctuary*; Davidson, *Convictions of the Heart*; Nepstad, *Convictions of the Soul*; Smith, *Resisting Reagan*.

15 Crittenden, *Sanctuary*, 21.

16 Crittenden, 21.

17 Leviticus 19:33–34.

18 Cunningham, *God and Caesar on the Rio Grande*, xi.

19 Crittenden, *Sanctuary*, 69–73.

20 Golden and McConnell, *Sanctuary*, 53.

21 Nepstad, *Convictions of the Soul*, 133–134.

22 Lorentzen, *Women in the Sanctuary Movement*, 15.

23 Bekemeyer, "The Acme of the Catholic Left," 5.

24 Quoted in Coutin, "Smugglers or Samaritans," 554.

25 "Leader in Movement to Harbor Aliens Is Convicted."

26 Cunningham, *God and Caesar on the Rio Grande*, 44–45.

27 Coutin, "Smugglers or Samaritans," 556.

28 Coutin, 556.

29 Coutin, 558.

30 Davidson, *Convictions of the Heart*.

31 Davidson, 89.

32 Coutin, "Smugglers or Samaritans," 562.

33 Yukich, *One Family under God*.

34 "Pledge to Resist Deportation and Discrimination through Sanctuary."
35 Yukich, *One Family under God.*
36 Brotherton and Kretsedemas, *Keeping Out the Other.*
37 Yukich, *One Family under God*, 24–25.
38 Yukich, 25–26.
39 Voss and Bloemraad, *Rallying for Immigrant Rights.*
40 Heredia, "From Prayer to Protest."

CHAPTER 6. EARTH ETHICS AND AMERICAN CATHOLIC
ENVIRONMENTALISM

1 Griswold, "How 'Silent Spring' Ignited the Environmental Movement."
2 Kline, *First along the River.*
3 Graham, *Environmental Politics and Policy.*
4 Rome, "The Genius of Earth Day."
5 Guhin, "Where Are the Catholic Environmentalists?"
6 Sicius, "Peter Maurin's Green Revolution," 1–14.
7 Novitsky, "Peter Maurin's Green Revolution," 83–103.
8 Sicius, "Peter Maurin's Green Revolution," 11.
9 Hamlin and McGreevy, "The Greening of America, Catholic Style," 464–465.
10 Hamlin and McGreevy, 469.
11 Hamlin and McGreevy, 480.
12 Callahan, "A Child over a Redwood," 21.
13 Quoted in Allitt, "American Catholics and the Environment," 268.
14 Allitt, 267.
15 Allitt.
16 White, "The Historical Roots of Our Ecological Crisis," 1203–1207.
17 Whitney, "Lynn White Jr.'s 'The Historical Roots of Our Ecological Crisis' after 50 Years," 396–410.
18 Ehrlich, *The Population Bomb.*
19 Ehrlich, 143.
20 Quoted in Allitt, "American Catholics and the Environment," 272.
21 Allitt, 276.
22 Quoted in Mich, *Catholic Social Teachings and Movements*, 388.
23 Mich, 390.
24 Pope, "If You've Seen One Redwood."
25 Allitt, "American Catholics and the Environment," 275.
26 Warner, "The Greening of American Catholicism," 119.
27 Mich, *Catholic Social Teachings*, 390–391.
28 Ellingson, *To Care for Creation.*
29 US Catholic Conference, *Renewing the Earth.*
30 US Catholic Conference.
31 Allitt, "American Catholics and the Environment," 277.
32 Christiansen and Grazer, *"And God Saw That It Was Good,"* 18n4.

33 Greeley, "Religion and Attitudes toward the Environment," 19–28; Guth et al., Faith and the Environment," 364–382.

34 Ellingson, *To Care for Creation*, 46.

35 National Religious Partnership for the Environment, "History," accessed December 14, 2017, www.nrpe.org.

36 Quoted in Ellingson, *To Care for Creation*, 95.

37 "Celebrating Our Creation Care Teams," Catholic Climate Covenant, accessed December 14, 2017, www.catholicclimatecovenant.org.

38 Pope Francis, *Laudato Si*, paragraph 68.

CONCLUSION

1 Terrell, "Dorothy Day's 'Filthy, Rotten, System' Likely Wasn't Hers at All."

2 Nepstad, *Religion and War Resistance in the Plowshares Movement*.

3 Although Willson is not Catholic, he was involved in the ecumenically based Pledge of Resistance organization.

4 Willson, *Blood on the Tracks*.

5 Kristensen and Norris, "United States Nuclear Forces, 2018."

6 Catholic Nonviolence Initiative, "About the Nonviolence and Just Peace Conference."

7 Thistlethwaite, *Interfaith Just Peacemaking*.

8 Catholic Nonviolence Initiative, "About the Nonviolence and Just Peace Conference."

9 Stephan, "What Happens When You Replace a Just War with a Just Peace."

10 "An Appeal to the Catholic Church to Re-commit to the Centrality of Gospel Nonviolence," 2.

11 Pope Francis, World Day of Peace Message, January 1, 2017.

12 Massaro, "From Industrialization to Globalization," 46.

13 Ellingson, *To Care for Creation*, 96.

REFERENCES

Akers, Keith. *The Lost Religion of Jesus: Simple Living and Nonviolence in Early Christianity*. New York: Lantern Books, 2000.

Alinksy, Saul. *Rules for Radicals: A Practical Primer for Realistic Radicals*. New York: Random House, 1971.

Allitt, Patrick. "American Catholics and the Environment, 1960–1995." *Catholic Historical Review* 84, no. 2 (1998): 263–280.

"An Appeal to the Catholic Church to Re-commit to the Centrality of Gospel Nonviolence." April 2016. Accessed June 26, 2018. ww.paxchristi.net.

Bainton, Roland. *Christian Attitudes toward War and Peace: A Historical Survey and Critical Reevaluation*. Eugene, OR: Wipf and Stock, [1923] 1960.

Bekemeyer, Aaron. "The Acme of the Catholic Left: Catholic Activists in the U.S. Sanctuary Movement, 1982–1992." Honors thesis, University of Michigan, 2012.

Berrigan, Daniel. "Swords into Plowshares." In *Swords into Plowshares: Nonviolent Direct Action for Disarmament*, edited by Arthur J. Laffin and Anne Montgomery, 54–65. San Francisco: Harper and Row, 1987.

Berrigan, Philip. *Fighting the Lamb's War: Skirmishes with the American Empire*. Monroe, ME: Common Courage Press, 1996.

———. *Prison Journals of a Priest Revolutionary*. New York: Ballantine Books, 1971.

Berryman, Phillip. "Basic Christian Communities and the Future of Latin America." *Monthly Review* 36 (July–August 1984): 27–40.

———. *Liberation Theology: The Essential Facts about the Revolutionary Movement in Latin America and Beyond*. New York: Pantheon Books, 1987.

———. *The Religious Roots of Rebellion: Christians in Central American Revolutions*. Maryknoll, NY: Orbis Books, 1984.

Bock, Edward C. *Wilhem von Ketteler, Bishop of Mainz: His Life, Times and Ideas*. Washington, DC: University Press of America, 1977.

Boff, Leonardo, and Clodovis Boff. *Salvation and Liberation: In Search of a Balance between Faith and Politics*. Maryknoll, NY: Orbis Books, 1984.

Bonino, Jose. *Doing Theology in a Revolutionary Situation*. Maryknoll, NY: Orbis Books, 1975.

Booth, John A., and Thomas W. Walker. *Understanding Central America*. Boulder, CO: Westview Press, 1993.

Braude, Ann. "A Religious Feminist: Who Can Find Her? Historiographical Challenges from the National Organization for Women." *Journal of Religion* 84, no. 4 (2004): 555–572.

Brett, Donna Whitson, and Edward T. Brett. *Murdered in Central America: The Stories of Eleven U.S. Missionaries.* Maryknoll, NY: Orbis Books, 1988.

Brett, Edward. "The Impact of Religion in Central America: A Bibliographic Essay." *The Americas* 49 (1983): 297–341.

Brock, Peter. *Varieties of Pacifism: A Survey from Antiquity to the Outset of the Twentieth Century.* Syracuse, NY: Syracuse University Press, 1999.

Brotherton, David, and Philip Kretsedemas, eds. *Keeping Out the Other: A Critical Introduction to Immigration Enforcement Today.* New York: Columbia University Press, 2008.

Browne, Henry. *The Catholic Church and the Knights of Labor.* Washington, DC: Catholic University of America Press, 1949.

Cabal, Hugo Latorre. *The Revolution of the Latin American Church.* Norman: University of Oklahoma Press, 1978.

Cadoux, C. John. *The Early Christian Attitude toward War.* London: Headley Bros., 1919.

Cahill, Edward. "The Catholic Social Movement: Historical Aspects." In *Readings in Moral Theology, No. 5: Official Catholic Social Teaching,* edited by Charles E. Curran and Richard A. McCormick, 3–31. New York: Paulist Press, 1986.

Callahan, Sidney. "A Child over a Redwood." *National Catholic Reporter,* May 8, 1970.

———. *The Illusion of Eve: Modern Woman's Quest for Identity.* New York: Sheed and Ward, 1965.

Campbell, Debra. "The Catholic Earth Mother: Dorothy Day and Women's Power in the Church." *CrossCurrents* 34, no. 3 (1984): 270–282.

Carroll, Denis. *What Is Liberation Theology?* Dublin: Mercier Press, 1987.

Castelli, Jim. *The Bishops and the Bomb: Waging Peace in a Nuclear Age.* Garden City, NY: Image Books, 1983.

Catholic Nonviolence Initiative. "About the Nonviolence and Just Peace Conference." 2016. Accessed June 26, 2018. https://nonviolencejustpeace.net.

Chávez, César. "Huelga! Tales of the Delano Revolution." *Ramparts,* July 1966.

———. "Nonviolent Trade Unionism." In *Nonviolence in America: A Documentary History,* edited by Staughton Lynd and Alice Lynd, 363–374. Maryknoll, NY: Orbis Books, 2009.

Christiansen, Drew, and Walter Grazer, eds. *"And God Saw That It Was Good": Catholic Theology and the Environment.* Washington, DC: US Catholic Conference, 1996.

Ciernick, Helen M. "A Matter of Conscience: The Selective Conscientious Objector, Catholic College Students, and the Vietnam War." *U.S. Catholic Historian* 26, no. 3 (2008): 33–50.

Cook, Guillermo. *The Expectation of the Poor: Latin American Basic Ecclesial Communities in Protestant Perspective.* Maryknoll, NY: Orbis Books, 1985.

Cooney, Terry. "There Are No Strangers among Us: Catholic Social Teaching and U.S. Immigration Law." *Catholic Lawyer* 40, no. 2 (2000): 105–164.

Cornell, Tom. "Nonviolent Napalm in Catonsville." In *The Universe Bends toward Justice,* edited by Angie O'Gorman, 203–208. Philadelphia: New Society Publishers, [1968] 1990.

Coutin, Susan Bibler. *The Culture of Protest: Religious Activism in the U.S. Sanctuary Movement*. Boulder, CO: Westview Press, 1993.

———. "Smugglers or Samaritans in Tucson, Arizona: Producing and Contesting Legal Truth." *American Ethnologist* 22, no. 3 (1995): 549–571.

Cox, Harvey. *Religion in the Secular City: Toward a Post-modern Theology*. New York: Simon and Schuster, 1984.

———. *The Silencing of Leonardo Boff*. Oak Park, IL: Meyer-Stone Books, 1988.

Crittenden, Anne. *Sanctuary: A Story of American Conscience and Law in Collision*. New York: Weidenfeld and Nicolson, 1988.

Cullather, Nick. *Secret History: The CIA's Classified Account of Its Operations in Guatemala, 1952–1954*. Palo Alto, CA: Stanford University Press, 1999.

Cunningham, Hillary. *God and Caesar on the Rio Grande: Sanctuary and the Politics of Religion*. Minneapolis: University of Minnesota Press, 1995.

Curran, Charles E. *American Catholic Social Ethics: Twentieth-Century Approaches*. Notre Dame, IN: University of Notre Dame Press, 1982.

Daly, Mary. *The Church and the Second Sex*. Boston: Beacon Press, 1968.

———. "Letter to the Editor." *Commonweal* 79 (1964): 603.

Davidson, Miriam. *Convictions of the Heart: Jim Corbett and the Sanctuary Movement*. Tucson: University of Arizona Press, 1988.

Davis, Tom. *Sacred Work: Planned Parenthood and Its Clergy Alliances*. New Brunswick, NJ: Rutgers University Press, 2005.

Day, Dorothy. "The Church and Work." *Catholic Worker*, September 1946, 1, 3, 7–8.

———. *Loaves and Fishes*. New York: Harper and Row, 1963.

———. *The Long Loneliness*. New York: HarperCollins, [1952] 2009.

———. "Suicide or Sacrifice?" *Catholic Worker Newsletter*, November 1965, 1, 7.

———. "To Our Readers." *Catholic Worker*, no. 1 (1933): 1. www.catholicworker.org.

Dillon, Michele. *Catholic Identity: Balancing Reason, Faith, and Power*. New York: Cambridge University Press, 1999.

Doggett, Martha. *Death Foretold: The Jesuit Murders in El Salvador*. Washington, DC: Georgetown University Press, 1993.

Dolan, Jay. *The American Catholic Experience: A History from Colonial Times to the Present*. Garden City, NY: Doubleday, 1985.

Domonoske, Camila, and Richard Gonzales. "What We Know: Family Separation and 'Zero Tolerance' at the Border." National Public Radio, June 19, 2018. www.npr.org.

Donahue, John R. "The Bible and Catholic Social Teaching: Will This Engagement Lead to Marriage?" In *Modern Catholic Social Teaching: Commentaries and Interpretations*, edited by Kenneth R. Himes, 9–40. Washington, DC: Georgetown University Press, 2005.

Dunn, David H. *The Politics of Threat: Minuteman Vulnerability in American National Security Policy*. New York: St. Martin's Press, 1997.

Ehrlich, Paul R. *The Population Bomb*. New York: Ballantine Books, 1968.

Ellingson, Stephen. *To Care for Creation: The Emergence of the Religious Environmental Movement*. Chicago: University of Chicago Press, 2016.

Ellis, Marc. "Peter Maurin: To Bring the Social Order to Christ." In *A Revolution of the Heart: Essays on the Catholic Worker*, edited by Patrick Coy, 15–46. Philadelphia: Temple University Press, 1988.

Erdozaín, Plácido. *Archbishop Romero: Martyr of El Salvador*. Maryknoll, NY: Orbis Books, 1980.

Evans, Eric J. *The Forging of the Modern State: Early Industrial Britain, 1783–1870*. London: Longman, 1996.

Exsul Familia Nazarethana. Apostolic Constitution of Pius XII, August 1, 1952.

Fiorenza, Elisabeth Schüssler. *Discipleship of Equals: A Critical Feminist Ekklesia-logy of Liberation*. New York: Crossroad, 1993.

Forest, Jim. *Love Is the Measure: A Biography of Dorothy Day*. Maryknoll, NY: Orbis Books, 1994.

Frank, Andre Gunder. *Latin America: Underdevelopment or Revolution*. New York: Monthly Review Press, 1969.

Friedan, Betty. *The Feminine Mystique*. New York: W. W. Norton, 1963.

Gaillardetz, Richard R. "The Ecclesiological Foundations of Modern Catholic Social Teaching." In *Modern Catholic Social Teaching: Commentaries and Interpretations*, edited by Kenneth R. Himes, 72–98. Washington, DC: Georgetown University Press, 2005.

Gallo-Cruz, Selina. "Negotiating the Lines of Contention: Counterframing and Boundary Work in the School of the Americas Protest." *Sociological Forum* 27, no. 1 (2012): 21–45.

Ganz, Marshall. "Resources and Resourcefulness: Strategic Capacity in the Unionization of California Agriculture, 1959–1966." *American Journal of Sociology* 105, no. 4 (2000): 1003–1062.

———. *Why David Sometimes Wins: Leadership, Organization, and Strategy in the California Farm Worker Movement*. New York: Oxford University Press, 2010.

Garcia, Matt. "Cesar Chavez and the United Farm Workers Movement." In *Oxford Research Encyclopedia of American History*. May 2016. http://americanhistory.oxfordre.com.

———. *From the Jaws of Victory: The Triumph and Tragedy of Cesar Chavez and the United Farm Workers*. Berkeley: University of California Press, 2012.

Gaventa, John. *Power and Powerlessness: Quiescence and Rebellion in an Appalachian Valley*. Urbana: University of Illinois Press, 1980.

Gerassi, John. *Revolutionary Priest: The Complete Writings and Messages of Camilo Torres*. New York: Random House, 1971.

Gibellini, Rosino. *The Liberation Theology Debate*. Maryknoll, NY: Orbis Books, 1988.

Gill, Lesley. *The School of the Americas: Military Training and Political Violence in the Americas*. Durham, NC: Duke University Press, 2004.

Golden, Renny, and Michael McConnell. *Sanctuary: The New Underground Railroad*. Maryknoll, NY: Orbis Books, 1986.

Gonzalez-Barrera, A., J. Krogstad, and M. Hugo Lopez. "Children 12 and under Are Fastest Growing Group of Unaccompanied Minors at U.S. Border." *Fact Tank*, July 22, 2014. Pew Research Center. www.pewresearch.org.

Graham, Otis L., Jr., ed. *Environmental Politics and Policy: 1960s-1990s*. University Park: Pennsylvania State University Press, 2000.

Greeley, Andrew. "*Quadragesimo Anno* after Fifty Years." *America*, no. 145 (August 8, 1981): 47.

———. "Religion and Attitudes toward the Environment." *Journal for the Scientific Study of Religion* 32 (1993): 19–28.

Griffin-Nolan, Ed. *Witness for Peace: A Story of Resistance*. Louisville, KY: Westminster/John Knox Press, 1991.

Griswold, Eliza. "How 'Silent Spring' Ignited the Environmental Movement." *New York Times*, September 21, 2012.

Guhin, Jeffrey J. "Where Are the Catholic Environmentalists?" *America*, February 13, 2006. www.americamagazine.org.

Guth, James L., John C. Green, Lyman A. Kellstedt, and Corwin E. Smidt. "Faith and the Environment: Religious Beliefs and Attitudes on Environmental Policy." *American Journal of Political Science* 39, no. 2 (1995): 364–382.

Gutierrez, Gustavo. *The Power of the Poor in History*. Maryknoll, NY: Orbis Books, 1983.

———. *A Theology of Liberation: History, Politics, and Salvation*. Maryknoll, NY: Orbis Books, 1973.

Guzder, Deena. *Divine Rebels: American Christian Activists for Social Justice*. Chicago: Lawrence Hill Books, 2011.

Hall, David D., ed. *Lived Religion in America: Toward a History of Practice*. Princeton, NJ: Princeton University Press, 1997.

Hamlin, Christopher, and John T. McGreevy. "The Greening of America, Catholic Style, 1930–1950." *Environmental History* 11 (2006): 464–499.

Handy, Jim. *Gift of the Devil: A History of Guatemala*. Boston: South End Press, 1984.

Harbury, Jennifer. *Bridge of Courage: Life Stories of the Guatemalan Compañeros and Compañeras*. Monroe, ME: Common Courage Press, 1995.

Henold, Mary Joanne. *Catholic and Feminist: The Surprising History of the American Catholic Feminist Movement*. Chapel Hill: University of North Carolina Press, 2008.

Heredia, Luis. "From Prayer to Protest: The Immigrant Rights Movement and the Catholic Church." In *Rallying for Immigrant Rights*, edited by Kim Voss and Irene Bloemraad, 102–122. Berkeley: University of California Press, 2011.

Hershberger, Guy F. *War, Peace, and Nonresistance*. Scottdale, PA: Herald Press, 1944.

Hess, Gary R. "South Vietnam under Siege: Kennedy, Johnson, and the Question of Escalation or Disengagement." In *The Columbia History of the Vietnam War*, edited by David L. Anderson, 143–167. New York: Columbia University Press.

Hinze, Christine Firer. "Commentary on Quadragesimo Anno (After Forty Years)." In *Modern Catholic Social Teaching: Commentaries and Interpretations*, edited by Kenneth R. Himes, Lisa Sowle Cahill, Charles E. Curran, David Hollenbach, and Thomas Shannon, 151–174. Washington, DC: Georgetown University Press, 2005.

Hollenbach, David. *Justice, Peace, and Human Rights: American Catholic Social Ethics in a Pluralistic Context*. New York: Crossroad Publishing, 1988.

Hornus, Jean Michel. *It Is Not Lawful for Me to Fight: Early Christian Attitudes toward War, Violence, and the State.* Scottdale, PA: Herald Press, 1980.

Hunt, Mary E. "Women-Church: Feminist Concept, Religious Commitment, Women's Movement." *Journal of Feminist Studies in Religion* 25, no. 1 (2009): 85–98.

Kaiser, David E. *American Tragedy: Kennedy, Johnson, and the Origins of the Vietnam War.* Cambridge, MA: Harvard University Press, 2002.

Katzenstein, Mary Fainsod. "Discursive Politics and Feminist Activism in the Catholic Church." In *Feminist Organizations: Harvest of the New Women's Movement,* edited by Myra Marx Feree and Patricia Yancey Martin, 35–52. Philadelphia: Temple University Press, 1995.

———. *Faithful and Fearless: Moving Feminist Protest Inside the Church and the Military.* Princeton, NJ: Princeton University Press, 1999.

Kaufman, Jason. "Rise and Fall of a Nation of Joiners." *Knights of Labor Revisited* 31, no. 4 (2001): 553–579.

Keller, Edward A. *Christianity and American Capitalism.* Chicago: Heritage Foundation, 1953.

King, Martin Luther, Jr. *Why We Can't Wait.* New York: Penguin Books, [1963] 2000.

Klejment, Anne. "The Spirituality of Dorothy Day's Pacifism." *U.S. Catholic Historian* 27, no. 2 (2009): 1–24.

———. "War Resistance and Property Destruction: The Catonsville Nine Draft Board Raid and Catholic Worker Pacifism." In *A Revolution of the Heart: Essays on the Catholic Worker,* edited by Patrick G. Coy, 272–309. Philadelphia: Temple University Press, 1988.

Klejment, Anne, and Nancy L. Roberts. "The Catholic Worker and the Vietnam War." In *American Catholic Pacifism: The Influence of Dorothy Day and the Catholic Worker Movement,* edited by Anne Klejment and Nancy Roberts, 153–169. Westport, CT: Praeger, 1996.

Kline, Benjamin. *First along the River: A Brief History of the U.S. Environmental Movement.* Lanham, MD: Rowman and Littlefield, 2011.

Kristensen, Hans M., and Robert S. Norris. "United States Nuclear Forces, 2018." *Bulletin of the Atomic Scientists* 74, no. 2 (2018): 120–131.

Kucinskas, Jaime. "The Unobtrusive Tactics of Religious Movements." *Sociology of Religion* 75, no. 4 (2014): 537–550.

Labarbera, Vince. "Dorothy Day: A Beautiful Legacy." *Today's Catholic News,* May 18, 2015. https://todayscatholic.org.

Lang, Marissa J., Julie Zauzmer, and Hannah Natanson. "Thousands March in Washington in Wilting Heat to Protest Trump's Immigration Policy." *Washington Post,* June 30, 2018. www.washingtonpost.com.

Lauer, Rosemary. "Women and the Church." *Commonweal* 79 (1963): 365–368.

"Leader in Movement to Harbor Aliens Is Convicted." *New York Times,* February 22, 1985. Accessed February 19, 2018. www.nytimes.com.

Lernoux, Penny. *Cry of the People.* New York: Penguin, 1980.

———. "The Long Path to Puebla." In *Puebla and Beyond*, edited by John Eagleson and Philip Scharper, 3–27. Maryknoll, NY: Orbis Books, 1979.

Lewis, Daniel. "Philip Berrigan, Former Priest and Peace Advocate in the Vietnam War, Dies at 79." *New York Times*, December 8, 2002, A36.

Lonsdale, David J. "Nuclear Strategy and Catholicism: A Reappraisal." *Journal of Military Ethics* 11, no. 3 (2012): 186–207.

Lorentzen, Robin. *Women in the Sanctuary Movement*. Philadelphia: Temple University Press, 1991.

Maron, Edward. "Interview with Mary Daly." *U.S. Catholic* 34, no. 5 (1968): 21–24. www.uscatholic.org.

Marx, Karl. *Critique of Hegel's "Philosophy of Right."* New York: Cambridge University Press, [1843] 1970.

Massaro, Thomas J. "From Industrialization to Globalization: Church and Social Ministry." In *Living the Catholic Social Tradition: Cases and Commentary*, edited by Kathleen Maas Weigert and Alexia K. Kelly, 41–58. Lanham, MD: Rowman and Littlefield, 2005.

———. *Living Justice: Catholic Social Teaching in Action*. Franklin, WI: Sheed and Ward, 2000.

McBrady, Jared. "The Challenge of Peace: Ronald Reagan, John Paul II, and the American Bishops." *Journal of Cold War Studies* 17, no. 1 (2015): 129–152.

McClory, Robert J. "Patty Crowley, Giant of Catholic Laity, Dies at 92." *National Catholic Reporter*, December 9, 2005. www.natcath.org.

McGuire, Meredith. *Lived Religion: Faith and Practice in Everyday Life*. New York: Oxford University Press, 2008.

McKenna, Kevin E. *A Concise Guide to Catholic Social Teaching*. Notre Dame, IN: Ave Maria Press, 2002.

McNeal, Patricia. *Harder Than War: Catholic Peacemaking in Twentieth-Century America*. New Brunswick, NJ: Rutgers University Press, 1992.

Meconis, Charles A. *With Clumsy Grace: The American Catholic Left, 1961–1975*. New York: Seabury, 1979.

Merton, Thomas. *Seeds of Destruction*. New York: Macmillan, 1964.

Mich, Marvin L. Krier. *Catholic Social Teachings and Movements*. Mystic, CT: Twenty-Third Publications, 1998.

Miller, William D. *Dorothy Day: A Biography*. San Francisco: Harper and Row, 1982.

Moon, Hellena. "Womenpriests: Radical Change or More of the Same?" *Journal of Feminist Studies in Religion* 24, no. 2 (2008): 115–134.

Moon, Penelope Adams. "'Peace on Earth: Peace in Vietnam': The Catholic Peace Fellowship and Antiwar Witness, 1964–1976." *Journal of Social History* 36, no. 4 (2003): 1033–1057.

Mooney, Margarita. "The Catholic Bishops Conferences of the United States and France: Engaging Immigration as a Public Issue." *American Behavioral Scientist* 49, no. 11 (2006): 1455–1470.

Muñoz, Ronaldo. "Ecclesiology in Latin America." In *The Challenge of Basic Christian Communities*, edited by Sergio Torres and John Eagleson, 150–160. Maryknoll, NY: Orbis Books, 1981.

National Conference of Catholic Bishops. *The Challenge of Peace: God's Promise and Our Response*. Washington DC: US Conference of Catholic Bishops, 1983.

Nepstad, Sharon Erickson. *Convictions of the Soul: Religion, Culture, and Agency in the Central America Solidarity Movement*. New York: Oxford University Press, 2004.

———. "Disruptive Action and the Prophetic Tradition: War Resistance in the Plowshares Movement." *U.S. Catholic Historian* 27, no. 2 (2009): 97–113.

———. *Nonviolent Revolutions: Civil Resistance in the Late 20th Century*. New York: Oxford University Press, 2011.

———. *Nonviolent Struggle: Theories, Strategies, and Dynamics*. New York: Oxford University Press, 2015.

———. "Popular Religion, Protest, and Revolt: The Emergence of Political Insurgency in the Nicaraguan and Salvadoran Churches of the 1960s–1980s." In *Disruptive Religion: The Force of Faith in Social Movement Activism*, edited by Christian S. Smith, 105–124. New York: Routledge, 1996.

———. *Religion and War Resistance in the Plowshares Movement*. New York: Cambridge University Press, 2008.

———. "School of the Americas Watch." *Peace Review* 12 (2000): 67–72.

Ngo, Anh D., Richard Taylor, Christine L. Roberts, and Tuan V. Nguyen. "Association between Agent Orange and Birth Defects: Systematic Review and Meta-analysis." *International Journal of Epidemiology* 35, no. 5 (2006): 1220–1230.

Novak, Michael. *The Catholic Ethic and the Spirit of Capitalism*. New York: Free Press, 1993.

Novitsky, Anthony. "Peter Maurin's Green Revolution: The Radical Implications of Reactionary Social Catholicism." *Review of Politics* 37, no. 1 (1975): 83–103.

Nuñez, Emilio A. *Liberation Theology*. Chicago: Moody Press, 1985.

Nuttall, Geoffrey. *Christian Pacifism in History*. New York: World Without War Publications, 1971.

O'Brien, David. *American Catholics and Social Reform: The New Deal Years*. New York: Oxford University Press, 1968.

O'Connor, June. "Dorothy Day's Christian Conversion." *Journal of Religious Ethics* 18, no. 1 (1990): 159–180.

O'Donovan, Oliver. *The Just War Revisited*. Cambridge: Cambridge University Press, 2003.

O'Gorman, Angie, and Patrick G. Coy. "Houses of Hospitality: A Pilgrimage into Nonviolence." In *Revolution of the Heart: Essays on the Catholic Worker*, edited by Patrick G. Coy, 239–272. Philadelphia: Temple University Press, 1988.

O'Gorman, Thomas, and Patty Crowley. "Interview with Patty Crowley, Co-founder of CFM." *U.S. Catholic Historian* 9, no. 4 (1990): 457–467.

Olson, Eric. "How to Address Child Migration from Central America." August 2014. Washington, DC: Wilson Center Publications. www.wilsoncenter.org.

Orsi, Robert A. "Is the Study of Lived Religion Irrelevant to the World We Live In? Special Presidential Plenary Address to the Society for the Scientific Study of Religion, Salt Lake City, November 2, 2002." *Journal for the Scientific Study of Religion* 42, no. 2 (2003): 169–174.

———. *The Madonna of 115th Street: Faith and Community in Italian Harlem, 1880–1950.* New Haven, CT: Yale University Press, 2002.

Pant, G. S. "Hiroshima: The Lingering Effects." *India International Centre Quarterly* 14, no. 2 (1983): 59–86.

"The Pastoral and the New Moment." *Commonweal* 291, no. 10 (May 20,1983): 291–292.

Paulhus, Normand. "Social Catholicism and the Fribourg Union." In *Selected Papers from the Annual Meeting (Society of Christian Ethics)*, 63–88. 1980.

Pawel, Miriam. *The Crusades of Cesar Chavez: A Biography.* New York: Bloomsbury Press, 2014.

Peterson, Anna L. *Martyrdom and the Politics of Religion: Progressive Catholicism in El Salvador's Civil War.* Albany: State University of New York Press, 1997.

Phan, Peter C., ed. *Social Thought: Messages of the Fathers of the Church.* Wilmington, DE: Michael Glazier, 1984.

"Pledge to Resist Deportation and Discrimination through Sanctuary." Accessed October 14, 2017. www.sanctuarynotdeportation.org.

Pontifical Council Cor Unum. 1987. "Refugees: A Challenge for Solidarity." Accessed December 29, 2018. www.vatican.va.

Pope, Carl. "If You've Seen One Redwood, You've Seen Them All—Not!" *Huffington Post*, July 12, 2006. www.huffingtonpost.com.

Pope, Stephen J. 2005. "Natural Law in Catholic Social Teachings." In *Modern Catholic Social Teaching: Commentaries and Interpretations*, edited by Kenneth R. Himes, 41–71. Washington, DC: Georgetown University Press, 2005.

Pope Francis. *Laudato Si: On Care for Our Common Home.* Vatican City: Libreria Editrice Vaticana, 2015.

———. *World Day of Peace Message.* January 1, 2017. https://w2.vatican.va.

Pope John XXIII. *Pacem in Terris: Encyclical of Pope John XXIII on Establishing Universal Peace in Truth, Justice, Charity, and Liberty.* April 11, 1963. https://w2.vatican.va

Pope Pius XII. *Papal Teaching: Women in the Modern World.* Boston: Daughters of St. Paul, 1959.

Prentiss, Craig R. *Debating God's Economy: Social Justice in America on the Eve of Vatican II.* University Park: Pennsylvania State University Press, 2008.

Quadragesimo Anno: After Forty Years (Pope Pius XI). In *Catholic Social Thought: The Documentary Heritage*, edited by David J. O'Brien and Thomas Shannon, 43–82. Maryknoll, NY: Orbis Books, 2010.

Randall, Margaret. 1983. *Christians in the Nicaraguan Revolution.* Vancouver, BC: New Star Books.

Ratzinger, Joseph, and Vittorio Messori. *The Ratzinger Report: An Exclusive Interview on the State of the Church.* San Francisco: Ignatius Press, 1985.

Rerum Novarum: The Condition of Labor (Pope Leo XIII, 1891). In *Catholic Social Thought: The Documentary Heritage*, edited by David J. O'Brien and Thomas Shannon, 12–40. Maryknoll, NY: Orbis Books, 2010.

Roberts, Nancy L. "Dorothy Day: Editor and Advocacy Journalist." In *A Revolution of the Heart: Essays on the Catholic Worker*, edited by Patrick G. Coy, 115–133. Philadelphia: Temple University Press, 1988.

Rodgers, Daniel T. *The Work Ethic in Industrial America, 1850–1920.* Chicago: University of Chicago Press, 1978.

Rome, Adam. "The Genius of Earth Day." *Environmental History* 15, no. 2 (2010): 194–205.

Rose, Margaret. "Traditional and Nontraditional Patterns of Female Activism in the United Farm Workers of America, 1962 to 1980." *Frontiers: A Journal of Women's Studies* 11, no. 1 (1990): 26–32.

Rostow, W. W. *The Stages of Economic Growth: A Non-Communist Manifesto.* Cambridge: Cambridge University Press, 1960.

Rue, Victoria. "Crossroads: Womenpriests in the Roman Catholic Church." San Jose State University ScholarWorks, 2008.

Ruether, Rosemary Radford. "A Catholic Mother Tells: Why I Believe in Birth Control." *Saturday Evening Post*, April 4, 1964, 12–14.

———. "Catholics and Abortion: Authority vs. Dissent." *Christian Century*, October 3, 1985.

———. "Male Chauvinist Theology and the Anger or Women." *CrossCurrents* 21, no. 2 (1971): 173–185.

———. "The Place of Women in the Church." In *Modern Catholicism: Aspects of Church Life since the Council*, edited by L. Adrian Hastings. New York: Oxford University Press, 1991.

———, ed. *Religion and Sexism: Images of Woman in the Jewish and Christian Traditions.* Eugene, OR: Wipf and Stock, 1998.

———. *Sexism and God-Talk: Toward a Feminist Theology.* Boston: Beacon Press, 1983.

———. "Should Women Want Women Priests or Women-Church?" *Feminist Theology* 20, no. 1 (2011): 63–72.

———. *Women-Church: Theology and Practice of Feminist Liturgical Communities.* San Francisco: Harper and Row, 1985.

Ryan, Cheney. "The One Who Burns Herself for Peace." *Hypatia* 9, no. 2 (1994): 21–39.

Ryan, John A. *Social Doctrine in Action: A Personal History.* New York: Harper and Brothers, 1941.

Ryder, Norman B., and Charles F. Westoff. *Reproduction in the United States: 1965.* Princeton, NJ: Princeton University Press, 1971.

Schäfer, Michael. "*Rerum Novarum*: The Result of Christian Social Movements 'From Below.'" In *Rerum Novarum: One Hundred Years of Catholic Social Teaching*, edited by John Coleman and Gregory Baum, 3–17. London: SCM Press, 1991.

Schlesinger, Stephen, and Stephen Kinzer. *Bitter Fruit: The Story of the American Coup in Guatemala.* New York: Doubleday, 1999.

Segers, Mary C. "Equality and Christian Anarchism: The Political and Social Ideas of the Catholic Worker." *Review of Politics* 40, no. 2 (1978): 196–230.

Segundo, Juan Luis. *A Theology for Artisans of a New Humanity: Evolution and Guilt.* Maryknoll, NY: Orbis Books, 1974.

Shah, Sural. "The Crisis in Our Own Backyard: United States Response to Unaccompanied Minor Children from Central America." *Harvard Public Health Review* 9 (April 2016). Accessed January 28, 2018. www.harvardpublichealthreview.org.

Sharkey, Stephen, ed. *Sociology and Catholic Social Teaching: Contemporary Theory and Research.* Lanham, MD: Scarecrow Press, 2012.

Sicius, Francis J. "Peter Maurin's Green Revolution." *U.S. Catholic Historian* 26, no. 3 (2008): 1–14.

Sirico, Robert A., and William E. LeMothe. *The Entrepreneurial Vocation.* Grand Rapids, MI: Acton Institute, 2001.

Smith, Christian. *The Emergence of Liberation Theology: Radical Religion and Social Movement Theory.* Chicago: University of Chicago Press, 1991.

———. *Resisting Reagan: The U.S.–Central America Peace Movement.* Chicago: University of Chicago Press, 1996.

Smith, Sydney D. *Grapes of Conflict.* Pasadena, CA: Hope Publishing House, 1987.

Sobrino, Jon. *Archbishop Romero: Memories and Reflections.* Maryknoll, NY: Orbis Books, 1990.

———. *Companions of Jesus: The Murder and Martyrdom of the Salvadoran Jesuits.* Nottingham, UK: Russell Press, 1990.

Stearns, Peter N. *The Industrial Revolution in World History.* Boulder, CO: Westview Press, 2013.

Steinfels, Peter. "The Life and Death of a Leading Lay Catholic." *New York Times,* December 31, 2005. www.nytimes.com.

Steinhoff, Uwe. *On the Ethics of War and Terrorism.* New York: Oxford University Press, 2007.

Stephan, Maria J. "What Happens When You Replace a Just War with a Just Peace: Can the Catholic Church Put an End to Centuries of Sanctioning War, and Start Promoting Peace Instead?" *Foreign Policy,* May 18, 2016. https://foreignpolicy.com.

Stock, Paul V. "The Perennial Nature of the Catholic Worker Farms: A Reconsideration of Failure." *Rural Sociology* 79, no. 2 (2014): 143–173.

Swidler, Leonard, and Arlene Swidler, eds. *Women Priests: A Catholic Commentary on the Vatican Declaration.* New York: Paulist Press, 1977.

Taylor, Ronald. *Chavez and the Farm Workers.* Boston: Beacon Press, 1975.

Tentler, Leslie Woodcock. *Catholics and Contraception: An American History.* Ithaca, NY: Cornell University Press, 2004.

———. "Souls and Bodies: The Birth Control Controversy and the Collapse of Confession." In *The Crisis of Authority in Catholic Modernity,* edited by Michael J. Lacey and Francis Oakley, 293–315. New York: Oxford University Press, 2011.

Terrell, Brian. "Dorothy Day's 'Filthy, Rotten, System' Likely Wasn't Hers at All." *National Catholic Reporter,* April 16, 2012. www.ncronline.org.

Thistlethwaite, Susan Brooks, ed. *Interfaith Just Peacemaking: Jewish, Christian, and Muslim on the New Paradigm of Peace and War*. New York: Palgrave Macmillan, 2011.

Topmiller, Robert. "The Buddhist Anti-war Movement." In *The War That Never Ends: New Perspectives on the Vietnam War*, edited by David L. Anderson and John Ernst, 143–167. Lexington: University Press of Kentucky, 2007.

"Top Voting Issues in 2016 Election." Pew Research Center, Politics and Policies. July 7, 2016. www.people-press.org.

US Catholic Conference. *Renewing the Earth: An Invitation to Reflection and Action on Environment in Light of Catholic Social Teaching*. Washington, DC: US Catholic Conference, 1991.

US Conference of Catholic Bishops. *Sharing Catholic Social Teaching: Challenges and Directions*. 1998. http://www.usccb.org.

———. "The U.S. Bishops on Peace and War," National Catholic Reporter, July 2, 1982, 1.

Voss, Kim, and Irene Bloemraad, eds. *Rallying for Immigrant Rights: The Fight for Inclusion in 21ˢᵗ Century America*. Berkeley: University of California Press, 2011.

Walzer, Michael. *Just and Unjust Wars: A Moral Argument with Historical Illustrations*. New York: Basic Books, 1977.

Warner, Keith Douglass. "The Greening of American Catholicism: Identity, Conversion, and Continuity." *Religion and American Culture: A Journal of Interpretation* 18, no. 1 (2008): 113–142.

Weaver, Mary Jo. "American Catholic Women since the Vatican II Council." In *Encyclopedia of Women in Religion*, edited by Rosemary Skinner Keller and Rosemary Radford Ruether, 200–208. Bloomington: Indiana University Press, 2006.

———. *New Catholic Women: A Contemporary Challenge to Traditional Religious Authority*. San Francisco: Harper and Row, 1985.

Webb, Sheila. "Dorothy Day and the Early Years of the 'Catholic Worker': Social Action through the Pages of the Press." *U.S. Catholic Historian* 21, no. 3 (2003): 71–88.

Weir, Robert E. *Beyond Labor's Veil: The Culture of the Knights of Labor*. University Park: Pennsylvania State University Press, 1996.

Westoff, Charles F., and Larry Bumpass. "The Revolution in Birth Control Practices of U.S. Catholics." *Science* 179 (January 5, 1973): 41–42.

White, Lynn. "The Historical Roots of Our Ecological Crisis." *Science* 155 (March 10, 1967): 1203–1207.

Whitney, Elspeth. "Lynn White Jr.'s 'The Historical Roots of Our Ecological Crisis' after 50 Years." *History Compass* 13, no. 8 (2015): 396–410.

Williams, Pete. "Sessions: Parents, Children Entering U.S. Illegally Will Be Separated." NBC News, May 7, 2018. www.nbcnews.com.

Willson, S. Brian. *Blood on the Tracks: The Life and Times of S. Brian Willson*. Oakland, CA: PM Press, 2011.

Wink, Walter. "Beyond Just War and Pacifism." In *War and Its Discontents: Pacifism and Quietism in the Abrahamic Traditions*, edited by J. Patout Burns, 102–121. Washington, DC: Georgetown University Press, 1996.

Wittner, Lawrence S. *Rebels against War: The American Peace Movement, 1941–1960.* New York: Columbia University Press, 1969.

Young, Alvin L., John P. Giesy, Paul D. Jones, and Michael Newton. "Environmental Fate and Bio-availability of Agent Orange and Its Associated Dioxin during the Vietnam War." *Environmental Science and Pollution Research* 11 (2004): 359–370.

Yukich, Grace. *One Family under God: Immigration Politics and Progressive Religion in America.* New York: Oxford University Press, 2013.

INDEX

Acton Institute, 13
Agricultural Workers Organizing Committee (AWOC), 40
Anti-Conscription League, 30
Aquinas, Thomas, 48, 84
Arbenz, Jacobo, 101–102
Arévalo, Juan Jose, 101–102
Augustine of Hippo, 9, 48

base ecclesial communities, 106–107, 111–112
Batterham, Forster, 30–31
Bernardin, Joseph, 69, 152–153
Berrigan, Daniel: and draft board raids, 62–63; and immolations, 60; and the Plowshares movement, 66–68
Berrigan, Philip: and draft board raids, 61–64; and the Plowshares movement, 66–68
Boff, Clodovis, 107, 110
Boff, Leonardo, 107, 109–110, 115
Bourgeois, Roy, 122–125
Butigan, Ken, 120–121

Cabat, Karl, 67–68
Callahan, Sidney, 81, 84–85
Câmara, Hélder, 103
Carson, Rachel, 146, 151
Casti Connubii, 90–91
Catholic Action, 77–78
Catholic Association for International Peace (CAIP), 52–53
Catholic Climate Covenant (CCC), 148, 158–160, 171

Catholic feminism: background, 74–80; and contraception, 77, 85–86, 170; female ordination, 85–88; theological themes, 80–86
Catholic Peace Fellowship, 58, 73
Catholics for Choice, 92
Catholic Social Teachings, 8. *See also* Catholic Social Thought
Catholic Social Thought: definition of, 3 3n3, 8; historical development of, 3–6; movements' influence on, 3, 166–171; sources and methods, 8–10; themes of, 6–8
Catholic Worker movement: background, 28–33; civil defense drills, 53–55, 59, 165; contributions of, 44–46; critiques of capitalism, 33–34; green revolution and farming communes, 12, 33, 37–38, 148–149; houses of hospitality, 32–33, 35–37; newsletter, 31–32; and pacifism, 53, 73; purposes of, 32–33; support for the United Farm Workers, 43; anti-Vietnam War activity, 58–61
Catonsville Nine, 63–65
Centesimus Annus, 13
Central America: history of, 95–98; immigration from, 2, 127
Central America solidarity movement, 116–126
Challenge of Peace, 71–72
Chávez, César: background, 38–39; contributions, 46; work with the UFW, 40–43
Chicago Religious Task Force on Central America, 136–137

Vatican II Council, 55, 103; and Latin America, 103, 113, 116–117, 126; and women's issues, 76, 79–80, 84, 93
Vietnam War, 47; 56–57

War Resisters League, 54
White, Lynn, 153

Willson, S. Brian, 165
Witness for Peace, 116–120, 165
Women-Church movement, 88–90
Womenpriests. *See* Roman Catholic Womenpriests
Women's Ordination Conference, 86–87

Zahn, Gordon, 55

ABOUT THE AUTHOR

Sharon Erickson Nepstad is Distinguished Professor of Sociology at the University of New Mexico, where she has also served as Director of Religious Studies. She is the author of *Convictions of the Soul: Religion, Culture, and Agency in the Central American Solidarity Movement*; *Religion and War Resistance in the Plowshares Movement*; *Nonviolent Revolutions: Civil Resistance in the Late 20th Century*; and *Nonviolent Struggle: Theories, Dynamics, and Strategies*. Two of these books received the Outstanding Book Award from the American Sociological Association's section on Peace, War, and Social Conflict.

Lightning Source UK Ltd.
Milton Keynes UK
UKHW040603031119
352780UK00011B/97/P